THE BYZANTINE LEGACY
IN THE
ORTHODOX CHURCH

THE BYZANTINE LEGACY IN THE ORTHODOX CHURCH

by

John Meyendorff

ST. VLADIMIR'S SEMINARY PRESS
CRESTWOOD, NEW YORK
1982

By the same author

GREGORY PALAMAS: Defense of the Holy Hesychasts
  Text and French translation (1959; 2nd ed. 1974)
THE ORTHODOX CHURCH (1961; 2nd ed. 1981)
A STUDY OF GREGORY PALAMAS (1964)
ORTHODOXY AND CATHOLICITY (1966)
MARRIAGE: AN ORTHODOX PERSPECTIVE (1971; 2nd ed.
  1975)
ST. GREGORY PALAMAS AND ORTHODOX SPIRITUALITY
  (1974)
BYZANTINE HESYCHASM: HISTORICAL, THEOLOGICAL
  AND SOCIAL PROBLEMS (1974)
CHRIST IN EASTERN CHRISTIAN THOUGHT (1975)
LIVING TRADITION (1978)
BYZANTIUM AND THE RISE OF RUSSIA (1980)

Library of Congress Cataloging in Publication Data

Meyendorff, John, 1926-
  The Byzantine legacy in the Orthodox Church.

  Bibliography: p.
  Includes index.
  1. Orthodox Eastern Church—Addresses,
essays, lectures. 2. Byzantine Empire—
Civilization—Addresses, essays, lectures.
  I. Title.
BX325.M49   281.9   82-797
ISBN 0-913836-90-7   AACR2

THE BYZANTINE LEGACY
IN THE
ORTHODOX CHURCH

ISBN 0-913836-90-7

PRINTED IN THE UNITED STATES OF AMERICA
BY
ATHENS PRINTING COMPANY
NEW YORK, N. Y.

Table of Contents

Introduction

A visitor to the Turkish city of Istanbul today can hardly recognize it as a major center of Christian tradition. Nevertheless this city—which used to be known as Byzantium to the ancient Greeks before being renamed "Constantinople" or "New Rome" by Emperor Constantine in the early fourth century—was once the cradle, the pattern and the admired center of Eastern Orthodox Christianity. St. Gregory the Theologian and St. John Chrysostom exercised their ministry there. The great temple of the Holy Wisdom, St. Sophia—still miraculously preserved after serving for five centuries as an Islamic mosque—was for over nine hundred years the place where the Orthodox liturgy took its present shape, where councils met to proclaim Orthodox dogma, and where canon law was defined.

From Constantinople, the Orthodox faith was carried to many countries. Following the model offered on the day of Pentecost, Byzantine missionaries made sure that the faith became accessible in various languages. The best example of this missionary spirit is offered by Sts. Cyril and Methodius, the apostles to the Slavs in the ninth century, who translated Scripture and the liturgy into the Slavic tongue. Their mission made possible the conversion of many Slavic nations, who from Byzantium accepted not only the Orthodox faith itself but also Byzantine Christian civilization. In Orthodox Byzantium they admired the icons, the music, the beauty of the liturgy. It was after they visited St. Sophia—where "they knew not whether they were in heaven or on earth"—that the ambassadors of the Russian prince, St. Vladimir of Kiev, were able to convince their master that the "Greek faith" was indeed the true religion.

This historical dependence of contemporary Orthodoxy upon its Byzantine past makes the study of Byzantium inevitable for a proper understanding of Orthodox tradition in all its forms: theology, spirituality, liturgy, canon law and religious art. The studies gathered in this volume under the general title of *The Byzantine Legacy in the Orthodox Church* were composed for different purposes and were addressed to different audiences. Nevertheless, they reflect a unity of purpose and inspiration. A general presentation of the Byzantine Church in its history and basic features opens the collection. Part II is composed of two articles discussing political structures, *i.e.,* essentially the Byzantine imperial ideology inherited from Rome. The lofty ideal of a "symphony" between church and state, as best formulated by Emperor Justinian—the builder of St. Sophia—is seen as an essentially positive inspiration, clearly distinct from "caesaropapistic" abuses. But Justinian's very failure to secure total religious unity of the Christian world raises the question of the theological legitimacy of his dream; could the empire really be identified with the Kingdom of God? Whatever answer one gives to this question, the fact remains that the universalist aspirations of Byzantium survived even in the midst of the catastrophes of the eleventh, twelfth and thirteenth centuries: the Turkish invasion and the challenge of the Western Crusades. It is precisely then that the Church was able to assume in its own name the universal task which had earlier been monopolized by the empire, and to prepare the further survival of Orthodoxy during the dark ages of Ottoman rule.

Part III approaches the "mind of Byzantium" from different angles: the defensive opposition to Islam, the liturgy as a tool of unity, the remarkable revival of spirituality and culture in the age of hesychasm (fourteenth century). Part IV contains two case studies of some essential issues in Byzantine theology, marking its peculiar identity in contrast with ideas which shaped Western Christian thought.

Finally, this collection of articles reflects their author's most intimate conviction, that faithfulness to the Byzantine legacy is legitimate only if it is accepted in the true spirit of the Orthodox understanding of the Church. It is not Byzantium which "made" Orthodoxy, but rather the opposite: the most valuable and lasting features of Byzantine Christian civilization are rooted in Christian Orthodoxy, so that today, faithfulness to Orthodoxy can not be identified with or reduced to a servile and mechanical preservation of Byzantine relics of the past. Christian tradition can only be authentic if it is a living tradition, and life always implies change. Byzantium itself changed much throughout the millenium of its history, and, since it fell in 1453, the world around has been transformed much more radically than ever before. It is in this totally new—and still rapidly changing—world that Orthodoxy is to develop, necessarily grounded in its Byzantine past but not bound by Byzantium's purely human and historically relative features.

In Part V, the first study recalls the remarkable recognition given in the Byzantine Christian world to a polarity between the "institution" and the "event," between "structure" and personal experience, between authority and responsible freedom. The polarity, well formulated by the greatest of the Cappadocian fathers of the fourth century, St. Basil of Caesarea, has remained since that time a necessary and sometimes puzzling aspect of Orthodox ecclesiology and Orthodox spirituality. Finally, in the same Part V, there appears a discussion of burning contemporary problems in the light of the Byzantine legacy: the poison of ecclesiastical nationalism, which transforms legitimate decentralization and pluralism into sinful divisiveness, and the possible forms which the universal primacy of the ecumenical patriarchate, inherited from Byzantium, could eventually take, if it is to assume the role assigned to it by sound ecclesiological thinking. In this case also, a blind and formal faithfulness to a dead past can transform a useful and necessary institution into a museum piece or—even worse—into a tool of secular ethnicism.

The study of church history—at least for Orthodox Christians—is primarily aimed at discovering the mechanisms, the rationale of continuity, and leads one to discover the *consistency* of tradition. But it would fail in its main purpose if it did not also help to destroy idols, to define the difference between what is absolute and what is relative in church life and, therefore, to exercise a salutary criticism without which the Christian faith would be in conflict with both truth and human intelligence.

— *John Meyendorff*

I

THE BYZANTINE CHURCH

The Byzantine Church*

The transfer of the capital of the Roman Empire to Constantinople in 324 and the imperial protection accorded to the Church by Emperor Constantine and his successors created an entirely new condition in Christendom. In the West, barbarian invasions soon greatly reduced the influence of the empire, but in the East it stood firm. Constantinople, the "New Rome," also called Byzantium—the name of the ancient city on the Bosphorus chosen by Constantine as the location of the new capital—survived as its capital until 1453. For over a millenium, it was the recognized center of Orthodox Christianity for much of Eastern Europe and the Middle East. The term "Byzantium" is used today to designate both the city of Constantinople and the Eastern Roman Empire itself, in order to distinguish them from the "Old Rome" and from the pagan empire. The role of the church of Constantinople in Christianizing the East is almost in every way similar to the achievements of the Roman church in the Latin West. One should note however that the name "Byzantine" was seldom used in the Middle Ages. The "Byzantines" spoke Greek and called themselves *Romans*. The Latin West also designated the empire as *Romania,* and the Muslims, as *Rum.*

1. Church and State

The survival of the empire in the East assured an active role of the emperor in the affairs of the Church. This does

*To appear, after 1983, in the *Dictionary of the Middle Ages,* published by Scribner's, New York, under the auspices of the American Council of Learned Societies.

not mean, however, that the relations between church and state in Byzantium can be expressed in any simple formula or concept, such as "caesaropapism." On the one hand, it is unquestionable that the Christian empire inherited from pagan times the administrative and financial routine of administering religious affairs, and this routine was applied to the Christian Church, almost automatically and without objections, by Constantine himself. But, on the other hand, the Christian faith was incompatible with the Hellenistic and Roman idea of the emperor as a divine being: Christ was the only king, the only *kyrios*. So, following the pattern set by Eusebius of Caesarea, who delivered a funeral oration at Constantine's death (337), the Byzantines rather thought of the emperor as a Christ's representative or messenger, "equal to the apostles" (*isapostolos*), responsible particularly for the propagation of Christianity among pagans and for the "externals" of the Christian religion, such as administration and finances (hence the title used by Eusebius, of ἐπίσκοπος τῶν ἐκτός).

This imperial role in the affairs of the Church never developed into a fixed, legally defined system. It was clearly conditioned by one decisive factor: the emperor's doctrinal orthodoxy. A heretical emperor was not to be obeyed. Numerous heroes of the faith—Athanasius of Alexandria (d. 373), John Chrysostom (d. 407), Maximus the Confessor (d. 662), John of Damascus (d. 750), Theodore of Studius (759-826) —were venerated as saints after their deaths because of their resistance to the imperial will; and the memory of many emperors, particularly Constantius I (337-361), Leo III (717-741), Constantine V (741-775) and Michael VIII (1250-1282), was formally cursed, because of their support for heterodox doctrines.

The text which comes closest to a theoretical definition of church-state relations in Byzantium is the Sixth *Novella* of Justinian (527-565), which defines the priesthood and the imperial dignity as "the two greatest gifts of God" to mankind and insists on their common divine origin. The ideal, as presented in the *Novella,* is a "harmony" between the two powers. The same idea of a joint responsibility to God of the emperor and the patriarch of Constantinople is also expressed in the *Epanagoge,* a legal compedium of the ninth century. These texts, however, sound more like pious exhortations than legal definitions. The Byzantines were well aware of the difficulty to express, in terms of the Christian faith, the dynamic and polarized relationship between the "earthly" and the "heavenly," the "old" and the "new," the "secular" and the "holy."

In court ceremonial and in official texts, the emperor was often described in terms of Old Testament kingship; but as David and Solomon anticipated the kingdom of the Messiah, so the emperor of the Christians was necessarily seen as an image of Christ. He convened councils and could always, if he wished, exercise a decisive influence in ecclesiastical appointments, including that of the patriarch of Constantinople and of those prelates who played an important diplomatic role in Byzantine foreign affairs (the archbishop of Ohrid, the metropolitan of Russia and others). It has been noticed that out of 122 patriarchs of Constantinople elected between 379 and 1451, thirty-six were forced to resign under imperial pressure.[1] But the relative dependence of the patriarchal office upon the emperor must be understood in the context of the permanent instability of the imperial office itself. Two-thirds of all Byzantine emperors were either killed or dethroned, and many had been, at least in part, the victims of their own religious policies.

2. The Eastern Patriarchates

As Christianity was becoming the official religion of the Roman state—a process which began under Constantine (324-337) and was completed under Theodosius I (379-395)—, the Church had no administrative structure on a universal scale. The Council of Nicaea (325) acknowledged only the authority of provincial episcopal synods, presided by their "metropolitans" and invested with the power of appointing

[1] E. Herman, in *Cambridge Medieval History* IV, 2 (Cambridge, 1967), p. 109.

new bishops (canons 4 and 5). However, it also recognized that some episcopal sees enjoyed traditional prestige which transcended the limits of a single province. The three sees mentioned specifically are those of Alexandria, Antioch and Rome (canon 6). In the East, both Alexandria and Antioch played a significant role in ecclesiastical affairs and theological controversies of the fourth century. They were then unquestionably the intellectual and cultural centers of Eastern Christendom, and by the fifth century their incumbents were generally using the title of "patriarch."

The archbishop of Alexandria—also designated as "pope" —headed a church which not only had its roots in early Christianity (cf. the prestige of the school of Origen in the third century) but also controled a vast and populous region— Egypt, Libya and Pentapolis—where the Christian faith had early won the popular masses. Missionaries from Alexandria also converted Ethiopia to the Christian faith (fourth century). Athanasius of Alexandria had been the hero of the anti-Arian struggle. His successor, Cyril, obtained the condemnation of Nestorius at the Council of Ephesus (431). However, Cyril's successor, Dioscorus, rejected the Council of Chalcedon (451). These theological developments were all expressing the typical Alexandrian concern for the divinity of Christ, even at the price of minimizing the reality of His humanity. The anti-Chalcedonian schism of the "Monophysites," who will always be a majority in Egypt, was instrumental not only in breaking permanently the religious unity of the Byzantine Empire but also in facilitating the Muslim conquest of Egypt.

In Antioch, the exegetical tradition was different from the Alexandrian, less philosophical and more oriented towards biblical history. There was a long resistence to the Nicaean (and Alexandrian) identification of Christ as of "one substance" with the Father, and, after the triumph of Nicaean orthodoxy, some Antiochenes defended a Christology which rather emphasized the genuine humanity of Jesus. Ecclesiastically, the "patriarchate" of Antioch, which included the civil "diocese" of the East, was less monolithic than Egypt. It included a mixed Greek and Syrian population and sent successful missions to Persia, Armenia and Georgia. After 431, some of its theologians—who followed the condemned teaching of Nestorius—emigrated to Persia. Divided in the fifth and sixth centuries between Chalcedonians and Monophysites, Antioch lost much of its prestige and influence before being overtaken by the Arabs.

In the decades which followed Nicaea (325), a third major ecclesiastical center developed in the East. It had nothing of the antiquity and prestige of Alexandria or Antioch, but closeness to the imperial court gave its bishop a singular advantage in influencing ecclesiastical affairs. Thus, in 381, as Theodosius I gathered the Second Ecumenical Council to finally settle the Arian dispute, the bishop of the new capital was formally recognized as having "priority of honor" after the bishop of Rome, because Constantinople was "the New Rome" (canon 3). The frankly political grounds for Constantinople's elevation were further emphasized in the famous canon 28 of Chalcedon (451), which became the charter of the capital's ecclesiastical rights:

> The fathers rightly granted privileges to the throne of Old Rome, because it was the imperial city. And one hundred and fifty most religious bishops [of Constantinople, 381], actuated by the same considerations, gave equal privileges to the most holy throne of New Rome, justly judging that the city which is honored with the presence of the emperor and the senate and enjoys equal [civil] privileges with the old imperial Rome should, in ecclesiastical matters also, be magnified as she is and rank next after her.

The text goes on to grant the bishop of Constantinople jurisdiction over the civil dioceses of Pontus, Asia and Thrace—creating a "patriarchate" comparable to those which were already *de facto* headed by Rome, Alexandria and Antioch—and also bestowing upon the bishop of the capital the right to send missionary bishops to "barbarian lands" situated beyond these dioceses.

Historically, the creation of a Constantinopolitan primacy

by the Councils of Constantinople and Chalcedon was directed primarily against what the emperors considered as an exaggerated power of Alexandria, which tended to impose its particular (and sometimes extremist) interpretation of the faith defined in Nicaea and in Ephesus. Indeed, the Councils of Constantinople and Chalcedon gave a definition of that faith which was more acceptable in Antioch and in Rome. However, the formulation of canon 28 of Chalcedon had even wider implications. It affirmed that the privileges of the "Old Rome" were, like the new privileges of Constantinople, granted by "the fathers," that, consequently, they were of human origin and had no connection with the *logia* of Christ addressed to the apostle Peter. In the fifth century, the idea that the Roman bishop enjoyed primacy because he was the successor of Peter was firmly implanted in Rome and served as the main argument of Pope Leo the Great (440-461) when he protested against the adoption of canon 28 at Chalcedon. Furthermore, the prevailing Roman interpretation of the Eastern primacies was that they were also created by Peter, who personally preached in Antioch (cf. Gal. 2) and, according to tradition, sent his disciple Mark to Alexandria. In this scheme, there was no place for any primacy of Constantinople. To the Easterners, however, the scheme seemed quite artificial. They did not consider that the apostolic foundation of a church involved jurisdictional rights, since so many Eastern cities—Jerusalem in the first place—could claim them, and interpreted all primacies, including those or Alexandria, Antioch and indeed Rome, in a pragmatic way, as a natural consequence of their being "major cities." Hence, the new role of Constantinople appeared quite natural to them.

The difference between the Eastern and the Western approach to the problem of primacies is best illustrated by the history of the church of Jerusalem. Mentioned under its Roman name of Aelia by the Council of Nicaea (canon 7), it remained in the orbit of Antioch until, using its prestige as a pilgrimage center, it acquired the status of a separate patriarchate, comprising the three provinces of Palestine, after 451, as a result of a clever manoeuvering of its bishop Juvenal (431-458). However, in the order of patriarchates, its apostolic or indeed divine foundation was never used to justify anything but a fifth place.

Thus, as Emperor Justinian embarked on a major attempt to restore the empire's universality by reconquest of the West, the Byzantine vision of the universal Church was that of a *pentarchy* of patriarchs—Rome, Constantinople, Alexandria, Antioch and Jerusalem—, united in faith, equal in rights, but strictly bound by an order of precedence enshrined in imperial law. The Monophysite schism, the Islamic conquest and, in the West, the rise of the papacy soon ended the pentarchy as a concrete historic reality, but it will survive as an ideal of the Byzantine vision of the Christian universe.

3. The "Great Church" of Constantinople

With the decline of ancient Rome and internal dissension in the other Eastern patriarchates, the church of Constantinople became, between the sixth and the eleventh centuries, the richest and the most influential center of Christendom. As a symbol and expression of this universal prestige, Justinian built a church which, even today, is seen as the very masterpiece of Byzantine architecture: the temple of the Holy Wisdom, "Haghia Sophia." Completed in the amazingly short period of four and a half years (532-537), it became the very heart of Christian Byzantium. The term of "Great Church," first applied to the building itself, designated also the patriarchate, whose cathedral church St. Sophia would remain for over nine centuries. In its main and most visible structure, it consists of an immense square hall covered by a wide dome. The light coming from all directions, the marble walls and the golden mosaics have often been felt as representing the cosmos upon which heaven itself had descended. The overwhelming impression produced by the building upon Greeks and foreigners alike is recorded in numerous contemporary texts.

Under John the Faster (582-595), the title of "ecumenical patriarch" was adopted by the archbishop of the capital. This title was interpreted by Pope Gregory the Great as a challenge to papal primacy, but, in fact, it did not imply a claim to universal jurisdiction but rather to a permanent and essentially political position in the *oikoumene, i.e.,* the *orbis christianorum,* ideally headed by the emperor. Together with the latter, the patriarch was responsible for the well-being of society, occasionally substituting for the emperor, as regent. This was the case, for example, with Patriarch Sergius (610-638) under Emperor Heraclius (610-641) and with Patriarch Nicholas Mysticus (901-907, 911-925) during the infancy of Emperor Constantine VII. The respective rights and duties of the dyarchy of emperor and patriarch are described in a legal compendium of the ninth century, known as the *Epanagoge.*

Ecclesiastical canons and imperial laws regulated the election of patriarchs. Justinian (*Novella* 174, issued in 565) required that an electoral college of clergy and "important citizens"—not unlike the college of cardinals in Rome—participate in the election; but laity, with the exception of the emperor, were soon eliminated from the process. According to Constantine Porphyrogenitus,[2] the metropolitans of the synod chose three candidates, so that the emperor could pick one, while reserving the option of making another choice as well. This openly admitted role of the emperor in patriarchal election—which formally contradicted canonical prescriptions against the choice of clerics by civil rulers—was perhaps understandable in view of the political functions of the "ecumenical" patriarch in the state itself.

Once enthroned in St. Sophia, the patriarch administered the church together with a "permanent synod" of metropolitans and a large staff. His jurisdiction covered the civil dioceses of Asia, Pontus and Thrace, which in the seventh century included 424 episcopal sees in Asia and Europe.[3] In the eighth century, the diocese of Illyricum and also southern Italy were included in the patriarchate, at the expense of the church of Rome. In addition, numerous missionary dioceses subject to the patriarchate existed in the Caucasus, the Crimea

[2]*De Ceremoniis* II, 14, ed. Reiske (Leipzig, 1751-54).
[3]*Ibid.* II, 54.

THE BYZANTINE CHURCH 21

and Slavic lands. A spectacular new expansion took place with the conversion of Russia (988).

Chosen mostly from among the secular clergy of Constantinople in the earlier period, more frequently from among the monastics after the thirteenth century, and sometimes promoted directly from the lay state, the patriarchs, with a few exceptions, were men of learning and, sometimes, authentic saints. Their list includes men like Gregory of Nazianzus (379-381), John Chrysostom (398-404), Tarasius (784-806), Nicephorus (806-815), Photius (858-867, 877-886), Arsenius Autorianus (1255-1259, 1261-1265), Philotheus Coccinus (1354-1355, 1364-1376). On the other hand, the often stormy politics of the court and the never-ending christological controversies necessarily involved the patriarchs. Some of them— like Nestorius (428-431)—entered history with the reputation of heresiarchs. Others, particularly during the reign of Heraclius and Constans II, followed the imperial policy of the moment and gave support to Monotheletism. This was the case of Sergius (610-638), Pyrrhus (638-641), Paul (641-653) and Peter (654-666). They were condemned as heretics by the Sixth Ecumenical Council (680).

The Roman popes never formally recognized the title of "ecumenical patriarch" for incumbents of the see of Constantinople, and they occasionally obtained from Constantinople verbal acceptance of their own "Petrine" interpretation of the Roman primacy. Nevertheless they could do nothing but acknowledge the real influence of the imperial church, especially during their visits to Constantinople. One of them, Pope Martin I (649-655), was even judged and deposed in Constantinople by an ecclesiastical tribunal presided over by the Monothelite Patriarch Peter.

Thus, the see of Constantinople, with its "equal privileges" with the "Old Rome," was an essential fact of history, but it certainly could not pretend to the charisma of doctrinal infallibility.

4. The Arab Conquest and Iconoclasm

In the seventh century, when the Islamic wave swept the ancient Christian and Byzantine provinces of Palestine, Syria, Egypt and North Africa, stopping only at the very gates of Constantinople, most Christians of those areas had already severed their ties with the imperial Orthodox Church. Egypt had been almost entirely Monophysite since the middle of the fifth century; so were the Armenian regions in eastern Asia Minor, and at least half of the population in Syria. The efforts of Justinian, and later the doctrinal compromises of Heraclius and his Monothelite successors, had failed to unify the empire religiously. Furthermore, the schism, which started with a dispute between Greek-speaking theologians concerning the true identity of Jesus Christ, had developed into cultural, ethnic and political antagonism. In the Middle East, the Chalcedonian Orthodox camp was now composed almost entirely of Greeks loyal to the empire, whereas the indigenous communities of Copts, Syrians and Armenians refused to accept the faith of the Council of Chalcedon and resented the brutal attempts of the imperial authorities to exile their leaders and impose religious conformity by force.

The Monophysite schism, followed by the Arab invasion, whose success was partially due to dissensions among Christians, left the patriarch of Constantinople alone as the foremost representative of Eastern Christianity within the borders of the empire. Of course, in Alexandria, Antioch and particularly in Jerusalem, there remained Orthodox (or "Melchite," i.e., "imperial") minorities, headed by their patriarchates, but they could have little influence in the universal Church. For them, during the long centuries of Islamic occupation, the problem would be one of survival, which they solved primarily by looking for and receiving cultural, psychological and material help from Constantinople.

Reduced in size to the limits of eastern Asia Minor, the southern Balkan peninsula and southern Italy, the Byzantine Empire found enough strength for a successful resistance to Islam. But during that struggle, between 726 and 843, Byzantine Christendom went through a major crisis which contributed much to its medieval shape: the crisis of iconoclasm and the eventual triumph of Orthodox iconodulia. The doctrinal, philosophical and theological background of Byzantine iconoclasm cannot be reduced to a simple scheme. The reluctance to use and venerate images in worship goes back to the prohibition of any representation of God in the Old Testament. Iconoclasm was also consistent with a certain Platonic spiritualism, popular among Greek Christians, which explains why trends hostile to images existed in early Christianity. It is beyond doubt, however, that the iconoclastic movement of the eighth century was started by imperial initiative and had political implications in the framework of the struggle of the empire against Islam. Indeed, the belief in the absolute transcendence and invisibility of God and sharp polemics against Christian "idolatry" were essential arguments of the Muslim anti-Byzantine propaganda. Emperors Leo III (717-741) and Constantine V (741-775), sponsors of iconoclasm, decided to "cleanse" the Christian Church from "idolatry" in order to fight Islamic ideology more successfully.

As images of Christ, the Virgin and the saints began to be removed from public places and churches by order of Leo III (beginning in 726), Patriarch Germanus (715-730)— and also Pope Gregory II (715-731)—stood up for the veneration of icons, and a theologian living in a Muslim-dominated area, John of Damascus, wrote treatises against iconoclasm. The argument was: God, though invisible by nature, can and must be represented in His human nature, as Jesus Christ. According to the Orthodox, iconoclasm amounted to a denial of the incarnation. An iconoclastic council, organized by Emperor Constantine V in 754, answered that a representation of Christ in His human nature implied either a denial of His divinity, which is inseparable from His humanity, or a Nestorian breaking-up of His one person into two beings. The debate continued—primarily on those christological grounds—for over a century. Iconoclastic repressions were severe, and the Orthodox counted many martyrs in their midst. Besides John of Damascus, two major Byzantine theologians stood for the veneration of icons: Theodore of Studius

(759-826) and Patriarch Nicephorus (806-815). Popular support for veneration was lead by the influential and numerous monastic communities, which faced imperial wrath. Finally, the Seventh Ecumenical Council (also known as Second Council of Nicaea) was gathered by Empress Irene in 787; it rejected iconoclasm and endorsed the *veneration (proskynesis)* of icons, carefully distinguishing it from *worship (latreia)*, which is due to God alone. After a second upsurge of iconoclasm, there was a final "Triumph of Orthodoxy" in 843.

The consequences of the crisis were both theological and cultural. In the Orthodox East, images were forever accepted as a major means of communion with God, so that art, theology and spirituality became inseparable. On another level, the struggle on behalf of the icons enhanced the prestige of monasticism, which was acknowledged, more than in earlier centuries, as an effective counter-weight in Byzantine society to the arbitrary rule of the emperors. But, at the same time, the iconoclastic crisis furthered the estrangement between the Eastern and the Western halves of Christendom. Fully involved in the struggle with Islam, the iconoclastic emperors neglected their power and influence in Italy. Furthermore, in retaliation against the pope's opposition to their religious policies, they transfered Illyricum, Sicily and southern Italy from papal jurisdiction to that of the patriarchate of Constantinople. Humiliated and abandoned by his traditional protectors and fearful of Lombard invasions, Pope Stephen II met with the Frankish King Pepin the Short in Ponthion (754), accepted the king's protection and obtained his sponsorship in the creation of a papal state in Italy made up of formed Byzantine territories.

5. Missions: The Conversion of the Slavs

The loss of the Middle East to the Arabs and the gradual estrangement between East and West could have led the patriarchate of Constantinople to become the center of a Greek church, limited ethnically and culturally. However, immediately following the end of iconoclasm, the church of Byzantium began a spectacular missionary expansion which led to the Christianization of Eastern Europe. In 860-861, two brothers from Thessalonica, Constantine and Methodius, successfully preached Christianity to the Khazars in the Crimea. In 863, they were sent to the Slavs of central Europe, since Rastislav, prince of the Moravians, had requested missionaries from Byzantium. The Moravian mission of the two brothers began with a complete and literal translation of Scripture and the liturgy into the language of the Slavs. In the process, the two brothers created a new alphabet and a vocabulary suitable for Christian usage. Furthermore, they justified the policy of translating essential Christian texts into the vernacular by reference to the miracle of Pentecost (Acts 3), when the apostles were given the gift of many languages. This policy was met with fierce opposition on the part of competing Frankish missionaries, with whom the two brothers had discussions in Moravia and, later, in Venice, and whom they accused of holding "the heresy of the three language" (*i.e.,* the belief that Christian worship is possible only in Hebrew, Greek and Latin). In a prologue to the Gospel of John, written in Slavic verse, Constantine (better known under his monastic name of Cyril) paraphrased St. Paul (I Cor. 14:19) in proclaiming the right of the Slavs to hear the Word in their own language: "I had rather speak five words that all the brethren will understand than ten thousand words which are incomprehensible."[4] Eventually, the Byzantine missionaries were forced by the Germans to leave Moravia. Travelling to Rome, they nevertheless received the formal support of Popes Hadrian II (867-872) and John VIII (872-882). After the death of Constantine-Cyril in Rome, Pope Hadrian consecrated Methodius as bishop of Sirmium and charged him with the mission to the Slavs. However, the authority of the pope was insufficient to secure the success of the mission. Methodius was tried and imprisoned by German bishops, and Moravia entered the orbit of Latin Christianity. Eventually, the entire medieval church of the West would

---

[4]Tr. R. Jacobson, "St. Constantine's Prologue to the Gospel," *St. Vladimir's Theological Quarterly* 7 (1963), pp. 15-18.

adopt the principle of accepting only Latin in the liturgy, in sharp contrast with the Byzantine missionary development, based upon translations and use of the vernacular. The Moravian disciples of Constantine-Cyril and Methodius found refuge in Bulgaria, particularly in the Macedonian center of Ohrid (St. Clement, St. Naum), where Slavic Christianity prospered in accordance with the Byzantine model. The conversion of Bulgaria was practically contemporary with the Moravian mission. As in Moravia and many other areas of Europe, the political leadership of the country was instrumental in the conversion, which had been prepared by missionaries and diplomats coming from Byzantium. Thus, in 865, Khan Boris of Bulgaria became a Christian, with Emperor Michael III acting as his godfather. After an attempt at joining the jurisdiction of Rome (866-869), Boris finally placed his country in the Byzantine religious orbit. His son and successor, Symeon (893-927), and later the Western-Bulgarian Tsar Samuel (976-1014) made their respective capitals of Preslav and Ohrid into important religious centers, where Byzantine liturgy, theology and religious culture were successfully appropriated by Slavs. And since Byzantine canon law admitted in principle a multiplicity of ecclesiastical centers, Bulgarian tsars created independent patriarchates in their capitals. However, as they also began to claim the imperial title for themselves, Byzantium, having regained its former military might, especially under Emperor Basil II (976-1025), put a temporary end to the independent existence of Bulgaria. However, it did not entirely suppress the principle and the practice of worship in the Slavic tongue.

Also contemporary was the Byzantine mission to the Russians. In 867, Patriarch Photius, in an encyclical to the eastern patriarchs, announced that the Russians had been converted and had accepted a bishop from Constantinople. This initial conversion concerned only a small group neighboring Byzantine cities in the Crimea. More significant was the conversion of the powerful princess of Kiev, Olga (957), who assumed the Christian name of Helen in honor of the reigning Byzantine empress, and, finally, the "conversion of Russia" which occurred in 988-989 under Prince Vladimir, who took the name of Basil and even married Emperor Basil II's sister, Anna. Under Vladimir, Byzantine Orthodoxy became the official religion of the Russian state, with its major centers in Kiev and Novgorod.

Finally, in the same period, Byzantine documents signal missionary activities in the Caucasus, particularly among the Alans, under the initiative of Patriarch Nicholas Mysticus (901-907, 911-925).

Thus, around the beginning of the second millenium, the Byzantine church exercised its ministry in a territory which extended from the polar regions to the Arab-occupied Middle East, and from the Adriatic to the Caucasus. Its center, Constantinople, seemed to have no rival not only in terms of power or wealth, but also in terms of intellectual, artistic and literary achievements.

6. Schism between East and West

A certain theological polarization between the Greek East and the Latin West goes back at least to the fourth century. For instance, trinitarian theology was formulated differently by the Cappadocian fathers on the one hand, and St. Augustine on the other, with a greater insistence on the Greek side upon personal distinctiveness, and a greater emphasis on the Latin side upon a philosophical definition of God as one simple essence. Also, Latins and Greeks often adopted divergent attitudes towards the Monophysites, with the Old Rome remaining much more rigidly attached to the very formula of the "two natures" adopted at Chalcedon, whereas Constantinople was more ready to remember that St. Cyril of Alexandria also spoke of "one incarnate nature." There was also increasing variety in disciplinary and liturgical practices.

However, more than any other difference, ecclesiological issues and, in particular, the increasingly divergent understanding of the primacy of Rome began to strain relations between East and West. As we have seen earlier, the leadership position of Rome—never denied in Byzantium—was explained (as also the eminence of the various eastern sees) in a pragmatic way without any decisive importance being attached to apostolicity. This pragmatic explanation was enshrined in conciliar legislation which the East considered as common tradition, even if Romans had in due time protested the publication of texts which denied that Rome had received its primacy from Christ, through the apostle Peter. Happily, both sides refrained for centuries from pushing these divergent positions to the point of final rupture. In the ninth, tenth and eleventh centuries, however, conflicts began to accumulate in which cultural and political elements were intermingled with doctrinal and disciplinary issues.

The issue of the *Filioque* became, in the iconoclastic and post-iconoclastic period, a major source of conflict. The creed of Nicaea-Constantinople, which served as the principle expression of faith in the universal Church, had been interpolated in the West with the Latin word *Filioque*. The interpolation, first made in Spain in the seventh century, affirmed that the Holy Spirit proceded from the Father *and the Son.* The interpolated text soon became popular—partly because it suited the Augustinian explanation of the Trinity better than the original uninterpolated version—and, in the eighth century, was used throughout Frankish Europe. Charlemagne and his theologians, who were looking for an opportunity to accuse the competing Eastern Empire with heresy, refused to accept the Acts of the Seventh Ecumenical Council (787) because they contained the original form of the creed and traditional Greek formulations of the trinitarian dogma. The so-called *Libri Carolini* addressed to the pope by Charlemagne to justify his position were thus the first written monuments in a polemic which would last for centuries. At first, the popes defended the Greek position and opposed the interpolation. Only in 866 did Pope Nichlas I sponsor in Bulgaria the activities of German missionaries, implicitly condoning the use of the interpolated creed among newly converted Bulgarians. Patriarch Photius, who considered Bulgaria as part of his jurisdiction, became the first Greek theologian to give a complete refutation of the *Filioque*. The conflict between Pope Nicholas and Photius, which concerned issues of authority as well as the *Filioque* problem, was eventually solved. In 879-880, a solemn council, with legates of Pope John VIII present, condemned the interpolation and sanctioned a reconciliation between Rome and Constantinople. However, Frankish influence upon the weakened papacy of the tenth century led to an almost routine acceptance of the *Filioque* in Rome (probably in 1014), which made the schism practically inevitable.

Other issues of discipline and liturgy contributed to the division. These included the use of unleavened bread ("azymes") in the eucharist by the Latins, the enforced celibacy of priests in the West (while the East allowed the ordination of married men), and differences in the rules of fasting. Such issues were particularly prominent during a famous incident which opposed the legates of Pope Leo IX to Patriarch Michael Cerularius (1054) and which is frequently —and mistakenly—seen as the beginning of the schism. In reality, it was rather an unsuccessful attempt at healing a division which existed already.

As polemics continued—and were greatly enhanced by national hatred after the sack of Constantinople by the Fourth Crusade in 1204—other issues were added to the list, such as the Latin doctrine of purgatory and the exact moment of consecration of the holy gifts in the eucharist (the "words of institution" in the Latin tradition, to which the Greeks opposed the existence in all Eastern liturgies of an invocation of the Holy Spirit, or *epiclesis*, after the words of institution). Each of these issues—as also the issue of the *Filioque*—could have been resolved if the two churches had been able to agree upon a criterion of authority. However, especially after the Gregorian reform of the eleventh century, the papacy could not allow its own unique authority to be questioned. On the Byzantine side, the official position of the church was always that differences between churches were to be solved only by councils, and that the honorary primacy of Rome did not exempt the pope from being answerable to conciliar judgment.

Numerous attempts at reunion took place in the late Byzantine period, initiated by the popes and by emperors of the Palaeologan dynasty (1261-1453). In 1274, representatives of Emperor Michael VIII were present at the Council

of Lyons, where his personal confession of faith, accepting the
Roman faith, was read. Motivated primarily by political reasons, Michael imposed a pro-union patriarch, John Beccus,
on the church of Constantinople. But such a union, imposed
basically by force, did not survive the death of Michael
(1381). In 1385, a council in Constantinople formally rejected it and approved a detailed—and in some ways open-
minded—refutation of the *Filioque,* drafted by Patriarch
Gregory of Cyprus (1383-1389). More union negotiations
took place throughout the fourteenth century, which saw the
personal conversion to Roman Catholicism of Emperor John
V (1369), a conversion which was not followed by the
church and which was tacitly renounced by John himself. It
is the Western conciliar movement which provoked a radical
change in the attitude of the papacy toward the idea of a real
council of union. After long preliminary negotiations with
Popes Martin V and Eugenius IV, Emperor John VIII, Patriarch Joseph and numerous Greek prelates came to Ferrara
and then to Florence, where the council finally took place
(1438-1439) as Byzantium stood under the immediate threat
of Turkish conquest. After months of debate, an exhausted
Greek delegation signed the decree of union, which accepted
the major doctrinal positions of the Roman Church. Only one
Greek bishop, Mark of Ephesus, refused to sign, but upon the
delegation's return to Byzantium, Mark's position was endorsed by the vast majority of the population and the clergy.
The fall of Constantinople in 1453 put an end to the union
itself and to further negotiations.

Provoked by gradual estrangement, the schism cannot be
formally associated with any particular date or event. Its
ultimate root, however, was clearly a different understanding
of doctrinal authority, which in the West had been concentrated in the person of the pope, whereas the East never
considered that truth could be formally secured by any particular person or institution, and saw no seat of authority
above the conciliar process, involving the bishops but also
requiring a popular consensus.

7. *Theology and Canon Law*

Throughout its entire history, Byzantium kept an uninterrupted tradition of learning going back to antiquity and to the Greek fathers of the Church. Although the imperial university of Constantinople and, particularly, the separate patriarchal school were training future officials of state and church, these institutions were neither the exclusive nor even the principal centers of theological development. Byzantium never witnessed the development of universities and formal scholasticism which played such an immense role in the West from the twelfth century onward. Most Byzantine theologians wrote in an ecclesiastical or monastic context. One should note also that theology never became a monopoly of clerics. Books on theology were published not only by bishops or monks but also by lay intellectuals.

The absence of a structured system of schools provides the probable explanation of why Byzantine theologians seldom undertook systematic presentation of their theology. St. John of Damascus (d. *ca.* 753) wrote an *Exact Exposition of the Orthodox Faith,* but this work is nothing but a short textbook faithfully adhering to formulations accepted in the past, not an original "system." In general, Byzantine theologians limited themselves to particular issues or denounced the heresies of their day. This lack of systematization, however, did imply that they did not believe in the effectiveness of theology. On the contrary, Byzantine spirituality, liturgy and thought always affirmed the possibility of communion with God, accessible to every Christian in the life of the Church. But this accessibility did not include the very *essence* of God, whose transcendence made intellectual or philosophical concepts—the basis for all structured theological "systems"—irrelevant or at least unconvincing. This simultaneous perception of divine transcendence and accessibility is well expressed by St. Gregory of Nyssa, one of the most influential fathers of the Greek church. "In speaking of God," he writes, "when there is question of His essence, that is *the time to keep silence* (cf. Eccles. 3:7). When, however, it is a question of His operation, a knowledge of which can come down even to us, that is *the time to speak* of His omnipotence by telling of His works and explaining His deeds, and to use words to this extent."[5]

The definition of the canon of Scripture—that basic source of all Christian theology—did not receive in the East its final form before the Synod in Trullo (692), which endorsed the so-called "longer" canon, including Old Testament books preserved in Aramaic and in Greek (also known as "apocrypha"). But several earlier fathers stood for the "shorter" (Hebrew) canon, and even John of Damascus in the eighth century considers Wisdom and Ecclesiasticus as "admirable" but does not include them in the canon proper. The Book of Revelation was generally omitted from the canon in the fourth and fifth centuries, and never entered liturgical usage in Byzantium.

The magisterium of the Church—which was obviously not limited by Scripture alone—found its most authoritative expression in the so-called "ecumenical" councils. Seven "ecumenical" council were formally accepted as such. These were the Councils of Nicaea I (325), Constantinople I (381), Ephesus I (431), Chalcedon (451), Constantinople II (553), Constantinople III (680) and Nicaea II (787). Formally, imperial convocation and approval gave the councils their authority in the empire, but for the Church a lasting consensus or "reception" was also necessary. Thus, several councils—Ephesus II (449), Hieria (753), Florence (1438-1439) —received imperial sanction, but were eventually rejected by the Church. Other councils, though not formally "ecumenical," were recognized as highly authoritative, for instance the Photian "Great Council of St. Sophia" (879-880) and the councils of 1341, 1347 and 1351, held in Constantinople, which endorsed the distinction between essence and energy in God in connection with the so-called "hesychast controversies."

The trinitarian theology of the Cappadocian fathers (fourth century) and Chalcedonian and post-Chalcedonian

[5]*On Eccles.* 7, ed. W. Jaeger (Leiden, 1962), p. 415.

Christology, as defined by the recognized ecumenical councils, provided the fundamental framework of all theological thought, as we have seen earlier in reference to iconoclasm. It is also in the same framework that the so-called "mystical theology" of the Byzantines must be interpreted.

The term "mystical theology" comes from the title of one of the treatises of Pseudo-Dionysius (fifth-sixth century) and reflects the notion that communion with God cannot be identified with any form of created knowledge, and that it is best expressed in negative or "apophatic" terms: God is *nothing* of what the created human mind is able to conceive. But, at the same time, the Greek patristic tradition affirms *deification (theosis)* as the goal of human existence, becoming accessible in the God-man, Jesus Christ. Best formulated by perhaps the most creative of all Byzantine theologians, St. Maximus the Confessor (*ca.* 580-662), who was also the main spokesman against Monotheletism, the doctrine of deification inspired a number of spiritual and mystical writers. The Byzantines generally recognized that, inasmuch as deification "in Christ" was not a doctrine reducible to rational categories, it was best expressed by those who experienced it. In general, Byzantine Christianity gave greater credit to saints or prophets as authorities in the field of theology than did the Latin West. Perhaps the greatest and the most striking of Byzantine prophets and mystics is Symeon the New Theologian (d. 1022). In some circles, particularly monastic, charismatic mysticism could even lead to a denial of the sacraments and of the institutional church. This sectarian form of charismaticism, repeatedly condemned, is known as Messalianism or Bogomilism.

One of the areas of intellectual and spiritual tension was, for Byzantine theology, the definition of relationships between the Christian faith and the legacy of ancient Greek philosophy. As a Greek-speaking civilization, Byzantium preserved the writings of ancient authors, and in every generation there were scholars and intellectuals enthusiastically committed to the traditions of ancient philosophy. Some of them, following the example of Origen (d. *ca.* 254), attempted to synthesize Greek philosophy and Christian revelation. While Origen and

Origenism were condemned (by the Fifth Ecumenical Council in 553), notions coming from Greek philosophy remained as necessary tools to express the basic dogmas of Christianity. But, at the same time, a great number of Byzantine theologians, particularly among the monks, insisted upon the basic incompatibility between "Athens" and "Jerusalem," the Academy and the Gospel. They were particularly opposed to Platonic idealism and spiritualism, which they considered as incompatible with the Christian doctrine of the incarnation. Sometimes they obtained from official church authorities the formal condemnation of Platonism (cf. particularly the case of John Italus, 1075-1077). Until the end of Byzantium, scholarly humanists (e.g., Michael Psellus, Theodore Metochites, Nicephorus Gregoras, Bessarion, Gemisthus Pletho and others) staunchly defended the heritage of antiquity, but they always did so against some opposition. The tension was never resolved, and in this respect the Byzantine Christian tradition can be easily contrasted with the contemporary Latin West, where, since the beginnings of scholasticism, a new synthesis between Greek philosophy and Christian theology was in the making.

As Byzantine theology avoided rationally structured systematization, so the Byzantine church never bound itself to an exhaustive code of ecclesiastical laws. The councils issued canons related to the structure and administration of the Church, and to discipline, but all these texts reflected the requirements of concrete situations. The canonical requirements were seen as absolute, inasmuch as they reflected the permanent norms of Christian doctrine and ethics, but in many cases the Byzantine church also recognized the possibility that these same norms could be preserved not by applying the letter of the law, but by exercising mercy or condescension. This latter attitude was identified as *oikonomia.* In the New Testament, this term is used to designate God's *plan* for the salvation of mankind (Eph. 1:9-10, 3:2-3), and also the *stewardship* entrusted to the bishops (I Cor. 4:1; Col. 1:24-25; Tit. 1:7). This biblical origin of the term helps to understand the Byzantine canonical notion of *oikonomia,* which was not simply an exception to established rules, but "an imitation of God's love for man,"[6] and implied repentence of the pardoned sinner. Thus, Patriarch Nicholas was ready to exercise *oikonomia* by recognizing the legitimacy of an imperial child born to Emperor Leo VI (886-912) of his uncanonical fourth marriage, but refused to legitimize the marriage itself.

The sources of Byzantine canon law, as they were included in the most standard and comprehensive compendium—the so-called *Nomocanon in Fourteen Titles,* published by Patriarch Photius in 883, and including imperial laws (*nomoi*) and church canons (*kanones*), include the so-called "apostolic canons" (a collection of rules reflecting the practice of the church in Syria in the fourth century), the canons of ecumenical councils, a collection of canons of "local" councils (mainly of the fourth century) and another collection of "canons of the fathers," *i.e.,* an anthology of opinions by prominent bishops of the early church. In many cases, these materials were to be used as authoritative precedents rather than formal rules. They were combined in the *Nomocanon* with imperial laws regulating disciplinary matters, setting guidelines for the election of bishops and defining borders of ecclesiastical provinces and patriarchates. Later, Byzantine canonists used these texts together with commentaries composed in the twelfth century (a period of development in canon law) by Balsamon, Zonaras and Aristenus.

8. Liturgy and Hymnography

The centrality of the liturgy in the life of Byzantine Christian society was perceived by the Byzantines themselves and by foreigners alike. Celebrated in the magnificent framework of St. Sophia—the "Great Church" built by Justinian—, it was remembered as a "heavenly" reality by the envoys of the Russian Prince Vladimir who came to Constantinople in 987. Its original forms were directly influenced by the traditions of the church of Antioch, which was closely connected with

[6]Patriarch Nicholas Mysticus, *Ep.* 32, ed. R.J.H. Jenkins and L.G. Westerink (Washington, D.C., 1973), I, p. 236.

the new capital in the late fourth and early fifth centuries. As Constantinople became the center of the entire Christian world, its practices became more eclectic. In the late medieval period, the *Typikon* (*Ordo*) of the Great Church was combined with the monastic traditions, particularly those of the monastery of Studius, and produced a synthetic system of liturgical celebrations which in turn integrated (in the thirteenth and fourteenth centuries) the liturgical traditions of the Lavra of St. Sabbas in Palestine.

By the ninth century, the two eucharistic canons in standard use in Byzantium were those attributed to St. Basil of Caesarea and St. John Chrysostom. Translated into many languages, they were adopted in the entire Orthodox world. The ancient liturgy attributed to St. James was also used locally. From the sixth century, the eucharistic liturgy—now celebrated in the huge cathedral of St. Sophia before big crowds—was embellished with a number of symbolic actions, losing some of its original communal character. Symbolic interpretations, inspired particularly by the book of Pseudo-Dionysius known as *Ecclesiastical Hierarchy,* presented the liturgy as an earthly representation of heavenly realities, standing between the individual Christian and God. Such ideas were primarily the result of an integration of Neoplatonic ideas into Christian thought. However, the original, mostly pre-Constantinian meaning of the liturgy was generally well preserved in the central parts of the rite itself, as distinct from its interpretations. Later commentators—for example Nicholas Cabasilas in the fourteenth century—recovered the christocentric, communal and sacramental dimensions of the eucharist.

Besides the central mystery of the eucharist, the Byzantine tradition also insisted upon the importance of *baptism* (always celebrated through triple immersion), of *chrismation* (the equivalent of the Western confirmation, but celebrated by a priest, who anoints the candidate with holy chrism), and of other sacraments which sometimes included in their number the rite of monastic tonsure and of burial.[7]

After the merger of the "cathedral" and the "monastic"

---

[7]Theodore of Studius, *Ep.* II, 165, PG 99, col. 1524.

liturgical traditions, the liturgical year always combined several cycles, each providing its own hymnographical material. The regular daily cycle, contained in a book called the *Horologion* (the "Book of Hours"), gives the text of the unchangeable structure of vespers, compline (*apodeipnon*), midnight prayer (*mesonyktikon*), matins (*orthros*) and the four canonical "hours." The feast of Easter is the changeable key for the yearly and weekly cycles. The Easter cycle includes the period of Lent, with proper hymns contained in a book known as the *Triodion,* and the festal period itself, with hymns contained in the *Pentekostarion.* A cycle of eight weeks repeats itself throughout the year, starting after Pentecost, with hymns contained in the *Oktoekhos* (the "Book of Eight Tones"). Finally, the twelve parts of the *Menaion* ("Book of Months") contain all the hymnographic material proper to the saints of every day. The detailed and highly complicated regulations about the various combinations, which depend on the changes of the date of Easter, are described in the *Typikon,* whose final shape is that of the fourteenth century.

Of all Christian medieval traditions, the Byzantine one is the richest in terms of its hymnographic legacy. Poetically and theologically, the Byzantine hymns constitute an immense literary corpus, which has often in history served as an effective substitute for both school and pulpit. Unfortunately, the Byzantine *neumes,* or musical signs, have not yet been deciphered except for the liturgical manuscripts of the later period (thirteenth-fourteenth centuries). It has been demonstrated, however, that Byzantine music has its roots in the traditions of the Jewish synagogue of the early Christian period and that its medieval shape was similar to—though probably richer than—Western Gregorian chant.

In composing their hymns, Byzantine hymnographers had to combine theological, poetic and musical skills. Their number include the great Romanus the Melode (sixth century) and many authors of the iconoclastic and post-iconoclastic period (Andrew of Crete, John of Damascus, Cosmas of Maium, Theodore of Studius). Romanus wrote *kontakia,* or poetic homilies, composed of metric stanzas sung by the cantor and accompanied by a refrain repeated by the congregation.

The most famous Byzantine kontakion is probably the so-called Akathistos Hymn to the Virgin Mary, whose popularity never diminished throughout the centuries. In the seventh and eighth centuries, however, the use of kontakia was, in most cases, replaced with a more structured and sophisticated form of liturgical poetry: the *canons*, which combined biblical odes, such as Exod. 15, Deut. 32 and the Magnificat (Luke 1) with newly composed hymns.

Hymnographic creativity, roughly following the models set in the eighth and ninth century, continued throughout the entire medieval period.

9. *The Legacy of Christian Byzantium*

Under the Palaeologan dynasty (1258-1453), the Byzantine Empire barely survived the steady advance of Turkish power in Asia Minor and, later, in the Balkans. During the same period, however, the patriarchate of Constantinople, adapting itself to the new political situation, succeeded not only in maintaining its jurisdiction over vast territories, but also in acquiring greater prestige and authority. As the Latins occupied Constantinople (1204-1261), the patriarch went into exile in Nicaea but continued to be recognized as the mother-church of the Orthodox Slavs. In exile he was more flexible and more generous towards them than his predecessors who resided in the imperial city at the height of its power had been. In 1219, he appointed St. Sava as the first archbishop of an independent Serbian church. In 1235, he recognized the Bulgarian patriarchate of Trnovo. In 1261, the patriarchate returned to Constantinople, which had been recaptured from the Latins. Throughout this entire period, Russia, destined to become the most powerful heir of Byzantine civilisation, remained firmly under the patriarch's ecclesiastical control. As most of Russian principalities were conquered by the Mongols (1237-1240), the "metropolitan of Kiev and all Russia," appointed from Byzantium and frequently a Greek by birth, remained as the single most influential power in Russia. Politically, his prestige was enhanced by the good diplomatic relations which existed between the Byzantine court and the Mongol khans residing in Sarai, on the lower Volga. Abandoning his traditional seat in Kiev, which had been destroyed by the Mongols, the metropolitan moved to northern Russia and established a residence first in Vladimir (1300), then in Moscow (1328), which eventually became both the political and the ecclesiastical capital of Russia. This rise of Moscow, supported by Byzantium, provoked centrifugal movements in the western dioceses of the Russian metropolitanate. For short periods in the fourteenth century, under the pressure of the grand prince of Lithuania and the king of Poland, the patriarch was forced to erect separate metropolitanates in Novgorodok (Lithuania) and Halich (Polish-occupied Galicia). However, by 1390 Byzantine ecclesiastical diplomacy succeeded in reuniting the metropolitanate again.

This extraordinary diplomatic activity of the patriarchate throughout Eastern Europe was not based any longer on the power of the emperor—now quite negligible—but on the prestige of Constantinople as a spiritual and intellectual center of a "commonwealth" of nations. A particular role in maintaining cultural ties was played by the monasteries. The "hesychast" revival, endorsed in Constantinople by a series of church councils (1341, 1347, 1351), had repercussions in all Orthodox countries. Mount Athos, the center of hesychast spirituality, was an international center where Greek, Slavic, Moldavian and Georgian monks received their spiritual formation, copied manuscripts, translated Greek texts into their own languages and frequently served as diplomatic emissaries of the patriarchate. They also frequently occupied episcopal sees throughout Eastern Europe.

However, Serbia (1389) and Bulgaria (1393) soon fell to the Ottoman Turks, and the harmonious relations between the mother-church of Constantinople and the daughter-church of Russia were broken by events connected with the Council of Ferrara-Florence (1438-1439). The Greek Isidore, a Byzantine appointee to the metropolitanate of Russia, signed the decree of union in Florence but was rejected by his flock upon his return to Moscow (1441). In 1448 Russian bishops elected a successor, Metropolitan Jonas, independently from Constantinople and interpreted the fall of Byzantium to the Turks (1453) as divine punishment for the betrayal of Orthodoxy perpetrated in Florence.

In spite of these tragic events, the intellectual and spiritual dynamism shown by the Byzantine church in the last years of its existence made possible the survival of what the French historian Charles Diehl called "Byzance après Byzance." Within the borders of the Ottoman Empire, a patriarchate of Constantinople continued to exist. The patriarch could not use his magnificent cathedral of St. Sophia, which was transformed into a mosque, but by decree of the sultan he became politically responsible for the entire Christian population of the empire, which gave him new powers not only over the Greeks but also over the Slavic and Romanian population of the Balkans. Preserving the full splendor of the Byzantine liturgy, maintaining the traditions of monastic spirituality, particularly on Mount Athos, the patriarchate was occasionally the victim of Muslim persecution and the corruption of the Ottoman court, but it carried on its Byzantine legacy into modern times.

In Russia, meanwhile, Grand Prince Ivan III married the niece of the last Byzantine emperor (1472), and Russians began to see in their powerful capital of Moscow a "new Constantinople" or a "third Rome." However, it is still from Turkish-held Constantinople that the Muscovite princes sought and obtained the recognition of their imperial title and, in 1589, the establishment of a patriarchate in Moscow. The Byzantine legacy remained valid even for them.

II
CHURCH AND STATE

1

Emperor Justinian, the Empire and the Church *

The age of Justinian has attracted for a long time and continues to attract the attention of historians. The understanding of Justinian's personality, his achievements and failures, are so overwhelmingly important for the history of Late Antiquity and Byzantium that analysts and syntheticists alike have produced an abundant literature on the subject.

Of particular significance are the questions raised by Justinian's dealings with the various groups of Christians in the East, questions involving both political, social and religious policy. What was Justinian's attitude toward religion, toward individual religious groups, toward the Church, and toward the theological problem of Christology, which produced in the fifth and sixth centuries the first major and lasting schism in Christendom? Two outstanding issues of Justinian's reign must be examined:

1. The issue of the emperor's role in the religious affairs of an empire which he extended again from Mesopotamia to Spain.

2. The theological issues existing between the official Chalcedonian position and the Monophysites in the sixth century.

*Paper originally presented at a symposium on "Justinian and Eastern Christendom," Dumbarton Oaks, May, 1967, and published in *Dumbarton Oaks Papers* 22 (1968), pp. 45-60.

1.

Reaching the imperial throne in 527, at the age of 45, a mature man with a reasonably long experience in government as principal adviser to his uncle and predecessor Justin, Justinian proceeded to the realization of a gigantic program of reconquest and restoration. His impressive successes in reconquering Africa, Italy and Spain not only bear witness to the military power and political skill of his government; they also manifest the extraordinary prestige of the imperial idea itself, in the eyes of both the local populations of the reconquered areas and the barbarian invaders. Throughout his entire reign Justinian showed constant awareness of this prestige. He was convinced that the strength of the empire lay not only in the success of its army, but also in permanent struggle against the forces of internal disintegration. While his armies were fighting in the West, the North and the East, he was constantly busy building the legal, administrative and economic foundation through which he hoped to ensure the permanence of an empire uniting forever the entire Christian *oikoumene*.

His religious policy obviously expressed the same concern. It was directed, on the one hand, toward the final liquidation of dissident groups—pagans, Samaritans, Christian heretics —which were small enough to be dealt with by simple administrative measures, and on the other toward a severe limitation in the civil rights of those whose simple annihilation was either impossible or undesirable. The Jews found themselves in the last category, but the Monophysites presented by far the major problem.

Professor Francis Dvornik in his article on "Emperors, Popes, and General Councils"[1] has brilliantly shown the political importance acquired by ecclesiastical councils in the post-Constantinian era. Gathered and regulated by the emperor, they were expected to produce definitions of faith which would be regarded as imperial law. However, it can be safely said that one of the major disappointments of Constantine

[1]*Dumbarton Oaks Papers* 6 (1951), pp. 1-23.

and his successors has been the legal ineffectiveness of the system. A law, when issued in a proper form by the proper authority, could not be questioned by law-abiding Roman citizens. Yet every single council gathered since the beginning of the Christian empire was challenged by a more or less substantial opposition: Nicaea by the vast majority of Eastern Christians, Constantinople by Alexandria and Rome, Ephesus by Antioch; not to speak of the various Arian councils, whose rejection by the Orthodox was, in the time of Justinian, glorified as a heroic confession of the true faith. And if Nicaea, Constantinople and Ephesus ended up by being recognized in the major centers of Christendom, this recognition was never unconditional. The East accepted Nicaea only when the Cappadocian fathers produced the necessary clarification of the *homoousion,* clarification which was long regarded as suspect of tritheism in the West. The West, meanwhile, accepted only tacitly the Council of Constantinople (381) and without really agreeing with either the doctrine of the "three hypostases" or the famous canon 3, which gave to the church of Constantinople "privileges equal" to those of Old Rome. The Council of Ephesus, finally, was accepted in Antioch only after a written "formula of union" could be agreed upon in 433.

There is no doubt that the emperors of the second half of the fifth century—especially Zeno and Anastasius—had these precedents in mind when they had to face the fierce opposition of vast numbers of Eastern Christians to the Chalcedonian definition. This is why, one after the other, they preferred to solve the ecclesiastical issues of the day themselves and, avoiding conciliar procedure, to publish decrees on the faith; the most important of those decrees, the *Henotikon* of Zeno (482), was legally enforced until 518, when it was officially rejected by Justin I, probably upon the advice, and certainly with the agreement, of his nephew Justinian. These imperial attempts—none of them successful—were directed at the pacification of the Eastern church, torn apart between the adherents and the opponents of the Council of Chalcedon. The rigid Chalcedonian policy of Marcian and Leo, a logical follow-up of the council itself, proved that coercion alone could not maintain Chalcedonian bishops in the major Oriental sees of Alexandria and Jerusalem. But the opposite policy, favoring Monophysitism, did not work either; the *Encyclical* of Basiliscus (475), disavowing Chalcedon, was successfully opposed by Acacius of Constantinople. And the *Henotikon* itself, the archetype of doctrinal compromise, in spite of a brief initial success in restoring unity between Constantinople and Egypt, soon proved unworkable. On the one hand, its essential ambiguity failed to prevent the continuation in the East itself of the old struggle between Dyophysites and Monophysites; on the other hand, its acceptance by the empire led to irreconcilable opposition on the part of the Christian West, led by the Roman bishop.

Thus, during the entire second half of the fifth century, while no one was prepared to deny in principle the established authority of the emperor in religious affairs, in fact all of the really convinced minorities of each theological party were eventually ready to challenge imperial will, if only it opposed their fundamental convictions. Neither did Marcian and Leo succeed in imposing their will upon Timothy Aelurus of Alexandria and the church of Egypt, nor could Anastasius force the patriarchs of his own capital to endorse his Monophysite interpretation of the *Henotikon*. However, both Monophysites and Chalcedonians were happy to enjoy imperial support against each other when such support was made available to them.

Thus, in 518, when Justinian, with his wide imperial ambitions, gathered up the reins of power under the patronage of his uncle Justin I, he had to face a rather paradoxical situation: as a result of the policy of Anastasius, two major ecclesiastical centers, Alexandria and Antioch, were solidly under Monophysite control and enjoyed the very able leadership of the best theologian of the post-Chalcedonian Greek East, Severus of Antioch. Constantinople and Palestine were the only reliable centers of Chalcedonian orthodoxy in the East. However, the church of the "New Rome" was deprived of the support which it could have expected from the pope of the "Old Rome" because the bishops of Constantinople, while solidly Chalcedonian and even suffering for their faith under

Anastasius, were keeping in the diptychs the name of Acacius, the architect of Zeno's unionist policy. Rejected as "Chalcedonian" by what looked very much like a majority of Eastern Christians, the bishops of the capital—who were supposed to occupy a central role in the policy of unifying the empire— were also rejected by Rome as not Chalcedonian enough. Divided in three major segments—Rome, the Chalcedonian East and the Monophysites—the imperial church could obviously not fulfill its function of unifying the Christian *oikoumene*. Justinian was thus faced with the apparently insurmountable task of bringing Rome, Constantinople and the Monophysites together.

To achieve his goal, the emperor used a variety of tactical methods ranging from direct coercion to free theological discussion with opposition groups. At no time was there in his mind any doubt that the Council of Chalcedon was to be considered a permanent expression of the Christian faith: in his *Novella* 131, issued in 545, he declared the canons of the four councils of Nicaea, Constantinople, Ephesus and Chalcedon to be imperial "laws" and the doctrinal definition of those councils to be "sacred writings." For Justinian, faithfulness to Chalcedon was not only a matter of theological conviction but also of urgent political expediency. During the reign of Justin, when Justinian was already in charge of ecclesiastical policy, and in the first years of his own reign which coincided with the reconquest of Africa and Italy, reconciliation with the Roman Church was obviously for him a concern of first priority. There is no doubt that in his own mind, the prestige of the "ancient Rome," and hence that of its bishops, was very great; but this prestige was also an essential aspect of his political plans in the West: the empire simply could not restore its control over its former Western territories unless the emperors and the bishops of Rome acted in unison.

On several occasions, especially in letters he addressed to the popes, Justinian mentioned Rome's "apostolicity." In writing to John II in 533, for example, the emperor "gives honor to the apostolic see," honors the pope as "his father," and "hastens to inform him about the state of the churches."[2] At no other time in the entire history of the Christian Church was the bishop of Rome able formally to impose upon the church of Constantinople the removal from the diptychs of two imperial names—those of Zeno and Anastasius—and of five successive Byzantine patriarchs; however, this is precisely what occurred in 519, when the Roman legates, met by the *comes* Justinian ten miles away from the city, restored communion between the "two Romes" on the basis of the strict adherence to the decrees of Chalcedon, which, according to the popes, had been betrayed by Zeno's *Henotikon*.

However, Justinian's attitude toward the church of Old Rome, which will be inherent in his dealings with the East as well, can be fully understood only against the general background of his view of the Christian *oikoumene*. And there is no alternative for me but to quote here the famous preamble of his edict—also known as the Sixth *Novella*—addressed on April 17, 535, to Epiphanius of Constantinople: "There are two greatest gifts which God, in his love for man, has granted from on high: the priesthood and the imperial dignity. The first serves (ὑπηρετουμένη) divine things, while the latter directs and administers human affairs; both, however, proceed from the same origin and adorn the life of mankind. Hence, nothing should be such a source of care to the emperors as the dignity of the priests, since it is for their (imperial) welfare that they constantly implore God. For if the priesthood is in every way free from blame and possesses access to God, and if the emperors administer equitably and judiciously the state entrusted to their care, general harmony (συμφωνία τις ἀγαθή) will result and whatever is beneficial will be bestowed upon the human race."[3]

To understand the full significance of this text it is important to remember that it is only a preamble to a longer

---

[2]*Codex Justinianus,* I, 1, 7, ed. P. Krueger, in *Corpus juris civilis* II (Berlin, 1929), p. 2.

[3]*Novella* VI, ed. R. Schoell, in *Corpus juris civilis* III (Berlin, 1928), pp. 35-36. Cf. the excellent analysis of this and parallel texts of Justinian in F. Dvornik, *Early Christian and Byzantine Political Philosophy: Origins and Background* 2 (Dumbarton Oaks Studies 9, 2, Washington, D.C., 1966), pp. 815-819.

constitution on church discipline where Justinian defines what he means by the "dignity of the priesthood"; the real object of the Sixth *Novella* is to legislate on the marital status of the clergy, on church property, on episcopal residence, on clergy selection and education, on obstacles to ordination, and on the legal status of the clergy. These legal measures, which constitute the real core of the Sixth *Novella,* are essential for the appreciation of what the preamble really means. Obviously, "human affairs," which the emperor considered as being within his imperial competence, included all the legal aspects of the Church's structure, while the "divine things" which were, according to the preamble, in the jurisdiction of the priesthood, consisted exclusively in "serving God," *i.e.,* in praying and in performing the sacraments. The "harmony" itself mentioned in the text is not a harmony between two powers or between two distinct societies, the Church and the State; rather, it is meant to represent the internal cohesion of one single human society, for whose orderly welfare on earth the emperor alone is responsible. In Justinian's *legal* thinking there is actually no place at all for the Church as a society *sui generis.* The Empire and the Church are one single body of the faithful administered by a twofold, God-given hierarchy;[4] theoretically, a duality is preserved between the *imperium* and the *sacerdotium,* but inasmuch as the priesthood's role is to deal with *divine* things, it has almost no *legal* expression; in Justinian's mind the law governs the entirety of *human* polity, and the emperor is sovereign in issuing laws. Ecclesiastical traditions and conciliar decisions are *made laws* by imperial decree, but they have no legal and binding existence by themselves.

Justinian's attitude toward the bishop of Rome is to be understood in this framework. He knows of the "Petrine" or "apostolic" theory of Roman primacy and has no difficulty in speaking about it precisely because—in his mind—only imperial authority can give it a binding force, relevant to "human affairs." And because the authority of the bishop of Rome

[4]A good general discussion of Justinian's thinking on this point in A. Schmemann, *The Historical Road of Eastern Orthodoxy* (New York, 1963), pp. 144-153.

is important for his political plans, he is ready in 519 to sacrifice the dignity of the patriarch of Constantinople to win the pope's support. Popes John I and Agapetus who visited Constantinople in 525 and 536 respectively in the rather humiliating capacity of ambassadors of the Arian Ostrogothic kings Theodoric and Theodahad, were the objects of the greatest attention and their primacy was recognized. The political mission with which the Goths had entrusted them failed in both cases, but their religious leadership was emphasized, as if to prepare the church of Rome for the role it would have to play in the Orthodox empire after the victory in Italy. Meanwhile, a few years later, when the pope was firmly integrated into the imperial system, Justinian has no scruples whatsoever in forcing the unfortunate Vigilius to comply with his policy of unifying Eastern Christendom. And actually, in his edict of 545 (*Novella* 131), he solemnly integrates in the laws of the empire the *political* principle of the precedence between the major sees, as opposed to the "apostolic" principle upon which, especially since St. Leo the Great, the popes were insisting. The edict of 545 confirmed canon 3 of Constantinople and canon 28 of Chalcedon, giving to the patriarch of Constantinople the second rank after the "Old Rome."[5] The principle obviously implied the politico-religious ideology expressed in the Sixth *Novella*: one single emperor and five patriarchs, ruling over one single society of Christians. It is with those five patriarchs that Justinian will attempt to solve the religious problems of his reign. His edict of 543 against Origen is thus addressed specifically to them,[6] and soon Byzantine texts will consider them as the "five senses" of the empire's body.

These and many other facts are plainly sufficient in themselves to accredit the view that the Byzantine theory on the relations between Church and State—or rather on the *absence* of such relations, since Church and State were integrated in each other—can be defined in terms of "caesaropapism."

However, the danger of associating a historical situation of the fifth or sixth century with the notion of "papism"—a

[5] *Corpus juris, ed. cit.,* p. 655.
[6] PG 86, cols. 945D, 981A.

Western Latin phenomenon which took final shape only in the eleventh—is rarely avoided by those who speak of Byzantine "caesaropapism." The notion of "papism" implies the acknowledged existence of a supreme religious power, invested with the legally recognizable right to define matters of faith and morals. Now, the autocracy of the Christian Roman emperors, to which Justinian gave legally its articulate and universal form, and which was shaped along the lines of an earlier Hellenistic tradition of sacralized political power, had constantly to face widespread opposition, especially in the East, from broad masses of Christian clergy and laity who failed to accept the idea that matters of religious faith were to be solved by a single infallible authority. To quote T. M. Parker, theological controversies in the East were "an inextricable mingling of politics and religion at all times, complicated by a participation of laity, as well as clergy, in doctrinal disputes to a degree rarely, if ever, to be found in the West."[7]

Any state, but especially the Roman Empire, and more especially under Justinian, naturally tends to establish, in all the spheres of human life it is able to control, an order governed by law. When he envisaged the empire and Church as one single society, Justinian could not avoid what for him was an obvious obligation, *i.e.,* to extend the competence of law to the sphere of religion. "Caesaropapism" was therefore *built in to* the *legal* scheme which was governing his legislative and political activity. But this scheme had not taken into consideration a fact which was especially true in the East: Christianity was not, in its very essence, a religion of legal authority. Even when the majority of the episcopate tended to follow imperial decrees, there could arise "a force of passive resistance which, if more amorphous than Western insistence upon the rights of the ecclesiastical power, was just as deadening to the blows of Erastianism."[8] This passive resistance is what kept Egypt essentially Monophysite, in spite

[7]*Christianity and the State in the Light of History* (London, 1955), p. 78; cf. also L. Bréhier, *Les institutions de l'Empire byzantin* (Paris, 1949), p. 195-200; F. Dvornik, "The Circus Parties in Byzantium," *Byzantina-Metabyzantina* 1, pt. 1 (New York, 1946), pp. 119-133.

[8]Parker, *op. cit.,* p. 74; cf. L. Bréhier, *op. cit.,* p. 441.

of violent imperial pressure, and it is also what kept Constantinople Chalcedonian under the reign of Anastasius. Both Monophysites and Dyophysites were in agreement on principle—to deny anybody's *absolute* authority in matters of faith. It is not my purpose to determine here whether their respective convictions were determined by true or false belief, by social or economic conditions, or by political factors, but the historical facts seem to lead unavoidably to the conclusion that there was no automatic, external and universally recognized criterion which in the time of Justinian could solve doctrinal disputes. The power of the emperor, in various forms, applied with various degrees of intensity and pressure, naturally claimed to be such a criterion, but imperial autocracy was moderated by the absence, among Christians, of any moral or theological obligation to believe that the emperor had the power to define Christian dogma.

Between the legal structure of the empire, under the absolute rule of the emperor, and the nature of the Christian religion itself, there remained a gap which texts like the Sixth *Novella* were unable to fill completely: what legal texts could do practically was to give to the emperor the absolute upper hand over the *management* of church hierarchy and institutions, but not power over the content of the faith. By appointing the right men in the right ecclesiastical positions, the emperor could certainly influence doctrinal definitions, but the definitions themselves, even when included by the emperors in the *corpus juris*, were not understood as *sources* of new religious beliefs, but as valid, or invalid, necessary, or unnecessary, expressions of a faith which, in principle, had to remain unchanged and was simply supposed to have been "handed down" from the apostles of Christ to later generations. There was, and there will always be in Byzantium, a *gap* between Roman law and Christian faith.[9]

The existence of such a gap is best illustrated by the

[9]In a sense, this gap coincides with the old Roman distinction between *potestas*, effective power, and *auctoritas*, moral prestige, as represented in the letters of Pope Gelasius to Anastasius I; cf. E. Caspar, *Geschichte des Papsttums* 2 (Tübingen, 1933), p. 65 ff., and F. Dvornik, *Early Christian and Byzantine Political Philosophy*, pp. 804-809.

difference with which the role of the emperor in church affairs was treated in the legal documents on the one hand and in theological literature on the other. While texts like the Sixth *Novella*, or the official court acclamations, or even the minutes of ecumenical councils convened by the emperors and run in accordance with legal procedures, emphasize the imperial power of judgement and decision, the writings of the theologians—to whatever theological faction they may belong—treat of the *doctrinal issues themselves* with practically no reference to imperial authority.

Certainly, imperial interventions in religious affairs may also have had a negative effect; non-theological, political or nationalistic motives may have contributed to place a particular geographic area or a group of sectarians in opposition to the imperial church. But A. H. M. Jones has shown in a way which, at least to me, seems convincing that "the evidence for nationalism of any kind in the later Roman Empire is tenuous in the extreme." "The nationalist and socialist theories" [explaining the schisms], he continues, "seem to me to be based on a radical misapprehension of the mentality of the later Roman Empire. Today religion, or at any rate doctrine, is not with the majority of people a dominant issue and does not arouse major passions. Nationalism and socialism are, on the other hand, powerful forces which can and do provoke the most intense feelings. Modern historians are, I think, retrojecting into the past the sentiments of the present age when they argue that mere religious and doctrinal discussion cannot have generated such violent and enduring animosity as that evinced by the Donatists, Arians, or Monophysites, and that the real moving force behind these movements must have been national or class feeling. . . . I would maintain that when the sectarians declared, as they did on our evidence declare: 'We hold the true faith and are the true Church; our opponents are heretics, and never will we accept their doctrine or communicate with them, or yield to the impious government which supports them,' they meant and felt what they said."[10]

[10]"Were Ancient Heresies National or Social Movements in Disguise?," *The Journal of Theological Studies*, N.S. 10 (1959), pp. 297-298.

Each party, one may add, readily used imperial authority
if it was aiding them against their opponents. Thus Monophysitism can hardly be defined simply as an anti-imperial
movement: Monophysite leaders even canonized Anastasius—
and also Theodora—for the help they received, and how gladly, from these imperial figures.

Here is one of the most obvious signs of true greatness
that cannot be denied to Justinian: he himself was, or became,
aware of the unavoidable limitations of his power in doctrinal
matters. Certainly, he fully used his authority at all times, as
had his predecessors; his doctrinal edicts, his ruthless dealing
with recalcitrant popes, patriarchs, bishops and any other
opponents prove it. But he did not stop there, as did Zeno
and Anastasius. He also tried to contribute to a solution of
the theological issues themselves, not by authority or repres-
sion alone, but by pushing Christian thought forward.

2.

The great council gathered in Chalcedon in 451 was the
largest Christian assembly ever held until then. Its proceedings were more orderly and regular than those of other councils; they allowed room for discussion, for study of texts in
commission, and they resulted in a christological formula
which has always been admired for having appropriated, in a
careful and balanced way, the positive elements found in both
the Alexandrian and the Antiochian Christologies.

Nevertheless, it was this balanced Chalcedonian definition
which also provoked the first major and lasting split in Eastern
Christianity. For, as is true of all dogmatic formulae and doctrinal definitions, it not only solved problems but created
new ones. Here are two of many possible examples:

1. The Nicaean Creed had spoken of the Son as "consubstantial" with the Father: Chalcedon, in order to affirm that
in Jesus Christ there were indeed two natures, the divine and
the human, proclaims that He was "consubstantial to the
Father according to His divinity and *consubstantial to us* according to His humanity." Implied in this definition was a

condemnation of Eutyches. In affirming that the Son with the Father had one substance, Nicaea was following the essential Biblical monotheism: there is *one God*. However, by saying that Christ was "consubstantial to us," was Chalcedon implying that there was also *one man?* Obviously, further clarification was needed on the point of how the three are one in God, but the many are not one in humanity.

2. The Council of Chalcedon took the crucial option of speaking of Christ as being *in two natures* (ἐν δύο φύσεσιν), while Dioscorus of Alexandria and the Monophysites were ready to accept the milder Cyrillian formula *of two natures* (ἐκ δύο φύσεων), which would actually permit them to say that in Christ the union "of two natures" resulted concretely in the *one nature* of the Word incarnate. The Chalcedonian option, which is really the dividing point between the Monophysites and the Orthodox, implies that divinity and humanity, while united in Christ, did not merge into each other, but retained their essential characteristics. However, the council was also very careful to maintain the Cyrillian intuition of the *one Christ:* the term ὁ αὐτός ("the same") is used eight times in the short crucial paragraph of the Definition in order to affirm that the *same one* was "born of Father before the ages" and "born of Mary the Theotokos" in the latter days. However, it is precisely the word "nature" (φύσις) that Cyril was using to designate this *identity* of Christ, and "nature" was interchangeable with another term —ὑπόστασις—when Cyril wanted to emphasize the concrete reality of Christ's person.[11] In Antioch meanwhile, the unity of Christ was designated by the word πρόσωπον: Theodore of Mopsuestia and, after him, Nestorius had spoken of the "prosopon of union" in which, or through which, divinity and humanity existed together in Jesus Christ. The Chalcedonian formula introduces a terminological revolution by identifying πρόσωπον and ὑπόστασις: the two natures of Christ, it proclaims, while preserving their properties, meet in one *prosopon* or *hypostasis*. This identification obviously aims at being faithful to Cyril, without shocking the Antio-

[11]Cf. A. Grillmeier, *Christ in Christian Tradition from the Apostolic Age to Chalcedon (451)*, tr. J. S. Bowden (New York, 1965), pp. 409-412.

chenes. However, what the formula does *not* say explicitly is whether the one *hypostasis* of Christ designates the pre-existing Logos, one of the divine *hypostaseis*—"the same one" born of the Father before the ages—or the Antiochian "prosopon of union," *i.e.,* the historical Jesus only.

These ambiguities of the Chalcedonian formula were to be exploited by the Monophysite theologians for almost a century. The tremendous success of Monophysitism would be due also to the surprising lack of major theological minds in the Chalcedonian party. Under the reigns of Leo I, Zeno, Anastasius and Justin I, no one among the Chalcedonians could even approach the theological brilliance of a Philoxenus of Mabbug or a Severus of Antioch, the leaders of the Monophysite party.

Thus, at the beginning of his reign, Justinian was faced by a number of different interpretations of the Chalcedonian formula. It seems to me that, for the sake of order, these interpretations can be reduced to four:

1. The "strict Dyophysites" (I prefer this term to the designation "strict Chalcedonians" used by Charles Moehler[12] and others, which implies an anticipated conclusion) considered Chalcedon as a sanction of Antiochian Christology. The first and greatest representative of this school of thought was Theodoret of Cyrus, the former friend of Nestorius and principal opponent of Monophysitism before and at Chalcedon. The council had lifted the excommunication which Dioscorus had launched against Theodoret at Ephesus in 449, and the latter survived Chalcedon for more than fifteen years, during which period he never stopped writing, and enjoyed increasing prestige. At Chalcedon he was forced, much against his will, to anathematize Nestorius, but he neither officially recanted his theological criticism of Cyril nor refrained from using a purely Antiochian Christology, with polemical anti-Cyrillian undertones. The continuous identity of his christological position is best illustrated by his attitude toward so-called "Theopaschite" formulae, *i.e.,* all expressions which

[12]"Le Chalcédonisme et le Néochalcédonisme en Orient de 451 à la fin du VIe siècle," in Grillmeier and Bacht, *Das Konzil von Chalkedon* 1 (Würzburg, 1951), pp. 637-720.

said, or implied, that the Logos, being "in the flesh," truly *died* on the cross, *e.g.*, that the *subject* of Christ's death was the Logos Himself.

"Theopaschism," however, was indeed the position of Cyril, which he actually read in the Nicaean Creed itself, where "passion" and "crucifixion under Pontius Pilate" are predicated to the Son of God. Consequently, in his Twelfth Anathematism against Nestorius, Cyril proclaims: "If anyone does not confess that the Word of God suffered in the flesh, was crucified in the flesh, tasted of death in the flesh and became first born of the dead, since He, as God, is life and life-creating, let him be anathema."[13] Theodoret's negative attitude toward Cyril's position on this remained constant before and after Ephesus as well as before and after Chalcedon: in his refutation of the Anathematisms, as well as in the synopsis of theology known as the *Haereticarum fabularum compendium* and published around 453, he rejects "Theopaschism" with the same virulence. An argument based on a Platonic concept of man—an immortal soul imprisoned in a mortal body—plays an important role in Theodoret's thought. The resurrection, he argues, was the resurrection of the body of Christ, not that of His soul or of divinity; for if the soul is immortal, how much more divinity? The death of Christ was a separation between the soul and the body; His resurrection, their reunion through the power of divinity which remained attached to both.[14] According to Theodoret, it is obviously inappropriate to speak of the "death of God." Maintaining contacts with the Nestorians in Persia, he explained to them his interpretation of Chalcedon: the concept of one *hypostasis* in Christ, he wrote, is used by the council in the sense in which Theodore of Mopsuestia used *prosopon,* and the definition is nothing else than the vindication of the old Christology of the school of Antioch.[15]

---

[13]*Acta conciliorum oecumenicorum,* ed. E. Schwartz, I, 1, p. 92.

[14]The refutation of Cyril's anathematisms, PG 76, cols. 404C, 449BC, etc. *Haer. fab. comp.* V, 15, PG 83, cols. 504B-505A.

[15]Letter to John of Aigaion, in F. Nau, "Documents pour servir à l'histoire de l'église nestorienne," *Patrologia Orientalis* 13 (Paris, 1919), pp. 190-191; cf. M. Richard, "La lettre de Theodoret à Jean d'Egées," *Les sciences philoso-*

Following Theodoret, an uninterrupted line of "strict Dyophysites" can be traced from the time of Chalcedon to the reign of Justinian. It includes several patriarchs of Constantinople, notably Gennadius (458-471) and Macedonius (495-511), and it is well represented in the polemics against the interpolated *Trisagion*. When Peter the Fuller, patriarch of Antioch, added to the famous hymn sung at Chalcedon, "Holy God, Holy Mighty, Holy Immortal, have mercy upon us" the sentence: "Who was crucified for us," he faced the fiercest opposition on the part of the Chalcedonians. The existence of this form of Chalcedonian Christology, which we call "strict Dyophysite" gave much ground to the contention of the Monophysites that Chalcedon was actually a Nestorian council.

2. The Monophysites, in their very opposition to the council, implied that it had totally betrayed the theology of Cyril of Alexandria. Actually, "strict Dyophysite" theologians like Theodoret and Gennadius, on the one hand, and a leader of Monophysitism like Severus of Antioch—whose views, as brilliantly defined by the classic study of Joseph Lebon,[16] were essentially identical to those of Cyril—on the other, were simply continuing the debate started between Cyril and Nestorius, as if the Council of Chalcedon had solved nothing.

The rational analysis of the incarnation, which we have described in Theodoret and upon which, in particular, the Dyophysite opposition to "Theopaschism" was based, was quite foreign to the Monophysite theologians. Their starting point was the personal identity of the pre-existing Logos and of the Logos incarnate of the Virgin and crucified on the cross. This identity, some Chalcedonians were saying, had been endorsed at Chalcedon. "But why then," the Monophysites asked, "don't you agree to say with us that 'the Word was crucified in the flesh'? If the 'one hypostasis' of the definition is the hypostasis of the Logos, *who else* than

phiques et théologiques (= *Revue des Sc. phil. et théol.*) 30 (Paris, 1941-1942), pp. 415-423.

[16]*Le Monophysisme sévérien: étude historique, littéraire et théologique sur la résistance monophysite au concile de Chalcédoine jusqu'à la constitution de l'église jacobite* (Louvain, 1909).

the Logos could die on the cross? For death can be the predicate of a person, not of a nature: only some*body* can die, not some*thing*. Besides, if Chalcedon has not disavowed Cyril, why did the council rehabilitate his opponents like Theodoret, and why doesn't the official, imperial, Chalcedonian church prevent the defenders of the council from contradicting so bluntly the Twelfth, and most important, Anathematism of Cyril against Nestorius, which proclaims that 'the Word was crucified in the flesh'?"

Thus, in the eyes of the Monophysites, the position of the Chalcedonian party was at least ambiguous, and this very ambiguity accredited in their eyes the belief that the council, in spite of the lip service it paid to Cyril, had in fact rehabilitated Nestorius. Their own traditional Christology, based upon the writings of Athanasius and Cyril—and also, unfortunately, upon works of Apollinaris attributed to Athanasius— was dominated by the concern for preserving the continuous identity of the Logos, before, during and after the incarnation. The formula of Cyril—"one nature incarnate of God the Word"—became their slogan and was much more powerful, in the eyes of the masses, than the more rational concern of Chalcedonian Christology to preserve in Christ the active role of an integral humanity.

Justinian himself and his theological advisers soon understood that the Monophysite criticisms would not be met with either negative or authoritarian answers alone. They became painfully aware of the fact that Chalcedon, as an independent formula, was not a final solution to the pending christological issue: that its meaning depended on interpretation. They had to have recourse to constructive interpretations of Chalcedon, the first of which was the Origenistic solution which supplied Justinian with a third possible exegesis of Chalcedon.

3. Concerning Origenism, I shall simply mention that after the publication of authentic works of Evagrius Ponticus[17] it can no longer be said that Justinian, in his condemnation— first through an edict, then at the Council of 553—of Origen and Origenism, was fighting phantom adversaries. What is

[17]Cf. A. Guillaumont, *Les Kephalaia Gnostica d'Evagre le Pontique et l'histoire de l'Origénisme chez les Grecs et les Syriens* (Paris, 1962).

even more interesting is that a connection seems to have existed between the problem of Origenism and the christological issue.[18] It may even be that the involvement of the Origenists in the debate over Chalcedon added to the effect of the well-known disturbances provoked by Origenist monks at St. Sabas' monastery in Palestine and attracted public and imperial attention to Evagrian doctrines. The solution to the christological problem proposed by the Origenists, whose main spokesman was Leontius of Byzantium, was based not upon the generally accepted concepts of "natures" but upon the Evagrian view that Christ was not the second person of the Trinity but an intellect (νοῦς) united essentially to the Logos. I mention the problem of Origenism only to stress that Origenistic Christology, very attractive intellectually, was far from the accepted criteria of Orthodoxy, and that Justinian and his advisers had to look elsewhere to find a way of expressing a universally acceptable formula of faith.

4. It was therefore a *fourth* interpretation of Chalcedon which would triumph in the imperial church in the sixth century, an interpretation which, since Joseph Lebon, is generally called "Neo-Chalcedonism." It essentially consisted in denying that Cyril and Chalcedon were mutually exclusive and in promoting the interpretation of the one by the other. According to the Neo-Chalcedonians, the term "one hypostasis" used by Chalcedon designated not what Theodore of Mopsuestia and Nestorius meant by the "prosopon of union," but what Cyril meant by "one nature." Consequently, Cyrillian terminology—including the expression "one incarnate nature of God the Word"—had to retain its value even after Chalcedon in an anti-Nestorian context, while the Chalcedonian formula on the "two natures" was essential to counteract Eutychian Monophysitism. In other words, none of the existing terminological systems is fully adequate to express the mystery of the incarnation of God becoming man, but the doctrinal positions of Cyril and Chalcedon each exclude a wrong interpretation of this central issue of the Christian faith without excluding each other.

[18]This connection is discussed by D. Evans, *Leontius of Byzantium, An Origenist Christology* (Dumbarton Oaks Studies 13, Washington, D.C., 1970).

This *negative* concern of the Neo-Chalcedonian position, which presupposes a necessary intellectual humility on the part of its defenders, should be kept in mind if one wishes to give full credit to the achievements of the reign of Justinian.

Neo-Chalcedonism, however, has not enjoyed great favor among historians in the last decades. It was considered simply as a state-imposed artificial scheme to please the Monophysites and a betrayal of the true Chalcedonian Christology. This critique of Neo-Chalcedonism was partially due to the widespread tendency to rehabilitate the great Theodore of Mopsuestia, teacher of Nestorius, and Nestorius himself. The discussion of these rehabilitations is obviously outside the scope of this paper. I would like to suggest, however, on purely historical grounds, that the Neo-Chalcedonian interpretation of Chalcedon would probably have found no opposition whatsoever in the minds of the Chalcedonian fathers themselves. This observation is suggested by my reading of the conciliar acts. The vast majority of the Council of 451 was Cyrillian. It almost approved the formula "of two natures," which was Cyrillian and which Dioscorus of Alexandria would have accepted. When the decisive influence of the famous Tome of Leo, addressed by the Pope to Flavian of Constantinople, in favor of the final Chalcedonian formulation began to gain ground at the second session, the faith it expressed was acclaimed by the assembly as the faith common "to Leo and to Cyril." And when representatives of Illyricum and of Palestine continued to object, the Tome of Leo was entrusted for five days to a special commission which made sure that it coincided with the doctrine of the Twelve Anathematisms of Cyril against Nestorius.[19]

It can, therefore, be said that the concern of the age of Justinian to consider Cyril and Chalcedon as one single continuous and coherent development in christological concepts is not a new idea but was present during the Chalcedonian debates themselves. In any case, the *Neo*-Chalcedonians of the sixth century would not interpret their own position otherwise, and would not accept that the prefix "Neo"

[19]*Acta conciliorum oecumenicorum*, ed. E. Schwartz, II, 1, pt. 2, pp. 82-83.

be used in a sense implying that the Chalcedonian doctrine was fundamentally modified by them.

The strength of Monophysitism, its appeal to the masses throughout the East, the well-deserved prestige of theologians like Philoxenus and Severus, and also the extreme weakness of Chalcedonian apologetics, which practically surrendered to the Monophysites the monopoly of Cyrillian orthodoxy, was the theological situation in the Christian East when Justinian came to power.

The policy of formal compromise with the Monophysites, practiced by Zeno and Anastasius, had failed not only on theological grounds but also because of rigid opposition from Rome. Even if Justinian had wanted to practice the same policy, he could not have afforded it, because the reconquest of Italy, Africa and Spain made it compulsory for him to espouse a religious policy acceptable to the Christian West. It is at this point that his great dream of a universal empire, united politically and religiously, as well as his personal theological mind which understood well the issues dividing Chalcedonians and Monophysites, were put at the service of a religious policy which led to the Second Council of Constantinople (553).

The first goal of this policy was to counteract the Monophysite accusation that Chalcedon had betrayed Cyril, and thereby exclude the possibility of interpreting it any longer in the "strictly Dyophysite" or Antiochian manner. But Justinian and his advisors were not moved exclusively by the concern of appeasing the Monophysites. They were also aware of the inner weakness and contradictions of the "strict Dyophysite" position itself, which, by denying for example, that it was possible to say that "the Logos *died* in the flesh," was opposing the doctrine of the "communication of idioms," or at least reducing it to purely verbal and nominal expression. For if the Logos, because of His divine nature, could not *die,* how could He be *born* of the Virgin? And if it is not He Himself who was born of Mary, how was she to be called *Theotokos?* The "strict Dyophysite" position was implicitly questioning not only the Monophysite position but also the Council of Ephesus. Thus, Justinian gave the greatest possible encouragement to those who, in the Chalcedonian camp, defended "Theopaschite" formulae: John the Grammarian, who had published between 514-518 an *Apology* of the Council of Chalcedon, John Maxentius and the "Scythian monks" and, later, Leontius of Jerusalem. The formula "One of the Holy Trinity suffered in the flesh" thus became the slogan of a policy and of a theology to which popes also gave support, since it was found in the Tome of Leo itself.[20] It was also included in the imperial confession of faith which opens the *Codex juris.*

The affair of the so-called "Three Chapters" created greater problems with the West. We have already seen how strong an argument the Monophysites made of the fact that two friends of Nestorius and critics of Cyril—Theodoret of Cyrus and Ibas of Edessa—had been admitted in communion by the Council of Chalcedon, and that the great father of Antiochian Christology, Theodore of Mopsuestia, was widely read in Chalcedonian circles. The question was a difficult one because it touched on the *legal* authority of the council: could one condemn these "chapters" and keep the council? It is specifically on these legal grounds—more than on grounds of theology—that Justinian encountered Western opposition to his project of condemnation.

He had to resort to rather "direct" means of action: the deposition of a pope, the installment of another—and face the unexpected six-year-long resistance of his and Theodora's candidate to the papacy, Vigilius. Finally, the papal confirmation once given, the West remained reticent for a long time still and perhaps never really appreciated the theological implications of the decisions of 553. However, the Fifth Council, formally, has not infringed on the authority of the Fourth: the acceptance of Theodoret and Ibas into communion was not put into question, but only their writings against Cyril. Theodore of Mopsuestia alone was the object of a personal posthumous condemnation.[21]

[20]"Filius Dei crucifixus dicitur et sepultus," in *Acta conciliorum oecumenicorum,* ed. E. Schwartz, II, 2, pt. 1, p. 28.

[21]I discuss at greater length the decisions of 553 and the entire christological problem under Justinian in my book on *Christ in Eastern Christian Thought* (Crestwood, N.Y., 1976).

Besides the condemnation of the "Three Chapters," the conciliar decisions formally endorse the essential positions of Cyril of Alexandria: unity of Christ's being, hypostatic identity between the Christ of history and the pre-existent Logos —this unity and identity being expressed in "Theopaschism." This endorsement of Cyril's theology obviously implied at least some accreditation of Cyril's theological vocabulary. Thus, the council formally admits that one may use such Cyrillian formulae as "of two natures" (ἐκ δύο φύσεων) and "one nature incarnate of God the Word" (μία φύσις Θεοῦ λόγου σεσαρκωμένη), provided that "one shall understand those expressions as the holy fathers [*i.e.,* of Chalcedon] have taught" (anathematism 8).

The implications of this decision are of great importance: the council, in fact, disengages theology from words and formulae and affirms that what matters is only their meaning. This attitude is in itself an important change from the usual practice of the post-Constantinian imperial church. The Monophysites are not requested to abandon overnight the theological vocabulary in which they are trained but simply to understand and accept *as well* the Chalcedonian concern for preserving in Christ the fulness of active and authentic humanity.

Unfortunately for Justinian, the Council of Chalcedon had become, for the Monophysites, and especially for the Egyptians, *a symbol* of both "Nestorianism"—whatever the content of that term may have been—and of the bloody repressions which had been directed against its opponents. Some of them would accept reconciliation only when, a century later, a really decisive concession was made by the Chalcedonians in the Monothelite *Ekthesis* of Heraclius (637) and the *Typos* of Constans II (647 or 648).

Thus, Justinian's dream of a universal empire, uniting both East and West into a "symphony" based upon one single faith, proved unworkable. Problems of religious faith proved to be *irreducible* to the legal structure of the state. Consequently, the persistence in Byzantium—and under another form, in the medieval West as well—of the utopian aspiration to identify Church and state, the kingdom of God with the earthly kingdom, dogma with law, political loyalty with religious truth, only favored and embittered divisions in Christendom.

It is against the background of this fundamental failure of the Justinianic imperial idea that his achievements also become discernible. The switch of emphasis from formulae to content, which we have just noted in the decisions of 553, was in itself an admission on the part of the emperor himself that theological issues could not be solved by state legalism. This content of Christian theology of the Justinianic age deserves, especially in our times, greater appreciation than it is generally given.

Our time become increasingly estranged from a theology which considers God and man as two distinct, philosophically definable entities, with incompatible characteristics, such as passibility and impassibility, capacity for change and changelessness, composition and simplicity. It becomes increasingly evident that these categories—at least when they are given absolute value—belong to a particular philosophy and are thus historically conditioned by the frame of mind which produced them. In order to understand the theological achievements of the age of Justinian, one has to give full credit to the Cyrillian and Justinianic conception of Christ: the God-man whose divine nature remains totally transcendent in itself and which therefore cannot be defined philosophically, but whose divine person or hypostasis somehow leaves the category of the transcendent and fully assumes a human nature and an immanent condition to the point of really "dying in the flesh." God Himself therefore ceases to remain "in heaven," bound by philosophical notions, a prisoner of His own transcendency; He becomes fully "compatible" with suffering humanity and makes it His own.

Obviously, Justinian failed to reconcile Eastern Christendom with the West and with itself. The social and political consequences of the final secession in the East of a vast majority of non-Greek-speaking Christians from the imperial church will be incalculable. But it is also important to recognize that the great debates of Justinian's reign were theologically among the most fruitful of Christian history, and may prove to be of special and rather unexpected relevance in the light of our own modern categories of thought.

2

Ideological Crises in Byzantium, 1071 to 1261*

The year 1071, marked by the battle of Mantzikert and the fall of Bari, saw the end of the imperial power of Byzantium as it had been built up by Basil II and his predecessors. More political catastrophes, particularly the coming of the Crusaders and the establishment of the Latin empire on the Bosphorus, were still to come. Nevertheless, Byzantium did not cease to play its long-standing role of intellectual and ideological leadership. Quite to the contrary, the weak state, headed by the Comnenians, the Angeli, the Lascarids of Nicaea and, later, the Palaeologi, exercised an intellectual influence sometimes greater than the powerful empire of the Macedonian dynasty upon the whole of Eastern Europe and upon the Latin West as well. Of course, Byzantium, having become weaker and less self-contained, was now not only preserving the heritage of its own past but also accepting the influence of the West. This process of give-and-take is particularly characteristic for the period under discussion.

During this period ideological trends in two areas appear to us as particularly significant for the understanding of Byzantine society and of its influence beyond the geographical and chronological limits which can be understood as properly "Byzantine": imperial theory and relations with the Latin West.

*Paper originally presented at the XV⁰ Congrès International d'Études Byzantines, Athens, 1976, and published in the proceedings of that congress.

1. Crisis in Imperial Ideology

At no time did Byzantium renounce the Roman ideal of a universal empire, which had been interpreted by Eusebius of Caesarea as a providential expression of the earthly power of Christ Himeself. Each year, on Christmas day, the hymn addressed to Christ and attributed to Emperor Leo VI proclaimed:

When Augustus reigned alone upon earth, the many
  kingdoms of man came to an end;
And when Thou wast made man of the pure Virgin,
  the many gods of idolatry were destroyed;
The cities of the world passed under one single ruler;
And the nations came to believe in one sovereign
  Godhead.[1]

This hymn—and many similar ones constantly repeated during the liturgical celebration of major church festivals—did certainly impress the average Byzantine, even more than the *novellae* of Justinian and other legal texts which reflected the same politcal ideology. The legal texts, however, continued to play their role in inspiring the official pronouncements of Byzantine officials concerning the nature of imperial power. As late as 1395, in his famous letter to the Russian Grand Prince Basil I, Patriarch Anthony, quoting the First Epistle of Peter (2:17): τὸν Θεὸν φοβεῖσθε, τὸν βασιλέα τιμᾶτε ("Fear God, honor the emperor"), emphasized that the emperor is and remains *one,* as God is one, "the emperor whose enactments and ordinances and commands are accepted in all the universe; the emperor of whom and of whom alone, Christians everywhere make mention."[2]

---

[1]*Menaion,* Dec. 25, vespers of Christmas eve; Eng. tr. in *The Festal Menaion,* tr. Mother Mary and K. Ware (London, 1969) p. 254.

[2]F. Miklosich and J. Müller, *Acta et diplomata graeca* 2 (Vienna, 1862), p. 192. Cf. the excellent survey of the Byzantine view of the *imperium* in D. M. Nicol, "The Byzantine View of Western Europe," *Greek, Roman and Byzantine Studies* 8 (1967), pp. 315-339 (repr. in D. M. Nicol, *Byzantium, Its Ecclesiastical History and Relations with the Western World* [London, 1972]).

There was, indeed, ideological *consistency* in Byzantium concerning the imperial function, but there was also, in the last centuries of the empire's existence, a permanent *crisis* which consisted in the ever-growing gulf separating myth and reality. Actually, the idea of a universal empire allied to a universal church was already a myth at the time of Constantine and Justinian, but Justinian—and also Basil II—had enough power and prestige to make their claim at least potentially plausible. After 1071, however, this potentiality itself disappeared, and in 1204 a rival myth of universality, led by the Roman papacy, had for all practical purposes won the day.

Historians have noted that the Byzantines, however inflexible in defending the idea of a unique and universal Christian empire as the norm for political theory, were in fact quite realistic and flexible in the practical application of the idea. For example, political realities forced them in the tenth century to recognize the existence of an "emperor of the Bulgarians" (βασιλεὺς Βουλγάρων), occupying a subsidiary place in the "family of nations" headed by the "emperor of the Romans" residing in Constantinople.[3] In the Comnenian period the flexibility had to be extended much further and integrate the Western principle of feudal allegiance. As a substitute for a formal recognition of his imperial power, Alexius I obtained from the leaders of the First Crusade an oath of fealty, based on a system of mutual obligations. These were understood quite differently by the two parties involved and, under such conditions, the relationship could not possibly last for long. Similarly, the feudal suzerainty which John II and Manuel I were able to exercise, for rather brief periods, over the crusader princes was certainly not the restoration of the former Roman rule in the Eastern Mediterranean but, implicitly, a gradual acceptance by the Byzantine emperors themselves of political pluralism inside the one Christian world.

[3] Cf. particularly G. Ostrogorsky, "Die byzantinische Staatenhierarchie," *Seminarium Kondakovianum* 8 (1936), pp. 41-61, and D. Obolensky, *The Byzantine Commonwealth, Eastern Europe, 500-1453* (London, 1971), p. 385.

Certainly, the Comnenian emperors did not forget the universalist claim of their predecessors and tried to realize it particularly through direct contacts with the papacy. In 1141, Emperor John II offered to Pope Innocent II to restore the political and religious unity of the Christian world under his and the pope's dual leadership.[4] This was, indeed, the Justinianic scheme, which, however, was taking into account the new monarchic consciousness of the medieval papacy and, thus, failing to mention the old "pentarchy" of patriarchs. Emperor Manuel I devoted much of his energy to the same cause of universal imperial unity, but for him, as for his father, this meant either a bilateral agreement with the German emperor (hence his alliance with Conrad III) or, in the face of the hostility shown to him by Conrad's successor, Frederick I Barbarossa, new offers to the pope, Alexander III, following the pattern of John II. But what a contrast between the Western and the Byzantine accounts of these diplomatic attempts! The *Liber Pontificalis* speaks of Manuel's anxiety "to unite his Greek church with the venerable Roman church, the mother of all the churches."[5] Meanwhile, the contemporary historian John Cinnamus, who was himself a secretary of Manuel (βασιλικὸς γραμματικὸς) and thus certainly reflected the thought and intentions of the Byzantine government, praises his master Manuel I for restoring Pope Alexander to his throne (of which he had been deprived by Frederick) and rhetorically reminds the pope that it does not belong to him "to install emperors" (βασιλέας προβεβλῆσθαι), but that rather he himself is indebted to Constantine and to his successors for his throne and his dignity.[6] Taking for granted the Byzantine view that the origin of Roman primacy lies with the *Donation of Constantine* and not with St. Peter, Cinnamus accuses the German emperor of

---

[4]Text in Sp. Lampros, "Αὐτοκρατόρων τοῦ Βυζαντίου χρυσόβουλλα καὶ χρυσᾶ γράμματα ἀναφερόμενα εἰς τὴν ἕνωσιν τῶν ἐκκλησιῶν," Νέος ʽΕλληνομνήμων 2 (1914), pp. 109-111; cf. F. Dölger, *Regesten* 2, 1302, 1303. On the date, see Ostrogorsky, *History of the Byzantine State* (rev. ed. New Brunswick, N.J., 1969), p. 385.

[5]*Liber Pontificalis* (Life of Alexander III by Cardinal Boso), ed. L. Duchesne (Paris, 1957) 2, p. 415.

[6]Cinnamus, *Historia* 5, 7, Bonn ed., p. 220.

usurping the imperial right of appointing popes.[7]

Thus, the Comnenian emperors, Alexius, John and particularly Manuel, were not pure utopists. They made repeated attempts at adjusting the Justinianic idea of a world Christian empire to the realities of the day. They tried feudal relationships with Western princes. When opportunity presented itself, they approached the German Empire with projects of world condominium. They also offered to grant some recognition to the new centralized and monarchic papacy, as it existed since the late eleventh century. All these attempts failed because the Byzantine idea of Roman and Christian universalism was ideologically incompatible with either one of the Western alternatives: the German and the papal.

Twelfth-century Byzantium was, of course, already too weak to have its own dreams of world political unity compete satisfactorily with the dreams of others, but it made a few last attempts at bridging the gaps and should be credited for it. It is only in 1182, with the massacre of the Latins in Constantinople and, finally, in 1204 that the dream had to face the test of ultimate defeat. It still survived, but only as a dream.

Who was the legitimate embodiment of the *imperium* of Constantine and Justinian after March 1204? It has been often recognized that the feudalization of the Byzantine countryside in the Comnenian period allowed for a rather smooth transition to Latin suzerainty. The economic system did not need radical political change. But what about the

---

[7]*Ibid.*, 228-229; on the *Donation* among the Byzantines, see P. J. Alexander, "The Donation of Constantine at Byzantium and its Earliest Use against the Western Empire," *Vizantoloshkog Instituta Zbornik Radova* 8 (Beograd, 1968), 12-25. As in the West, the *Donation* was interpreted either in favor of imperial power over the priesthood (as is the case in Cinnamus), or in defense of the inalienable privileges of the Church. The latter was the case with Patriarch Michael Cerularius (cf. Th. Balsamon, in Rhalles and Potles, Σύνταγμα κανόνων 1, p. 147); cf. also the remarkable eleventh-century cross which may have belonged to Cerularius and which is decorated with images of Constantine and Pope Sylvester, representing in reality Isaac Comnenus and Michael Cerularius. The cross is now at Dumbarton Oaks; see publication and commentary by R. J. H. Jenkins and E. Kitzinger, *Dumbarton Oaks Papers* 21 (1967); on Cerularius' view of his own role and dignity see particularly N. Suvorov, *Vizantiiskii Papa* (Moscow, 1902); on his use of the *Donation*, see pp. 114-115, 127-130.

72 THE BYZANTINE LEGACY IN THE ORTHODOX CHURCH

ideological content of the new political system which now prevailed in the territories of the Byzantine Empire? Very few Greeks or Balkan Slavs ever took as legitimate the election of Baldwin of Flanders. Many more of them, however, were ready to accept—at least tentatively—the idea of the universal political monarchy of the Roman pope, which was, in principle, the official ideology of the Latin West. In 1204, Caloyan of Bulgaria was crowned king by a Roman cardinal, and his example was followed in 1217 by Stephen *Prvovencani* of Serbia. As late as 1253, the Russian Prince Daniel of Galich also received a crown from Innocent IV. No theological element at all entered in these arrangements, which were caused exclusively by "political motives": "neither the Bulgarians, nor the Serbs, nor the West Russians seem to have been seriously disposed to renounce the Orthodox Faith which their ancestors had received from Constantinople."[8] A similar *de facto* acceptance of the new political realities was equally evident among some Greeks. In 1206, a letter of the Greek clergy of Constantinople, written by Nicholas Mesarites and addressed to the pope, envisaged the possibility of having the name of Innocent III commemorated in Greek churches at the end of the service, when it was usual to chant the *polychronismos* of the emperor (Ἰννοκεντίου δεσπότου πάππα τῆς πρεσβυτέρας Ῥώμης πολλὰ τὰ ἔτη). This would express the political *imperium* of the pope. The commemoration of his name in the liturgical *anaphora* itself, however, would have to wait until an ecclesiastical and doctrinal union is achieved.[9]

The short-sightedness of the papal policies, the weakness and ineptitude of the Latins who ruled Constantinople, soon made these practical agreements ineffective. Imperial succession will then be claimed by the Grand Comneni of Trebizond, the Angeli of Epirus and the Lascarids of Nicaea. If one discounts the first of these claims, which will never

[8]D. Obolensky, *op. cit.,* p. 240.

[9]PG 140, col. 297 C; cf. P. L'Huillier, "La nature des relations ecclésiastiques gréco-latines après la prise de Constantinople par les Croisés," *Akten des XI. Internationalen Byzantinisten-Kongress* 1958 (München, 1960), pp. 317-318.

achieve more than local importance, one faces the interesting and ideologically quite important contest between Epirus and Nicaea. The conclusion of the contest resulted in a new political situation, in which the respective roles of the emperor and the Church were substantially modified in favor of the Church, which will to a large degree replace the emperor as the focus of unity between the Orthodox nations of Eastern Europe.

Probably since Leo I (457-474), Byzantine emperors were crowned at their accession by the patriarch of Constantinople.[10] By the eleventh century, some claimed that imperial legitimacy was inseparable from the patriarchal crowning.[11] However, since the appointment of the patriarchs themselves largely depended upon the emperors, the old Roman criterion —proclamation by the army and the senate—was still *de facto* a more decisive criterion, to which the patriarchal crowning was only giving sanction.[12] In the thirteenth century, the competition between the Lascarids and the Angeli made things more complicated. In 1208, Theodore I Lascaris was not only crowned but also anointed with holy chrism (μύρον) by Patriarch Michael Autoreianus in Nicaea.[13] The practice was probably introduced in emulation of the Latin emperors of

[10]Cf. G. Ostrogorsky, *op. cit.,* p. 61, following W. Ensslin, "Zur Frage nach der ersten Kaiserkrönung durch den Patriarchen und zur Bedeutung diese Aktes im Wahlzeremoniell," *Byzantinische Zeitschrift* 42 (1942), pp. 101 ff.

[11]So, for example, Patriarch Alexius Studites (1025-1043) challenged his detractors, who denied his own personal canonicity, by saying that, if he was not the legitimate patriarch, neither were the emperors he had crowned— Constantine VIII, Romanus III and Michael IV[81]legitimate emperors (Skylitzes-Cedrenus, Bonn ed., 2, pp. 517-518); cf. N. Skaballanovich, *Vizantiiskoe gosurdarstvo i tserkov v XI veke* (St. Petersburg, 1884), pp. 369-370.

[12]Cf. P. Charanis, "Coronation and its Constitutional Significance in the Later Roman Empire," *Byzantion* 15 (1940-1941), pp. 49-66.

[13]The texts which mention the anointment are sometimes interpreted metaphorically, cf. M. Angold, *A Byzantine Government in Exile: Government and Society Under the Lascarids of Nicaea (1204-1261)* (Oxford, 1975), pp. 43-44. However, in view of the controversy between Demetrius Chomatianus of Ohrid and Patriarch Germanus II (see below) about the power of consecrating the holy chrism, there is no doubt that the chrism was used in Nicaea (but not in Thessalonica) for the anointment of emperors.

Contantinople,[14] but it also implied a personal sanctification and consecration of the emperor's *person* by the Church in a sense which was not stressed in the earlier periods of Byzantium. Anointment with the "holy chrism," normally used only *once* at baptism, was now used *a second time* at the emperor's coronation. The weakening of the political power and prestige of the emperors was leading to a new emphasis upon their religious and mystical role, and therefore to a greater reliance upon the carrier of this mystical power, *i.e.,* the Church.

As is well known, after his capture of Thessalonica in 1224, the Despot Theodore Angelus, ruler of Epirus, was crowned "emperor of the Romans" by Demetrius Chomatianus, archbishop of Ohrid.[15] It was certainly not the first time in Byzantine history that the imperial crown was disputed between several pretenders. It is the first time, however, that such a dispute took the form of a theological and canonical debate, which concerned not only the source of imperial legitimacy, but also the authority of the "ecumenical patriarch." The ancient canonical texts define the power of the archbishop of Constantinople as stemming exclusively from the political importance of the imperial capital,[16] but, in the thirteenth century, the situation is reversed. Theodore Lascaris, in Nicaea, receives his imperial legitimacy from his coronation by a patriarch-in-exile. In this event the dyarchic relationship between the emperor and the patriarch is certainly reaffirmed, but their respective importance is modified in favor of the patriarch. The meaning and implication of the event were

[14]G. Ostrogorsky, "Zur Kaisersalbung und Schilderhebung im spätbyzantinischen Krönungszeremoniell," *Historia* 4 (1955), pp. 246-256.

[15]On the exact date of this event, see L. Stiernon, "Les origines du despotat d'Épire," *Actes du XIIe Congrès d'Études Byzantines, Ohrid* 2 (Beograd, 1964), pp. 197-202; and A. Karpozilos, "The Date of Coronation of Theodore Doukas Angelos," Βυζαντινά 6 (1974), pp. 253-261.

[16]See particularly the famous canon 28 of the Council of Chalcedon (451): "The fathers rightly granted privileges to the throne of Old Rome, because it was the imperial city. And one hundred and fifty most religious bishops [of Constantinople, 381], actuated by the same considerations, gave equal privileges to the most holy throne of New Rome, justly judging that the city, which is honored with the presence of the emperor and the senate and enjoys equal privileges with the old imperial Rome, should, in ecclesiastical matters also, be magnified as she is and rank next to her."

challenged with competence and energy by learned canonists supporting the cause of Michael Angelus of Epirus.

There is no possibility to develop here the details of the controversy.[17] The major spokesman of the Epirote cause, Demetrius Chomatianus, archbishop of Ohrid, made the following main points:

1) The crowning of emperors and the appointment of patriarchs in Nicaea is no less an irregularity than the crowning of an emperor in Thessalonica by the autocephalous archbishop of Ohrid.[18]

2) The patriarch of Constantinople has no exclusive right to bless the holy chrism, used both for baptism and the anointment of emperors. Any bishop (Chomatianus rightly refers to canon 7 of Carthage and to Pseudo-Dionysius, *Ecclesiastical Hierarchy*) has the power to perform the blessing,[19] and, in any case, at the crowning of Michael Angelus the baptismal holy chrism (μύρον) was not used—because such was not the traditional practice—but special holy oil (ἔλαιον).[20]

3) In the normal exercise of his powers, the patriarch of Constantinople has no right to infringe upon the territories

[17]See D. Nicol, "Ecclesiastical Relations between the Despotate of Epirus and the Kingdom of Nicaea in the Years 1215 to 1230," *Byzantion* 22 (1952), pp. 206-228; and *The Despotate of Epiros* (Oxford, 1957), pp. 24-102, where the episode is exaggeratedly presented as a real "schism," whereas in fact no breach of communion actually ever occurred between Nicaea and the "bishops of the west" (*i.e.*, those of Epirus and of the autocephalous archbishopric of Ohrid); cf. also J. H. Erickson, "Autocephaly in Orthodox Canonical Literature to the Thirteenth Century," *St. Vladimir's Theological Quarterly* 15 (1971), pp. 28-41, and particularly A. Karpozilos, *The Ecclesiastical Controversy Between the Kingdom of Nicaea and the Principality of Epirus (1217-1233),* (Thessaloniki, 1973).

[18]Chomatianus, Letter 104, to Germanus II (1225), ed. J. B. Pitra, *Analecta sacra et classica spicilegio solesmensi parata* (Paris-Rome, 1891), col. 489-490.

[19]The Byzantine practice of reserving to the patriarch alone the privilege of blessing the chrism is not older than the ninth century. Cf. L. Petit, "Le pouvoir de consacrer le saint chrême," *Echos d'Orient* 3 (1899-1900), pp. 1-7, E. Herman, "Wann ist die Chrysmaweihe zum Vorrecht der Patriarchen geworden?" *Sbornik P. Nikov* (Sofia, 1940), pp. 509-515.

[20]Οὐδὲ τοῦ ἐπικρατοῦντος ἔθους ἐστὶ μύρῳ χρίεσθαι τὸν εἰς τὴν βασίλειον ἀνάρρησιν προκαλούμενον, ἐλαίῳ δὲ ἱεροῖς ἁγιαζομένῳ ἐπάσμασι. Πῶς οὖν ᾧπερ οὐκ ἐχρησάμεθα πρὸς κατηγορίαν ἡμῶν προέτεινας, *ed. cit.*, col. 493.

belonging to the jurisdiction of other autocephalous churches —particularly that of Ohrid[21]—and, even within the geographical limits of his own patriarchate, he should care for spiritual unity, rather than for his legal power to appoint metropolitans.[22]

It is noteworthy that the "western" bishops, in spite of their opposition to the policies of Nicaea, never denied the legitimacy of the exiled patriarchate. This legitimacy was actually challenged nowhere in the Orthodox world and proved to be the trump card in the diplomatic game of the time, which was played successfully by Nicaea. In a series of brilliant moves, Nicaea recognized an autocephalous archbishop of Serbia, in Pec, and a new patriarchate of Bulgaria in Trnovo.[23] It thus acknowledged the political realities of the thirteenth century (rather than the legitimate but abstract

[21]Ohrid had been the residence of the Bulgarian patriarch at the time of Tsar Samuel (974-1014). Upon the destruction of Samuel's empire by Basil II, the patriarchate was suppressed, but the "archbishop" of Ohrid remained autocephalous (cf. particularly B. Granic, "Kirchengeschichtliche Glossen zu den von Kaiser Basileios II. dem autokephalen Erzbistum von Achrida verliehenen Privilegien," *Byzantion* 12 [1937] p. 215 ff.) even if the now Greek archbishops were *de facto* quite dependent upon Constantinople (cf. the remarks by Chomatianus: ἐταπείνωσαν τοῦτο [the prestige of Ohrid] οἱ ἀπὸ τῆς μεγάλης ἐκκλησίας τῆς τοῦ Θεοῦ λόγου Σοφίας κατὰ καιροὺς προβαλλόμενοι ἀρχιεπίσκοποι, ἐφ' οἷς τρόφιμοι ταύτης ὄντες, καὶ τὴν σύμφυτον τούτοις ὑποταγὴν πρὸς τοὺς πατριάρχας Κωνσταντινουπόλεως, καὶ μετὰ τὴν ἀρχιερωσύνην τηροῦντες ἀνόθευτον συνεταπείνωσαν, Letter to Germanus II, *ed. cit.*, col. 495). For Chomatianus, however, the prestige and rights of Ohrid are not only a sequel of Bulgarian separatism, but a venerable canonical establishment, enacted by Justinian himself when he granted ecclesiastical independence to Justiniana Prima, the place of his birth, with jurisdiction over most of the Balkan peninsula (*Novella* 131); hence his official title: ἀρχιεπίσκοπος πρώτης Ἰουστινιανῆς καὶ πάσης Βουλγαρίας (*ed. cit.*, col. 479, 481, *etc.*); cf. V. N. Zlatarski, "Prima Justiniana im Titel des bulgarischen Erzbischofs von Achrida," *Byzantinische Zeitschrift* 30 (1929-1930), pp. 484-489.

[22]Πατριάρχην ἔχειν ἡμᾶς κοινὸν φροντιστὴν καὶ μὴ διαιροῦντα τὸ σῶμα τῆς Ἐκκλησίας ἀλλ' ἐνοῦντα μᾶλλον καὶ συμβιβάζοντα, Pittakion of the Synod of Bishops meeting in Arta (1225), ed. V. Vasilievsky, "Epirotica," *Vizantiiskii Vremennik* 3 (1896), pp. 484-489.

[23]In both cases, the patriarchate transgressed the formal rights claimed by Chomatianus since both Pec and Trnovo were located upon the territory of the archbishopric of Justiniana Prima and of the former patriarchate of Ohrid; cf. the protests of Chomatianus: ἡ Σερβία ὑπὸ τὴν ἐπαρχίαν

traditional privileges claimed by Chomatianus in favor of his "Bulgarian" archbishopric of Ohrid). These moves indicate that the patriarchate was actually abandoning the policies of ecclesiastical centralism, which were uninforceable in the thirteenth century, and in this respect was following some of the advice given by Chomatianus and the "western" bishops, even if its moves were directed against the latter.

Politically, the fortunes of Epirus soon vanished and with them, the claims of the archbishop of Ohrid. But ideologically the issues raised by Chomatianus were real. The disintegration of an οἰκουμένη ruled by one emperor and one patriarch was irreversible, and a pluralism of "empires" and "patriarchates," an inevitable process. The bishops of the "west" (i.e., of Epirus and Macedonia), when in 1225 they rhetorically express their indignation against the Nicaean readiness to recognize imperial titles for the Latins and the Bulgarians but not for Theodore Angelus of Thessalonica, reflect this new political ideology. "So let the azymite," they write, "who ascribes the imperial dignity to Constantinople alone, the one who is corrupt in his faith, be called basileus, and also let the Scythian Asen who took over the Balkans be called "most high basileus" in word and in writing, but let the one who received the imperial dignity from his forefathers [i.e., Theodore Angelus] and who therefore justifiably claims the title, be neglected!"[24]

In the midst of this pluralism of empires, which in fact were nation-states, the "emperor of the Romans" could exercise only a preeminence of honor and be the titular head of a "commonwealth." Gradually, he himself became accustomed to consider himself primarily as the head of the Greek nation. In Nicaea, the terms Ἑλλάς, Ἑλληνίς, Ἕλλην, and also Γραικὸς became increasingly frequent, not only in the narrow circle of sophisticated humanists, but also in official documents and histories, to designate the "Roman" Empire

τοῦ θρόνου τῆς Βουλγαρίας τελεῖ, Letter to St. Sava, ed. cit., col. 384; μέρος γὰρ τῆς καθ' ἡμᾶς ἐπαρχίας ὁ Τέρνοβος, Letter to Germanus II, ed. cit., col. 496.

[24]Ed. V. Vasilievsky, op. cit., p. 292.

and its inhabitants.[25] The learned monk Nicephorus Blemmydes, influential friend of John Vatatzes and tutor of Theodore II Lascaris, sternly and successfully objected against ecclesiastical sanctions to be taken against Epirus, assuming Epirus to have an equal right to existence with the Nicaean state,[26] and wrote his "Model of an Emperor" (Βασιλικὸς Ἀνδριάς), a pedagogical instruction addressed to Theodore II, without reference to imperial universalism and using examples primarily from classical and biblical history applicable to any national ruler.[27]

However, the idea of a universal Christian world did not disappear in the thirteenth century. In Nicaea and, after 1261, in recovered Constantinople, its witness and carrier will be the patriarchate, rather than the empire itself. If the direct administrative power of the patriarch was now reduced, particularly in the Balkans (although it still extended to large areas beyond the Danube and to the whole of Russia!), it was still seen in Serbia, in Bulgaria, in Trebizond, in the Caucasian area, as well as in the Moslem-held Middle East as the center of the Orthodox world. The emperor still possessed the last word in appointing patriarchs, but the patriarchate as an institution had a greater moral power and a much wider field of action than the imperial chancery. It frequently proclaimed its supranational and universal responsibility.[28] Occasionally, it took upon itself the role of the emperor's ideo-

[25]On this development a good survey of sources and literature in M. Angold, op. cit., pp. 28-33; cf. also A. Vakalopoulos, The Origins of the Greek Nation (New Brunswick, N.J., 1970).

[26]Nicephori Blemmydae curriculum vitae et carmina, ed. A. Heisenberg (Leipzig, 1896), pp. 45-46.

[27]Oratio de regis officiis, PG 142, col. 611-674. The basic monograph on Blemmydes is by V.T. Barvinok, Nikifor Vlemmid i ego sochineniya (Kiev, 1911); cf. other bibliography in H.G. Beck, Kirche und theologische Literatur im Byzantinischen Reich (Munich, 1959), pp. 671-673.

[28]See, for example, the claim made by Germanus II, patriarch in Nicaea (1222-1240), to exercise authority among Crimeans, Armenians, Georgians, Russians and Christians in Jerusalem: R. Loenertz, "Lettre de Georges Bardanes, métropolite de Corcyre, au patriarche œcuménique Germain II," Ἐπετηρὶς Ἑταιρείας Βυζαντινῶν Σπουδῶν 33 (1964), pp. 96-97. For the continuing supra-national role of the patriarchate in the fourteenth century, see Part III, Chapter 3, below.

logical advocate.[29] The ideological and practical consequences of this situation are essential for the understanding of East European history in the fourteenth and fifteenth centuries, as well as of the survival of "Byzance après Byzance."

2. Crisis in Relations with the Latin West

In the past few decades, historical research on the origin and significance of the ecclesiastical schism between Byzantium and Rome has rightly emphasized the Crusades and the sack of Constantinople in 1204 as the points when national and cultural animosity between Latins and Greeks made the schism an irreversible reality. Certainly, neither the quarrel between Patriarch Photius and Pope Nicholas I—which was healed at the Union Council of 879-880[30]—nor the incident of 1054 can be considered as the dates of the schism. In 1089, when Emperor Alexius I, interested in breaking the alliance between the papacy and the Normans, received legates of Urban II and consulted the synod of Constantinople concerning the status of relations between the churches, no official documents on the schism were found in the archives of the patriarchate and Patriarch Nicholas III addressed a letter to Rome offering to restore relations on the basis of the pope's confession of Orthodox faith.[31] Obviously, in the eyes of the Byzantines, there was no formal "schism" between the churches, but only an estrangement which could be healed

---

[29]See, for example, the letter of Patriarch Anthony quoted above.

[30]On this point, F. Dvornik's studies, basically confirmed by V. Grumel and others, are in essence unchallengeable. See F. Dvornik, *The Photian Schism, History and Legend* (Cambridge, 1948); cf. also the significant thesis of J. Meijer, *The Synod of Union. A Theological Analysis of the Photian Synod of 879-880* (Thessalonica, 1974), and our remarks on the same subject, "Églises-soeurs: Implications ecclésiologiques du Tomos Agapis," *Istina* (1975) no. 1, pp. 35-46.

[31]Cf. the documents on this episode in W. Holtzmann, "Unionsverhandlungen zwischen Kaiser Alexis I und Papst Urban II im Jahre 1089," *Byzantinische Zeitschrift* 28 (1928), pp. 38-67; cf. V. Grumel, *Les Régestes des Actes du patriarcat de Constantinople* 1 (Paris, 1947), no. 953, pp. 48-49, and B. Leib, "Les patriarches de Byzance et la politique religieuse d'Alexis Comnène (1081-1118)," *Recherches de science religieuse* 40 (1951-1952 = Mélanges Jules Lebreton II), pp. 214-218.

through the simple, but official, removal of the *Filioque* from the Latin Creed. The more enlightened Byzantine ecclesiastics (Peter of Antioch, Theophylact of Ohrid) agreed that the disciplinary and liturgical issues raised by Michael Cerularius —such as the Latin use of azymes in the eucharist—were not really important.

However, if one considers the period between 1071 and 1261 as a unit, is there not a definitely *ideological* factor, which—in addition to national, cultural and political factors connected with the Crusades—made ecclesiastical reconciliation critically more difficult than ever before? It is obvious that this *new* factor did indeed exist. It consisted in the theory and practice of the "reformed" papacy of Gregory VII and Innocent III.

We have already noticed that, during the Comnenian period, Byzantine imperial diplomacy was aware of the change which had occurred in the West, in terms of the new political claims of the papacy, and was ready to reconcile itself with them inasmuch as they concerned the Latin West only. One would even assume that the Byzantine preferred to deal with the pope, as the *de facto* "emperor of the West," than with the more offensive German *imperium*. The major difficulty and the constant source of misunderstanding resided, however, in the fact that the reformed papacy understood its power as theologically based on the idea of Petrine succession in Rome, as established by divine decree (and not by the *Donation of Constantine*, as the Byzantines would readily admit) and that, therefore, its power could not be limited geographically to the Latin West alone.[32]

It is not the task of historians but of theologians to determine whether this new development of the medieval papacy was a legitimate outcome of the early Christian structure of the Church; or whether the Byzantine reaction to it was a legitimate conservative instinct, or an act of schismatic rebellion. It is, however, a historical fact that in 1204, "it was

---

[32]The contrast between the terms of the *Dictatus papae* of Gregory VII and what the Byzantine considered as "normal" relations with the West is well underlined by F. Dvornik, *Byzantium and the Roman Primacy* (New York, 1966), p. 137.

the first time that the Greeks had been treated to the direct application of the papal theory of universal supremacy."[33] Never before had the pope either confirmed an emperor of Constantinople or appointed a patriarch in the New Rome. Innocent III, however shocked he may have been morally by the Crusaders' performance in the city, considered it to be his divine right to exercise jurisdiction in the East. His views on this point are clear: "[The pope], in virtue of his pontifical authority, appoints patriarchs, primates, metropolitans and bishops; in virtue of his royal power, he names senators, prefects, judges and notaries."[34] Between this ideology and that of the Byzantines there was obvious incompatibility. The age-old polemics between Greeks and Latins took a new direction, finally acknowledging—after centuries of argument about the *Filioque* and issues of discipline—the underlying problem of church authority.

Historians generally recognize today that very early in the history of Christianity—and certainly already in the fourth century—there were different trends, in the East and in the West, in determining which local churches should enjoy primacy. The West insisted on the idea of apostolic foundation, which meant in practice that Rome was the only "apostolic see" in the West, since the apostles of Jesus were not reported as having founded any other church in the Western part of the Mediterranean world. The East, meanwhile, where "apostolic foundation" could be claimed by dozens of local communities (Antioch, Ephesus, Corinth and, certainly, Jerusalem itself), the adoption of "apostolicity" as criterion for primacy would have been meaningless. The actual power of some churches over others was thus determined by the requirements of history (frequently determined by the emperor) and sanctioned by conciliar decrees. Such is, certainly, the origin of the primacy of Constantinople, the "New Rome."[35]

[33]D. Nicol, "The Fourth Crusade and the Greek and Latin Empires, 1204-1261," *The Cambridge Medieval History* IV, 1 (Cambridge, 1967), p. 302.

[34]"Sermo VII in festo S. Silvestri pontificis maximi," quoted in A. Fliche et al., *La Chrétienté romaine (1198-1274)*, in A. Fliche and V. Martin, *Histoire de l'Église* 10 (Paris, 1950), pp. 34-35.

[35]Council of Constantinople 381, convened by Theodosius I. The best description of the opposition between the "apostolic" notion of primacy and

It is remarkable, however, that these two ideas of primacy, even if they frequently clashed with each other during numerous ecclesiastical conflicts in the first millenium, were never debated for their own sake. The bishops of the "Old Rome" clearly lacked the power to impose their view upon the Easterners, while the Byzantines seemed to ignore the true implications of the "Petrine idea," while frequently using it rhetorically in their relations with the bishop of Rome when this was in their interest.

In 1204, the evidence asserted itself with catastrophic and deplorable violence. It has been assumed that 1204 marks the real beginning of the direct discussion, by Byzantine polemicists, of the issue of Roman primacy.[36] In fact, discussions on the primacy did already take place in the twelfth century, as early as 1112, on the occasion of the visit to Constantinople of Peter Grossolanus, archbishop of Milan, and on several later instances.[37] It is obvious, however, that the two parties did not confront each other directly and explicitly on this issue before the emergence of the reformed papacy in the late eleventh century, and that the events of 1204 precipitated the debate even more dramatically. And since these events—and particularly the appointment of a Latin patriarch, as well as the establishment of a Latin hierarchy in the Crusaders' states —were justified by the divine right of the pope as successor of Peter, it was unavoidable that the debate would touch upon this theological basis invoked by the Latins.

There is no possibility to discuss here the exegetical, ecclesiological and canonical arguments used by the Greek polemicists. Not all of them, of course, are of equal value and relevance. It is noteworthy, however, that the main stress of the Byzantine polemic is not directed against the idea of the

the Byzantine idea of empirical "accommodation" can be found in F. Dvornik, *The Idea of Apostolicity in Byzantium and the Legend of the Apostle Andrew* (Cambridge, 1958); cf. by the same author *Byzantium and Roman Primacy*, pp. 27-54, and also my own book, *Orthodoxy and Catholicity* (New York, 1966), pp. 49-78.

[36]See our article on "St. Peter in Byzantine Theology" in J. Meyendorff et al., *The Primacy of Peter in the Orthodox Church* (London, 1963).

[37]J. Darrouzès, "Les documents byzantins du XIIe siècle sur la primauté romaine," *Revue des Études Byzantines* 23 (1965), pp. 42-88.

apostle Peter's primacy among the apostles of Jesus, as reported by the New Testament accounts, but against the Latin idea of Peter's *succession* in Rome alone, which, of course, has no scriptural basis. This succession is seen by the Byzantines as being present *in every local church* which confesses the faith of Peter. "You try to present Peter as the teacher of Rome alone," says Nicholas Mesarites in 1206. "While the divine fathers spoke of the promise made to him by the Savior as having a *catholic* meaning and as referring to all those who believed and believe, you force yourself into a narrow and false interpretation, ascribing it to Rome alone. If this were true, it would be impossible for every church of the faithful, and not only that of Rome, to possess the Savior properly, and for each church to be founded on the Rock, *i.e.,* on the doctrine of Peter, in conformity with the promise."[38] This idea of the succession of Peter in *every* church implies, of course, that if *one church* is elevated in honor or in power it is not because of Peter but because of historical circumstances, and Rome is not an exception.

Remarkably, the crisis of 1204 and its sequels did not close all the doors to dialogue on Roman primacy between Greeks and Latins. Although much of the polemics was now marked with acerbity and national animosity, there were also instances when Byzantine churchmen accepted to speak of a Petrine succession as being conditioned by the restoration of the *faith* of Peter (hence the continual return to the *Filioque* question, which the Byzantine saw as opposed to the "faith of Peter") and as being localized in Rome through a consensus of eccle-

[38]Ed. A. Heisenberg. "Neue Quellen zur Geschichte des lateinischen Kaisertums und der Kirchenunion, II. Die Unionverhandlungen 30. Aug. 1206," *Bayerische Akademie der Wissenschaften, Philos.-philolog. und hist. Klasse, Abhandlungen* (1923), pp. 34-35. Cf. many other similar texts in our study "St. Peter in Byzantine Theology," *op. cit.* pp. 7-29; also in *Byzantine Theology. Historical Trends and Doctrinal Themes* (New York, 1974), pp. 91-115. Perhaps the most striking and articulate critique of the Latin view that the Roman bishop has the exclusive privilege of being the only successor of Peter is found in the letters of Patriarch John Camaterus to Pope Innocent III, which were written before the capture of Constantinople, in 1200; the original text of the letters has been published by A. Papadakis and A. M. Talbot, "John X Camaterus Confronts Innocent III: An Unpublished Correspondence," *Byzantinoslavica* 33/1 (1972), pp. 26-41.

siastical tradition rather than by a divine decree. This consensus, says Symeon of Thessalonica as late as in the fifteenth century, can be restored if unity of faith is first reestablished.[39]

Conclusions

A full survey of the intellectual life in the empire between 1071 and 1261 would have to cover the issues debated and solved during the Comnenian period, especially those which were included in the *Synodikon of Orthodoxy*.[40] In the past few years, publications of texts and analytical studies of these issues have abounded. These include:

1) The constant preoccupation of the Byzantine civil and ecclesiastical authorities with the spiritualist and "enthusiastic" movements, which appear under the name of "Messalians," "Bogomils" or, even, "Paulicians," and whose doctrines and attitudes are sometimes undistinguishable from those held by some mystical circles of orthodox monasticism.[41]

2) The continuous debate on christological issues and related topics, such as the "deification" of man and its foundation in the liturgical and sacramental life of the Church, expressed in the condemnation, by the Synod of Constantinople, of Eustratius of Nicaea, Soterichus Panteugenus, Constantine of Corfu and John Eirenicus.[42]

---

[39]*Dialogus contra haereses* 29, PG 155, col. 120-121.

[40]This basic document on the ecclesiastical and intellectual life of Byzantium is now available in a critical edition and with an excellent commentary by J. Gouillard, "Le Synodikon de l'Orthodoxie: edition et commentaire," *Travaux et mémoires* 2 (1967), pp. 1-316.

[41]Cf. on this point the new and comprehensive monograph by Milan Loos, *Dualist Heresy in the Middle Ages* (Prague, 1974), where earlier bibliography is quoted. See particularly J. Gouillard, "L'hérésie dans l'Empire byzantin des origines au XIIe siècle," *Travaux et Memoires* 1 (1965), pp. 312-324; D. Angelov, *Bogomilstvoto v Bulgarija* (Sofia, 1969); N. Gersoyan, "Byzantine Heresy: A Reinterpretation," *Dumbarton Oaks Papers* 25 (1971), pp. 85-113; "L'abjuration du Moine Nil de Calabre," *Byzantinoslavica* 34/1 (1974), pp. 12-26; and earlier, S. Runciman, *The Medieval Manichee: A Study of the Christian Dualist Heresy* (Cambridge, 1947), and D. Obolensky, *The Bogomils* (Cambridge, 1948).

[42]On these debates, see particularly J. Gouillard, *Synodikon,* and also our study *Christ in Eastern Christian Thought* (rev. ed. New York, 1975), pp. 196-203.

3) The equally continuous debate on the significance of ancient Greek philosophy, and particularly Platonism, in Christian thought. The trials of John Italus (1076-1077, 1082), the successor of Michael Psellus as ὕπατος τῶν φιλοσόφων, which resulted in a stern condemnation of Platonism, included in the *Synodikon*, was a high point of a polarity opposing scholarly humanists to conservative ecclesiastics.[43] The negative attitude towards Greek philosophy which this decision implied is in clear contrast with the revival of philosophical studies which marked the beginning of the great scholastic period in the West. Byzantine Christianity would not accept a new synthesis between philosophy and the faith apart from the synthesis realized by the fathers of the fourth-seventh centuries.

Further discussion of these issues must wait. We limit ourselves here to briefly mentioning them because the study of the major *crises* in the Byzantine ideological outlook—and particularly the crisis of imperial ideology and the acute confrontation with the Latin West—must be seen against the more general background of the Byzantine intellectual outlook. It is remarkable that all three issues mentioned above—"Messalian" spiritualism, the christological issue, and the Christian view of Hellenism—reflected debates which started already in the fourth century. Whatever its concern with the reality of the twelfth and thirteenth centuries, Byzantium also remained an embodiment of permanence and continuity with its past.

---

[43]Bibliography and commentary in J. Gouillard, *Synodikon*, pp. 188-202.

III
CHURCH AND CULTURE

1

Byzantine Views of Islam*

No knowledge of the Islamic teachings is evident in Byzantine literature before the beginning of the eighth century. We know that the spiritual and intellectual encounter of Muhammad and the first generations of his followers with Christianity involved not the imperial Orthodox Church, but the Monophysite and Nestorian communities which made up the majority of the Christian population in Arabia, Egypt, Syria and Mesopotamia. Until the end of the Umayyad period, these Syrian or Coptic Christians were the chief, and practically the only, spokesmen for the Christian faith in the caliphate. And it was through the intermediary of these communities—and often by means of a double translation, from Greek into Syriac, and from Syriac into Arabic—that the Arabs first became acquainted with the works of Aristotle, Plato, Galen, Hippocrates and Plotinus.[1] Among the Monophysites and Nestorians, the Arabs found many civil servants, diplomats and businessmen who were willing to help in the building of their empire, and who often preferred, at least in the beginning, to accommodate themselves to the Moslem yoke rather than suffer oppression which in the Orthodox Chalcedonian empire of Byzantium was the fate of all religious dissidents.

The first encounter of Islam with Orthodox Christianity

*Paper originally presented at a symposium on "The Relations between Byzantium and the Arabs," Dumbarton Oaks, May, 1963, and published in *Dumbarton Oaks Papers* 18 (1964), pp. 115-132.

[1] Cf. L. Gardet, "Théologie musulmane et pensée patristique," *Revue Thomiste* 47 (1947), pp. 51-53.

took place on the battlefield, in the wars which since the seventh century opposed the Arabs to the Greek emperors. Both civilizations thus confronted were, to a large extent, shaped by their respective religious ideologies, and each side interpreted the attitudes and actions of the other as motivated by religion. If the Qurran appealed to a holy war against "those who ascribe partners to God"—i.e., Christians who believe in the Trinity[2]—the Byzantine retaliated, after the example of St. John of Damascus, by considering Islam as a "forerunner of Antichrist" (πρόδρομος τοῦ ᾿Αντιχρί-στου).[3] But, however abrupt were these statements of mutual intolerance, however fanatical the appeals to a holy war, a better mutual appreciation was gradually brought about by the requirements of diplomacy, the necessity of coexistence in the occupied areas, and the cool reflection of informed minds.

My purpose here is to examine the encounter between Byzantium and Islam in the sphere of religion. Limitations of space do not permit me to do more than offer a few selected examples illustrating various attitudes of the Byzantines towards the Moslem faith. These examples will be drawn from four categories of documents:

1. Polemical literature
2. Canonical and liturgical texts
3. Official letters sent by Byzantine dignitaries to their Moslem counterparts
4. Hagiographical materials.

1.

The name of John of Damascus usually heads every list of Christian anti-Moslem polemicists.[4]

[2]Sura IX, 5, 5.
[3]De haeresibus, PG 94, col. 764A.
[4]On the Byzantine anti-Islamic polemics, see C. Güterbock, Der Islam im Lichte der Byzantinischen Polemik (Berlin, 1912); W. Eichner, "Die Nachrichten über den Islam bei den Byzantinern," Der Islam 23 (1936), pp. 133-162, 197-244; and H.-G. Beck, Vorsehung und Vorherbestimmung in

According to traditional accounts, John belonged to the wealthy Damascene family of Sergius Mansur, an official of the Byzantine financial administration of Damascus, who negotiated the surrender of the city to the Arabs in 635, preserved his civil functions under the new regime, and transmitted his office to his descendants. John, according to this tradition, was his grandson. After exercising his duties for a while, he retired to the monastery of St. Sabbas in Palestine and became one of the most famous theologians and hymnographers of the Greek Church.

If we are to believe this traditional account, the information that John was in the Arab administration of Damascus under the Umayyads and had, therefore, a first-hand knowledge of the Arab Moslem civilization, would, of course, be very valuable. Unfortunately, the story is mainly based upon an eleventh-century Arabic life, which in other respects is full of incredible legends. Earlier sources are much more reserved. Theophanes tells us that John's *father* was a γενικὸς λογοθέτης under the Caliph Abdul-Melek (685-705),[5] which probably means that he was in charge of collecting taxes from the Christian community. Such a post would not necessarily imply deep acquaintance with the Arab civilization. The Acts of the Seventh Council seem to suggest that John inherited his father's post, for they compare his retirement to St. Sabbas to the conversion of the Apostle Matthew, who, before he became a follower of Christ, was a "publican," *i.e.,* a "tax-collector."[6]

Since the information available to us on John's life is very meager, it is only from his writings that we can form an accurate idea of his thoughts and his views on Islam. Unfortunately, a close examination of his work reveals very few writings connected with Islam. Johannes M. Hoeck, in his critical analysis of the Damascene's manuscript tradition,[7]

der theologischen Literatur der Byzantiner (Orientalia Christiana Analecta 114, 1937), pp. 32-65. None of these studies goes further than to give a list of authors and to present a selection of their major arguments.

[5]*Chronographia,* Bonn ed. I, p. 559.

[6]Mansi 13, col. 357B; cf. Matt. 9:9.

[7]"Stand und Aufgaben der Damaskenos-Forschung," *Orientalia Christiana Periodica* 17 (1951), pp. 18, 23-24.

mentions four works connected with John's name which deal with Islam:

1. A chapter of the *De haeresibus*,[8] a catalogue of heresies, which is part of John of Damascus' main work, the *Source of Knowledge* (Πηγὴ γνώσεως) and is based on a similar compilation drafted in the fifth century by St. Epiphanius of Cyprus. Islam, rather surprisingly, is treated as a Christian heresy and bears the number 101 in the printed edition. It follows a description of the sect of the Αὐτοπροσκόπται (a peculiar deviation of Christian monasticism) and preceeds the paragraph on the Iconoclasts. In some manuscripts Islam figures under No. 100 and follows immediately after the Monothelites (No. 99).

2. *A Dialogue between a Saracen and a Christian,* a combination of two *opuscula,* both of which are to be found also under the name of Theodore Abu-Qurra, an author who will be mentioned later in this paper. The *Dialogue* has been published twice under the name of John of Damascus, once by Lequien and once by Gallandus, both editions being reprinted in Migne.[9] In each of these editions, the two original *opuscula* are in reverse order, which underlines the inconsistency of the Damascene's manuscript tradition on this point and strongly suggests that the *Dialogue* is a compilation of Abu-Qurra's writings, attributed to John of Damascus by later scribes.[10]

3. Another dialogue, formally ascribed to Abu-Qurra in the title, which, however, specifies that Theodore had written διὰ φωνῆς 'Ιωάννου Δαμασκηνοῦ. The expression διὰ φωνῆς, and equivalent of ἀπὸ φωνῆς, is a technical expression, recently and convincingly studied by M. Richard[11]: it means "according to the oral teaching" of John of Damas-

---

[8]PG 94, cols. 764-773.

[9]*Ibid.,* cols. 1585-1596 (Lequien); 96, cols. 1335-1348 (Gallandus). The text corresponds almost verbatim to the *Opuscula,* 35 (*ibid.,* cols. 1586A-1592C) and 36 (97, cols. 1592CD) of Abu-Qurra.

[10]H.-G. Beck, while still tending to accept John' authorship, mentions a manuscript where the *Dialogue* is anonymous and another where it is ascribed to Sisinnius the Grammarian (*Kirche und theologische Literatur im byzantinischen Reich* [Munich, 1959], p. 478).

[11]"Ἀπὸ φωνῆς," *Byzantion* 20 (1950), pp. 191-222.

cus. The real author here is obviously Abu-Qurra, and, as a matter of fact, the *Dialogue* is also found in some manuscripts under his name, without any mention of John of Damascus.[12]

4. The fourth anti-Islamic writing ascribed to John is an unpublished Arabic *Refutation* which has never been studied.

Out of all these texts, the chapter on Islam in the *De haeresibus* appears, therefore, to be the only reliable one. But even in this instance, doubts have been expressed concerning its authenticity and the quotations from the Qurʾān are considered by some scholars to be a later interpolation.[13]

Therefore, whatever the result of further critical investigation of the anti-Islamic writings attributed to John of Damascus, it appears that his contribution to the history of Byzantine polemics against Islam is slight. If one admits the authenticity of these writings even in part, it will be seen below that chronologically they were not the earliest to have been written on the subject by a Byzantine author. Theologically, they do not add much to the unquestionable glory of John of Damascus, defender of the veneration of icons, author of the first systematic *Exposition of the Orthodox Faith,* and one of the most talented hymnographers of Eastern Christianity. The study of the liturgical texts ascribed to John of Damascus strongly confirms the impression first gained from reading the chapter on Islam in the *De haeresibus*—that of John living in a Christian ghetto which preserves intact the Byzantine political and historical outlook. In his hymns he prays for "the victory of the emperor over his enemies";[14] he hopes that through the intercession of the Theotokos, the *basileus* "will trample under his feet the barbarian nations."[15] He never fails to mention the "cross-bearing sovereign (σταυροφόρος Ἄναξ)" as the shield protecting Christ's inheritance from the "blasphemous enemies."[16] And there is no ambiguity concerning the identity of these enemies: they

[12]Cf. PG 97, col. 1543.
[13]A. Abel, in *Byzantion* 24 (1954), p. 353 n. 2.
[14]*Octoechos,* Sunday Matins, Tone 1, canon 1, ode 9, Theotokion.
[15]*Ibid.,* Tone 3, canon 1, ode 9, Theotokion.
[16]*Ibid.,* Tone 4, canon 2, ode 9, Theotokion.

are "the people of the Ishmaelites, who are fighting against us" and whom the Theotokos is asked to put under the feet of the piety-loving emperor ('Ισμαηλίτην λαὸν καθυπο-τάττων τὸν πολεμοῦντα ἡμᾶς φιλευσεβοῦντι βασι-λεῖ).[17]

In mind and in heart John still lives in Byzantium. The fact that the Byzantine emperor—whose victorious return to the Middle East he is hopefully expecting—has actually fallen into the iconoclastic heresy is, for him, a matter of greater concern than are the beliefs of the Arab conquerors. And he is certainly much better informed about the events in Constantinople than about Islam.

Even if it is eventually proved that the last part of chapter 101 of the De haeresibus, which contains quotations from the Qurran, is not a later interpolation, this would not provide clear evidence that John had, in fact, read the Qurran.[18] Any knowledge of Islam, direct or indirect, which is betrayed by John, relates to four suras only—the second, the third, the fourth and the fifth—and to the oral Islamic traditions, especially those connected with the veneration of the Ka'aba in Mecca, which give John a pretext to deride the Islamic legends about Abraham's camel having been attached to the sacred stone. The knowledge of oral Arab traditions, sometimes more ancient than Islam, displayed by John and by other Byzantine polemicists is perhaps one of the most interesting aspects of the type of literature which we are studying; yet, at the same time, it illustrates the casual and superficial character of their acquaintance with Islam. Legendary commonplaces about the origins of Islam are repeated by different authors in different ways. I shall mention but one example, one which shows that John is neither original nor better informed than other Greeks in this matter. John refers to a pre-Islamic Meccan cult of Aphrodite, named Χαβὲρ or Χαβὰρ by the Arabs, which survived in the form of the

---

[17]Ibid., Tone 8, canon 2, ode 9, Theotokion.

[18]J. R. Merrill, "On the Tractate of John of Damascus on Islam," Muslim World 41 (1951), p. 97; cf. also P. Khoury, "Jean Damascène et l'Islam," Proche Orient chrétien 7 (1957), pp. 44-63; 8 (1958), pp. 313-339.

veneration of a sacred stone, the *Ka'aba*.[19] The same account is also mentioned by Constantine Porphyrogenitus in the *De administrando imperio*. This is what Constantine writes: "They pray also to the star of Aphrodite which they call Κουβάρ, and in their supplication cry out 'Αλλᾶ οὐὰ Κουβάρ, that is, God and Aphrodite. For they call God 'Αλλᾶ; and οὐὰ they use for the conjunction *and* and they call the star Κουβάρ. And so they say 'Αλλᾶ οὐὰ Κουβάρ."[20]

It is for the Arabists to inform us how much of this imperial excursion into the field of etymology, which is obviously parallel to, though independent of, the Damascene's text, is of any value. The traditional Islamic invocation *Allahu akbar*—"God is very great"—which is obviously referred to here, puzzled the Byzantine authors from the eighth century onwards. About 725, that is before the time of John of Damascus, Germanus of Constantinople also mentions that "the Saracens, in the desert, address themselves to an inanimate stone and make an invocation to the so-called Χοβὰρ (τήν τε λεγομένου Χοβὰρ ἐπίκλησιν)."[21] John of Damascus identifies Χαβὰρ or Χαβὲρ (he uses the two forms) with both Aphrodite herself, and with the *Ka'aba*, which according to him represents the head of the pagan goddess.[22] In the ninth century, Nicetas also speaks of the "idol of Χουβὰρ" (προσκυνεῖ τῷ Χουβὰρ εἰδώλῳ) said to represent Aphrodite.[23] That some cult of the Morning Star existed among the Arabs before the rise of Islam seems certain, and this was known to the Byzantines, who attempted, of course, to find traces of paganism in Islam itself. However, the example of the page on Aphrodite proves that John of Damascus did not add anything substantial to the information on Islam already available to the Byzantines of his time,[24] and

[19]PG 94, cols. 764B, 769B.
[20]Constantine Porphyrogenitus, *De administrando imperio*, I, 14, ed. Moravcsik, tr. R.J.H. Jenkins (Budapest, 1949), pp. 78-79.
[21]Letter to Thomas of Claudiopolis, PG 98, col. 168D.
[22]*De haeresibus*, PG 764B, 769B.
[23]*Refutatio Mohamedis*, PG 105, col. 793B.
[24]It should be noted, however, that the Damascene gives a *translation* of the word χαβάρ, and interprets it as meaning "great" in the feminine

that he merely made use of an accepted argument which conveniently confirmed the Byzantine belief that the Arabs "were devoted to lechery."[25]

We have already noted, on the other hand, that John lists Islam among the Christian heresies. This attitude toward Islam was based on the fact that the Qurran admits the revealed character of both Judaism and Christianity. John and his contemporaries tended, therefore, to apply to Islam the criteria of Christian orthodoxy and to assimilate Islam with a Christian heresy *already* condemned. Thus Muhammad was an Arian, because he denied the divinity of the Logos and of the Holy Spirit; hence, probably, the legend of Muhammad being instructed in the Christian religion by an *Arian* monk.[26] In fact, the contact of early Islam with Christianity involved the Monophysite and the Nestorian communities, certainly not the Arians, and the appellation ascribed by John to the Moslems—κόπται τοῦ Θεοῦ ("cutters of God")[27]—because they cut away from God the Logos and the Spirit, is but a reply to the Moslem accusation directed against Christians that they are ἑταιριασταί—"those who admit partners of God."[28]

Together with these polemical arguments dealing with the opposition between the absolute monotheism of Islam and the Christian doctrine of the Trinity, John touches upon another acute point of disagreement—the question of free will and of predestination—and his whole argument is supported by the most violent epithets which he applies to Muhammad, the "pseudo-prophet," the "hypocrite," the "liar," and the

form (ὅπερ σημαίνει μεγάλη—col. 764B). This has led G. Sablukov to see the origin of the form used by Nicetas and Constantine (κουβὰρ or χουβὰρ) in the *feminine form of akbar-koubra*, and to infer that the Byzantines knew of a pre-Islamic Arab invocation of Aphrodite—*Allata koubra* ("Zametki po voprosu o vizantiiskoi protivomusul'manskoi literature," *Provoslavnyi Sobesednik* 2 [1878], pp. 303-327; cf. also a similar etymological argument put forward by Georgius Hamartolus, ed. de Boor, II, p. 706).

[25]B. Lewis, in Constantine Porphyrogenitus, *De administrando II, Commentary* (London, 1962), p. 72.

[26]PG 94, 765A.

[27]*Ibid.*, 768D.

[28]*Ibid.*, 760B.

"adulterer." All this was, of course, later taken up at length by other polemicists.

Two names deserve quite special mention in the history of early Byzantine polemics against Islam. One is that of an Arabic-speaking bishop, Theodore Abu-Qurra, who lived in Moslem-occupied territory, mainly in Syria, in the second half of the eighth century. The other is that of Nicetas Byzantius, a scholar from the entourage of Photius. Although they wrote in very different styles and were involved in different situations, both Theodore and Nicetas were much better acquainted with Islam than was John of Damascus; Theodore, because he lived side by side with the Moslems and engaged them in dialogue, and Nicetas, because he had studied the entire text of the Qurran.

Abu-Qurra wrote in both Greek and Arabic. Of his fifty-two short Greek treatises, most were composed in the form of dialogues with various heretics encountered by the author (Nestorians, Monophysites, Origenists) and seventeen are directed against Islam. It is from these short *opuscula*[29] that one can sense the true nature of the relations which existed between Moslems and Christians in the eighth century. The dialogues of Theodore maintain, it is true, a strictly negative attitude towards the faith of Islam and towards the person of Muhammad, an Arianizing false prophet (1560 A), possessed by an evil spirit (1545 B-1548 A). But the arguments used are conceived in such a way as to be understood by the opponents; they correspond to an attempt at real conversation. Here are some examples: the Arabs refuse to believe in the trinitarian doctrine, because it brings division to God. But the Qurran is one, even if many copies can be made of it; in the same way, God is one and three (1528 C D). A short dialogue is entirely devoted to the Christian doctrine of the eucharist, which, of course, was difficult for Moslems to understand; here Theodore relies on medical images familiar to both sides: the descent of the Holy Spirit on bread and wine which are thereby changed into the body and blood of Christ is similar to the action of the liver which assimilates

[29]The Greek treatises of Abu-Qurra are published in PG 97, cols. 1461-1609.

food through the emission of heat (1552 D-1553 C). In a question which was unavoidable in any conversation between a Moslem and a Christian, that of polygamy, Theodore adopts a pragmatic attitude, which he knows will be better understood by his opponent than any reference to high morality or to the sacrament of marriage. "A woman," Theodore writes, "marries a man for the sake of pleasure and childbirth." But can one imagine a greater human pleasure than that which Adam and Eve enjoyed in Paradise, where, however, they were under a regime of monogamy? And when the Moslem still maintains that he prefers polygamy because it secures quicker multiplication of the human race, Theodore answers that since God did not care for a quick multiplication of men when man was *alone* on earth, he certainly does not desire too great a proliferation today. . . . And he concludes the argument by reminding the Moslem of the unavoidable quarrels and scenes of jealousy which occur in a harem (1556 A-1558 D).

The pragmatic character of some of Abu-Qurra's dialogues does not preclude the use of more technical theological arguments. Theodore is a trained Aristotelian, and he is well aware of all of the refinements of Byzantine trinitarian doctrine and Christology. When the Moslem objects to the doctrine of the death of Christ—the person of Christ is made up of a body and a soul, their separation would mean the disappearance of Christ as a person—Theodore answers by referring to the Orthodox doctrine of the hypostatic union which is based upon the unity of Christ's *divine* hypostasis which is and remains, even in death, the unifying factor of all the elements composing the God-man. This is why the body of Christ remained uncorrupted in the grave (1583-1584).

The discussion very often touches on the doctrine of predestination, which was promoted in orthodox Islam and was often discussed in the Moslem world. It is, of course, refuted by Theodore in a series of arguments which reflect actual conversations on a popular level: if Christ had to die voluntarily, says the Moslem, then the Christians must thank the Jews for having contributed to the realization of God's will, since *everything* which happens is in accordance with His will. Theodore replies: since you say that all those who die in the holy war against the infidels go to heaven, you must thank the Romans for killing so many of your brethren (1529 A). But the discussion on predestination runs also on a more philosophical and theological level: Theodore explains the Christian doctrine of the divine creative act, which was completed in the first six days and which, since then, has given to human free will the opportunity to act, to create and to choose; if any predestination toward good exists, it is derived from baptism, which is a new birth and which should be freely accepted and followed by good works (1587 A-1592 C).[30]

Many of the theological points touched upon by Theodore are also discussed in the lengthy treatise written by Nicetas Byzantius and dedicated to the Emperor Michael III.[31] Nicetas writes in Constantinople and has probably never spoken to a Moslem, but he has a complete text of the Qurran and gives a systematic criticism of it, with exact quotations of various suras under their titles and numbers. (The latter do not always correspond to those used in the modern editions of the Qurran.) Nicetas' book is in two parts:

1. An apologetical exposition of the Christian faith, concentrated mainly on the doctrine of the Trinity (673-701).

2. A systematic refutation of the Qurran in thirty chapters (701-805). Nicetas' refutation is purely academic and scholarly in character; it is an intellectual exercise of the kind one might expect from the learned circle of scholars gathered around Photius and financed by the Caesar Bardas and the court of Michael III. Basically it reflects the impression produced by the Qurran on a Byzantine intellectual of the ninth century who has been given the assignment of refuting the new faith. He performs his task carefully, but without any real concern for an eventual Moslem auditor or reader.

Comparing the Qurran with Christian Scripture, he speaks of the "most pitiful and the most inept little book of the Arab Muhammad (τὸ οἴκτιστον καὶ ἀλόγιστον τοῦ

---

[30]This passage on predestination is reproduced verbatim in the *Dialogue* attributed to John of Damascus, PG 96, cols. 1336-1340.
[31]PG 105, cols. 669A-805.

Άραβος Μωάμετ βιβλίδιον), full of blasphemies against the Most High, with all its ugly and vulgar filth," which does not have even the appearance of any of the biblical *genres* and is neither prophetical, nor historical, nor juridical, nor theological, but all confused. How can this, he asks, be sent from heaven? Nicetas does not know Arabic himself and uses several different translations of the Qurran. This is apparent, for example, in his treatment of the famous sura CXII, directed against the Christian trinitarian doctrine, which is thenceforth an inevitable subject in every discussion of faith between Christians and Moslems:

> "Say, 'He is God alone!
> God the Eternal!
> He begets not and is not begotten!
> Nor is there like unto Him any one!' "
> (*Palmer's translation*)

The Arabic word *samad* which means "solid," "massive," "permanent"—rendered here by the English *eternal*—is at first, at the beginning of Nicetas' book, translated by the Greek ὁλόσφαιρος, *i.e.*, "all-spherical," which gives Nicetas an opportunity of ridiculing such a material conception of the divinity (708 A). Later, he corrects his translation and renders *samad* by ὁλόσφυρος, which evokes a solid metallic mass, beaten by a hammer, and which is closer to the concrete image of God given by the Coranic text (776 B).

Another example of a misunderstanding due to a faulty translation: Nicetas accuses the Qurran of teaching that man comes "from a leech" (ἐκ βδέλλης—708 A). In fact, the Arabic text (sura XCVI, 2) speaks of a particle of congealed blood.

I have chosen these examples, among many others in the Nicetas text, because they are repeated by many other Byzantine authors and occupy a central place in later polemics. They illustrate the permanent misunderstanding between the two cultures and the two religious mentalities, but also show the positive knowledge of Coranic texts on the part of some Byzantines. Nicetas Byzantius, for example, had obviously studied the Qurran, even if in faulty translations, which were probably unavoidable at this early stage of Byzantine-Arab relations. On the other hand, it can be asked whether, in some instances, such Byzantine interpretations of Islam doctrine as the alleged belief in the spherical shape of God or the leech as the origin of man, did not, in fact, come from some forms of popular Arab religion—distinct, of course, from orthodox Islam—which were known to the Byzantines.

A complete survey of the Byzantine literature directed against Islam should, of course, include the study of many Byzantine documents belonging chronologically to later periods which are outside the scope of our paper. It will be sufficient to mention here that, from the eleventh to the fifteenth century, the knowledge of Islam gradually increases in Byzantium. A thirteenth-century writer, Bartholomew of Edessa,[32] already shows some knowledge of the role of Othman and Abu-Bakr after the death of Muhammad. In the fourteenth century, the retired Emperor John Cantacuzenus gathers an even richer documentation. He composes four *Apologies* of Christianity directed against the Moslems, and four treatises (λόγοι) refuting the Qurran.[33] In addition to earlier Byzantine sources, he uses the Latin *Refutation of Islam* by a Florentine Dominican monk, Ricaldus de Monte Croce (d. 1309), translated by Demetrius Cydones.[34] Cantacuzenus seems to have regarded the publication of his anti-Islamic writings as a major event in his life: in the well-known, beautiful copy of his theological works, ordered for his private library by Cantacuzenus himself and which is now in Paris (*Paris. gr.* 1242), the ex-emperor had himself represented holding a scroll with an inscription Μέγας ὁ Θεὸς τῶν Χριστιανῶν which is the *Incipit* of his work against Islam. Although his general method of refutation remains rather academic and abstract, there is no doubt that Cantacuzenus is better aware than many of his predecessors of the new situation in which he lives. He faces the Islamic challenge

[32]"Ελεγχος 'Αγαρηνοῦ, PG 104, cols. 1384-1448; for the date, see Eichner, *op. cit.*, pp. 137-138.

[33]PG 154, cols. 373-692.

[34]Translation published in PG 154, 1035-1152.

realistically and shows readiness to seek information and arguments in any source, even in the work of a Latin monk. (He quotes his source: "a monk of the Order of Preachers—τῆς τάξεως τῶν Πρεδικατόρων, ἤτοι τῶν κηρύκων—of the name of Ricaldus, went to Babylon . . . and, having worked much, learned the dialect of the Arabs."[35]) And his prayers are not only for the destruction, but also for the conversion of the Moslems.[36] All this proves that he took Islam much more seriously than did the authors of the eighth and the ninth centuries. It is perhaps worth recalling here that a friend of Cantacuzenus, the famous hesychast theologian and archbishop of Thessalonica, Gregory Palamas, describes in 1354 his journey to Turkish-occupied Asia Minor in a rather optimistic tone, hoping, like Cantacuzenus, for a subsequent conversion of Moslems and implying the acceptance, for the time being, of a friendly coexistence.[37]

2.

Byzantine polemical literature has largely determined the official canonical attitude of the Church towards Islam, an attitude which is reflected in the rites of the reception of Moslem converts to Christianity. One such very ancient rite contains a series of twenty-two anathemas against Moslem beliefs.[38] The convert is required to anathematize Muhammad, all the relatives of the Prophet (each by name) and all the

[35]PG 154, col. 601.

[36]Ibid., col. 584.

[37]On this episode, see J. Meyendorff, Introduction à l'étude de Grégoire Palamas (Paris, 1959), pp. 157-162.

[38]This rite has been published by F. Sylburg (Heidelberg, 1595). Sylburg's edition has been reprinted as a part of the Thesaurus Orthodoxae fidei of Nicetas Choniates in PG 140, cols. 123-138. A new edition of the rite has been issued by F. Montet, "Le rituel d'abjuration des Musulmans dans l'Église grecque," Revue de l'histoire des religions 53 (1906), pp. 145-163, with a French translation of the anathemas. This new edition does not replace Sylburg's, which is more complete. Cf. observations on Montet's edition in S. Ebersolt, "Un nouveau manuscrit sur le rituel d'abjuration des Musulmans dans l'Église grecque," in the same Revue de l'histoire des religions 54 (1906), pp. 231-232; Cf. Clermont-Ganneau, "Ancien rituel grec pour l'abjuration des

caliphs until Yezid (680-683). The fact that no later caliph is mentioned has led Fr. Cumont to conclude that the rite dates from the early eighth century. However, since the list lacks any chronological order (the name of Yezid is followed by that of Othman, the third caliph), the argument does not seem altogether conclusive.

Other anathemas are directed against the Qurʾan; the Moslem conception of paradise, where all sorts of sins will take place "since God cannot be ashamed"; polygamy; the doctrine of predestination, which leads to the idea that God Himself is the origin of evil; the Moslem interpretation of the Gospel stories and the Qurʾan's treatment of the Old Testament. The anathemas repeat many of the arguments used by polemicists: the Arab worship of Aphrodite, called Χαβάρ, and the theory that has man issuing from a leech are mentioned, and the convert to Christianity is required to renounce them formally.

The author of the rite obviously knew more about Islam than did John of Damascus. He probably made use of Nicetas' treatise and also of other contemporary sources. It seems reasonable, therefore, to place the composition of the rite in the ninth century, at a time when similar rituals for the admission of Jews and Paulicians were composed. At any rate, this particular rite was still in use in the twelfth century because Nicetas Choniates gives a detailed account of a conflict which opposed the Emperor Manuel I to the patriarchal synod and in which Eustathius, metropolitan of Thessalonica, played a leading role.[39] In 1178, Manuel published two decrees, ordering the deletion of the last anathema from the rite, starting with the copy in use at the Great Church of St. Sophia. The anathema, quoted from sura CXII, reads as follows: "I anathematize the God of Muhammad about whom

---

Musulmans," *Recueil d'archéologie orientale* 7 (Paris, 1906), pp. 254-257; Fr. Cumont, "L'origine de la formule grecque d'abjuration imposée aux Musulmans," *Revue de l'histoire des religions* 64 (1911), pp. 143-150.

[39]Nicetas Choniates, *Historia*, Bonn ed., pp. 278-286; on the whole episode, see C. G. Bonis "Ὁ Θεσσαλονίκης Εὐστάθιος καὶ οἱ δύο "τόμοι" τοῦ αὐτοκράτορος Μανουὴλ Α´ Κομνηνοῦ (1143/80) ὑπὲρ τῶν εἰς τὴν χριστιανικὴν ὀρθοδοξίαν μετισταμένων Μωαμεθανῶν," in Ἐπετηρὶς Ἑταιρείας Βυζαντινῶν Σπουδῶν 19 (1949), pp. 162-169.

he says: 'He is God alone, God the Eternal [the Greek text reads ὁλόσφυρος—of "hammer-beaten metal"], He begets not and is not begotten, nor is there like unto Him any one.' "

The reason for this measure was that the emperor was afraid to scandalize the converts by obliging them to anathematize not only the beliefs of Muhammad but also "the God of Muhammad," for this seemed to imply that Christians and Moslems did not, in fact, believe in one and the same God. The imperial measure provoked strong opposition on the part of the patriarch and the synod. Eustathius of Thessalonica, who acted as the Church's spokesman in this matter, proclaimed that a God believed to be "of hammer-beaten metal" is not the true God, but a material idol, which should be anathematized as such. After some argument between the palace and the patriarchate, a compromise solution was found. The emperor withdrew his original decree; the twenty-second anathema was retained in the ritual, but now it read simply: "Anathema to Muhammad, to all his teaching and all his inheritance." This text was preserved in the later editions of the *Euchologion.*

The episode is significant inasmuch as it clearly illustrates the existence in Byzantium of two views on Islam: the extreme and "closed" one, which adopted an absolutely negative attitude towards Muhammadanism and considered it a form of paganism, and another, the more moderate one, which tried to avoid burning all bridges and to preserve a measure of common reference, in particular, the recognition of a common allegiance to monotheism.

Manuel I belonged to this second group, and in this respect he followed the tradition which seems to have been predominant in official governmental circles of Byzantium. One can see this from the next category of documents which we shall examine—the letters addressed by the Byzantine emperors and officials to their Arab colleagues.

3.

First, and historically most important, is a letter of Leo III to the Caliph Omar II. Omar II reigned for only three years (717-720), and the letter can, therefore, be dated with relative precision. I cannot discuss here in detail the problem of its authenticity. The fact that there was some correspondence on questions of faith between Leo and Omar is explicitly attested by Theophanes,[40] but the original Greek text of Leo's letter (or letters) is lost. A short Latin version has been published by Champerius, who quite wrongly attributes the letter to Leo VI.[41] This attribution is accepted without question by Krumbacher and Eichner. A much longer Armenian version has been preserved by the historian Ghevond. It reproduces the original text, possibly with some minor additions.[42]

The document is interesting in more than one respect: 1. It emenates from the first iconoclastic emperor, but precedes the iconoclastic controversy itself and thus provides valuable evidence on Leo's views about icon veneration at this early period; this evidence is confirmed, as we shall see later, in other contemporary sources. 2. It is the first known Byzantine text which refutes Islam, and it shows a knowledge of the subject much wider than that of other contemporary polemicists.

Leo's letter is a reply to a solemn appeal by Omar to send him an exposition of the Christian faith. In fact, it was customary for the early caliphs, at their enthronement, to send such requests to infidel princes, denouncing their beliefs and calling upon them to join Islam. Omar asks Leo to furnish him with the arguments that make Leo prefer Christianity to any other faith, and puts several questions to him: "Why

[40]*Chronographia*, Bonn ed., II, p. 399.

[41]This version is reproduced in PG 107, cols. 315-24.

[42]English translation, commentary and bibliography in A. Jeffrey, "Ghevond's Text of the Correspondence between Umar II and Leo III," *Harvard Theological Review* 37 (1944), pp. 269-332. Jeffrey offers a convincing amount of internal and external evidence in favor of the letter's authenticity, in opposition to Beck, *Vorsehung und Vorherbestimmung*, pp. 43-46, who thinks that the letter could not be earlier than the late ninth century. Cf. also A. Abel's recent suggestion that Leo the Mathematician is possibly the author (*Byzantion* 24 [1954], p. 348 n.1). Among earlier believers in the authenticity of the letter, see B. Berthold, "Khalif Omar II i protivorechivyia izvestiia o ego lichnosti," *Khristianskii Vostok* 6, 3 (1922), p. 219.

have the Christian peoples, since the death of the disciples of Jesus, split into seventy-two races? . . . Why do they profess three gods? . . . Why do they adore the bones of apostles and prophets, and also pictures and the cross? . . ."[43]

Leo's answers are all based on sound exegesis of both the Bible and the Qurran. For him there is no question of relying on popular legends or misrepresentations. He does not feel the need of condemning the alleged cult of Aphrodite in Islam or of having Omar renounce the doctrine which claims that man's origin was the leech. He does not doubt that he and his correspondent believe in the same God, that the latter accepts the Old Testament as revealed truth. Is Omar looking for arguments in support of the true religion? But there are numerous prophets and apostles who affirmed the divinity of Jesus, while Muhammad stands alone. . . . And how can one say that the Qurran is above all criticism? "We know," Leo writes "that it was 'Umar, Abu Turab and Solman the Persian, who composed [the Qurran], even though the rumor has got round among you that God sent it down from the heavens. . . ." And we know also that "a certain Hajjaj, named by you Governor of Persia, replaced ancient books by others, composed by himself, according to his taste. . . ."[44] And is not Islam, the younger of the two religions, torn apart by schisms even more serious than those which beset the comparatively ancient Christianity? These divisions occurred in Islam, Leo continues, although it arose among only one people, the Arabs, all of whom spoke the same tongue, while Christianity from the beginning was adopted by Greeks, Latins, Jews, Chaldeans, Syrians, Ethiopians, Indians, Saracens, Persians, Armenians, Georgians and Albanians: some disputes among them were inevitable![45]

A large part of Leo's letter is devoted to the problems of cult and worship, in reply to Omar's attack on the Christian doctrine of the sacraments. The Byzantine emperor's criticism of the Ka'aba cult has nothing of the mythical exaggeration of the other polemicists. He writes: "The region to which the

[43]A. Jeffrey, op. cit., pp. 277-278.
[44]Ibid., p. 292.
[45]Cf. ibid., p. 297.

prophets turned when they made their prayers is not known. It is you alone who are carried away to venerate the pagan altar of sacrifice that you call the House of Abraham. Holy Scripture tells us nothing about Abraham having gone to the place. . . ."[46] And here is an interesting passage concerning the veneration of the cross and the icons: "We honor the cross because of the sufferings of the Word of God incarnate. . . . As for pictures, we do not give them a like respect, not having received in Holy Scripture any commandment whatsoever in this regard. Nevertheless, finding in the Old Testament that divine command which authorized Moses to have executed in the Tabernacle the figures of the cherubim, and, animated by a sincere attachment for the disciples of the Lord who burned with love for the Savior Himself, we have always felt a desire to conserve their images, which have come down to us from their times as their living representations. Their presence charms us, and we glorify God who has saved us by the intermediary of His Only-Begotten Son, who appeared in the world in a similar figure, and we glorify the saints. But as for the wood and the colors, we do not give them any reverence."[47]

This text clearly reflects a state of mind which was predominant at the court of Constantinople in the years which preceded the iconoclastic decree of 726. The images are still a part of the official imperial orthodoxy, but Leo does not attach to them anything more than an educational and sentimental significance; the veneration of the cross is more pronounced, and we know that it was preserved even by the iconoclasts themselves. The use of images is justified explicitly by Old Testament texts, but no reverence is due to the "wood and colors." An attitude similar to that of Leo can be found in contemporary letters of Patriarch Germanus,[48] who, around 720, still represented the official point of view on images. The fact that it is expressed in the text of the letter, as preserved by Ghevond, is a clear indication of its authenticity, for neither the iconoclasts nor the orthodox

[46]*Ibid.*, p. 310.
[47]*Ibid.*, p. 322.
[48]Cf., for example, his letter to Thomas of Claudiopolis, PG 98, col. 173D.

were capable, at a later date, of adopting towards the images so detached an attitude. The orthodox, while still condemning the veneration of "wood and colors" in themselves, were to invoke the doctrine of the incarnation in support of a sacramental—and not purely educational—approach to images, while the iconoclasts were to condemn any image representing Christ and the saints.

Leo's text represents, therefore, an interesting example of Christian apologetics, based upon minimizing the role of images, and one can clearly see the importance of this apologetical attitude towards Islam in the early development of Iconoclasm. The iconoclastic edict of 726 was merely the next and decisive stage of this development. As André Grabar has pungently remarked,[49] a "cold war" of propaganda and blackmail was carried on, side by side with the armed conflict which permanently opposed Byzantium to the caliphate, throughout the second part of the seventh century and the beginning of the eighth. Sacred images played an important role in this cold war, sometimes as a symbol of Christianity against the Infidel, sometimes as a proof of the Christians' idolatry. And, as in the cold war of today, the opponents often tended to use each other's methods. The correspondence between Leo III and Omar is an interesting phenomenon in the gradual emergence of the issues at stake.

The other extant letters of Byzantine officials relevant to our subject belong to the ninth and tenth century and are less important historically. About 850, the Emperor Michael III received a letter ἐκ τῶν Ἀγαρηνῶν, "from the Arabs," and asked Nicetas Byzantius, the polemicist whose major work we have already examined, to answer them in his name. It is justifiable to suppose that the epistle that Michael III had received from the caliph was similar to the one that Omar had sent to Leo III; in this case the caliph would have been Al-Mutawakkil (847-861). The two answers written by Nicetas are concerned entirely with an exposition of the Christian doctrine of the Trinity which, the writer asserts, does not essentially contradict monotheism.[50] In his first refu-

---

[49]*L'iconoclasme byzantin; dossier archéologique* (Paris, 1957), p. 47.
[50]PG 105, cols. 807-821, 821-841.

tation Nicetas repeats part of his polemical treatise dedicated
to a positive *exposé* of Christian faith, but omits the direct
polemics and criticism of the Qurran. We do not know
whether Nicetas' writings were actually communicated to the
emperor's correspondent, but one can see at this point that,
already in the ninth century, a significant difference existed
between the internal use made of polemics and the requirements of diplomatic courtesy.

There is no doubt that the latter was observed in the correspondence between Photius and the caliph, the existence of
which is mentioned by his nephew, the patriarch Nicholas
Mysticus.[51] Nicholas himself corresponded with the caliph on
political matters and three of his letters have been preserved.
From them we learn that a good deal of mutual tolerance
did, in fact, exist between Moslems and Christians, especially
when the opponents were able to exercise retaliation in case
of abuse. Since, according to the patriarch's letter, the Arab
prisoners could pray in a mosque in Constantinople without
anyone obliging them to embrace Christianity, the caliph
should also cease to persecute Christians.[52] And Nicholas refers to those laws of Muhammad himself that favor religious
tolerance.[53] In another letter, he expresses in strong terms the
belief in a single God which is shared by both Christians and
Moslems: all authority comes from God and it is "from this
unique God that we all received the power of government,"
and "the two powers over all powers on earth, *i.e.,* that of
the Arabs and that of the Romans, have preeminence [over
all] and shine as the two big lights of the firmament. And
this in itself is a sufficient reason for them to live in fraternal
fellowship."[54]

One wonders whether, side by side with these official diplomatic letters, one may not justifiably mention here an infamous

[51]Letter 2, ed. Jenkins-Westerink (Washington, D.C., 1973), p. 12.
[52]Letter 102, *ed. cit.,* pp. 376-380.
[53]*Ibid.,* p. 381.
[54]Letter 1, *ed. cit.,* p. 2; on the true nature of this letter, addressed not to an
"emir of Crete," as the present superscription states, but to the caliph himself,
see R.J.H. Jenkins, "The Mission of St. Demetrianus of Cyprus to Bagdad,"
Annuaire de l'Institut de Phil. et d'Hist. Orient. et Slaves 9 (1949), pp. 267-
275.

and tasteless pamphlet composed about 905-906 in Constantinople and wrongly ascribed to Arethas, bishop of Caesarea, a famous scholar and a disciple of Photius. The pamphlet consists essentially of a number of jokes in poor taste about the Moslem conception of Paradise. As Professor R. J. H. Jenkins has recently shown, the real author of the pamphlet is a certain Leo Choirosphactes,[55] whom Arethas ridicules in a dialogue entitled Χοιροσφάκτης ἢ Μισογόης.[56] For us, interest in this document resides in the fact that it shows that Byzantine anti-Islamic polemics could be pursued simultaneously at very different levels, and that diplomatic courtesy and intellectual understanding at the government level did not prevent slander and caricaturization at others.

4.

In the early eighth century, John of Damascus describes with horror the heresy which appeared "in the time of Heraclius": "the deceptive error of the Ishmaelites, a forerunner of Antichrist." And six centuries later, John Cantacuzenus, in almost the same terms, refers to the same cataclysm "which appeared under Heraclius." There was an abyss between the two religions which no amount of polemics, no dialectical argument, no effort at diplomacy, was able to bridge. Insurmountable on the spiritual and the theological level, this opposition from the very beginning also took the shape of a gigantic struggle for world supremacy, because both religions claimed to have a universal mission, and both empires world supremacy. By the very conception of its religion, Islam was unable to draw a distinction between the "political" and "spiritual," but neither did Byzantium ever want to distinguish

---

[55]The "letter to Arethas" has been published by J. Compernass, *Denkmäler der griechischen Volkssprache* 1 (Bonn, 1911), pp. 1-9; French tr. by A. Abel, "La lettre polémique 'd'Arethas' à l'émir de Damas," *Byzantion* 24 (1954), pp. 343-370; another edition by P. Karlin-Hayter in *Byzantion* 29-30 (1959-1960), pp. 281-302; for the definitive word, see R. J. H. Jenkins, "Leo Choerosphactes and the Saracen Vizier," *Vizant. Institut, Zbornik radova* (Belgrade, 1963), pp. 167-318.

[56]Ed. J. Compernass, *Didaskaleion* 1 fasc. 3 (1912), pp. 295-318.

between the universality of the Gospel and the imperial universality of Christian Rome. This made mutual understanding
difficult and led both sides to consider that holy war was,
after all, the normal state of relations between the two empires.

One may, nevertheless, be permitted to ask what the situation was on the popular level. What was the attitude of the
average Christian towards the Moslem in their everyday relations both in the occupied lands and inside the limits of the
empire where Arab merchants, diplomats and prisoners were
numerous? Hagiography seems to be the best source for a
possible answer to this question. My cursory observations in
this area have shown, however, that here too the solution
cannot be a simple one. On the one hand, we have a great
number of the lives of martyrs with the description of massa-
cres perpetrated by Moslems—that of the monks of St. Sabbas,[57] that of sixty Greek pilgrims to Jerusalem in 724, whose
death marked the end of a seven-year truce between Leo III
and the caliphate,[58] that of the forty-two martyrs of Amorium
captured during the reign of Theophilus,[59] that of numerous
Christians who, having succumbed to pressure, adopted Islam,
but later repented and went back to the Church, as did for
example, two eighth-century saints—Bacchus the Young and
Elias the New.[60] No wonder then that in popular imagination
the Moslem, any Moslem, was a horrible and an odious being:
in the life of St. Andrew the *Salos* (the "fool for Christ's
sake") Satan himself appears in the guise of an Arab merchant.[61] Furthermore, Arabs who played a role in the Byzantine imperial administration had an extremely bad reputation
among the people; such was the case with the "Saracens"

[57]Ed. A. Papadopoulos-Kerameus, *Pravoslvnyi Palestinskii Sbornik* (1907),
pp. 1-41.

[58]The two versions of this life were published by A. Papadopoulos-Kerameus, *Pravoslavnyi Palest. Sbornik* (1892), pp. 1-7 and *ibid.* (1907), pp. 136-
163.

[59]Several versions of their martyrium in Greek and in Slavonic were published by V. Vasil'evski and P. Nikitin in *Akademiia Nauk, Istoriko-filolo-
gicheskoe otdelenie, Zapiski,* 8th ser., 7, 2 (St. Petersburg, 1905).

[60]Chr. Loparev, "Vizantiiskiia Zhitiia Sviatykh," *Vizantiiskii Vremmenik*
19 (1912), pp. 33-35.

[61]PG 111, col. 688.

who, according to the life of St. Theodore and St. Theophanes the *Graptoi,* were at the service of Emperor Theophilus,[62] or with Samonas, the *parakeimomenos* of Leo VI. In occupied areas Christians often lived in closed ghettos, avoiding any intercourse with the Moslem masters of the land: when St. Stephen, who was a monk at St. Sabbas and a man of great prestige among both Christians and Moslems, learned that Elias, Patriarch of Jerusalem, had been arrested, he refused to go and intercede for him, because he knew that it would be of no avail.[63]

Occasionally, the lives of saints reproduce discussions which took place between Christians and Moslems, and in such cases they make use of the polemical literature examined above: in Euodius' account of the martyrdom of the forty-two martyrs of Amorium, the problem of predestination is mentioned as a major issue between the two religions.[64] Among documents of this kind, the richest in content and the most original is an account of a discussion which took place about 850, in which Constantine, imperial ambassador to Samarra and future apostle of the Slavs, was involved. It is recorded in the Slavonic *Vita Constantini.* The attitude of the "Philosopher" Constantine is altogether apologetical: he defends the Christians against the accusation, mentioned above, of being "cutters of God,"[65] he quotes the Qurran (sura XIX, 17) in support of the Christian doctrine of the Virgin birth, and, as did Abu-Qurra, refutes the Moslem contention that the division of Christianity into various heresies and sects is proof of its inconsistency.[66] He counterattacks with the accusation of moral laxity among the Moslems—the standard Christian objection to the Islamic pretense of being a God-revealed religion—and, finally, expresses the classical Byzantine claim that "the empire of the Romans" is the only one

[62]PG 116, cols. 673C, 676C.

[63]*Acta Sanctorum, Jul.* III, col. 511.

[64]*Ed. cit.,* pp. 73-74; cf. Abu-Qurra, *Opuscula* 35, PG 97, col. 1588AB; Nicetas Byzantius, *Refutatio Mohammedis* 30, PG 105, col. 709; Bartholomew of Edessa, *Confutatio Agareni,* PG 104, col. 1393B.

[65]*Vita* 6, 26, ed. F. Grivec and F. Tomsic, *Staroslovenski Institut, Radovi* 5 (Zagreb, 1960), p. 104.

[66]*Ibid.,* 6, 16, p. 104.

blessed by God. He finds even a Biblical basis for this claim: in giving to His disciples the commandment to pay tribute to the emperor and in paying that tax for Himself and for others (Matthew 17:24-27; 22: 19-21), Jesus had in mind the Roman Empire only, not just *any* state; there is, therefore, no obligation for Christians to accept the caliph's rule. The Arabs have nothing to be proud of, even in the fields of arts or sciences, for they are only the pupils of the Romans. "All arts came from us" (*ot' nas' sout' v'sa khoudozh'stvia ish'la*), Constantine concludes.[67] Fr. Dvornik is certainly right when he sees in this attitude of Constantine a typical Byzantine approach to all "barbarians," Latin or Arab, as expressed in several ninth-century documents issued by Michael III, Basil I, or the Patriarch Photius himself.[68] A cultural and national pride of this kind did not, of course, contribute much to mutual understanding between Christians and Moslems.

However, here and there, in the hagiographical writings, a more positive note is struck. In another passage of the life of St. Stephen we are told that the saint "received with sympathy and respected everyone, Moslems as well as Christians."[69] The holiness, the hospitality of some Christian saints are said to have favorably impressed the Saracens, who are then described in more generous terms in the lives. This occurs, for example, in the early tenth century, when the Arabs invading the Peloponnesus are impressed by the holiness of St. Peter of Argos, and at once accept baptism.[70] At approximately the same time a Cypriot bishop, Demetrianus, travelling to Bagdad, is received by the caliph and obtains the return to Cyprus of a number of Greek prisoners.[71] Another significant story recounts that, under Michael II, after an attack on Nicopolis in Epirus, an Arab of the retreating Moslem army remains in the mountains and lives there for several years in complete isolation, afraid to mingle with the

[67]*Ibid.*, 6, 53, p. 105.
[68]*Les légendes de Constantin et de Méthode vues de Byzance* (Prague, 1933), pp. 110-111.
[69]*Acta Sanctorum, Jul. III,* col. 511.
[70]Mai, *Nova Patrum Bibliotheca* 9, 3, 1-17.
[71]Life of St. Demetrianus, ed. H. Grégoire, *Byzantinische Zeitschrift* 16 (1907), 232-233.

population. During these years, however, he manages to be baptized. One day a hunter kills him by mistake. He then is entered into the local *martyrologium* under the name of St. Barbaros, for even his name was not known. Again, Constantine Acropolites, starting his thirteenth-century account of St. Barbaros' life, begins with a quotation from St. Paul: "there is no barbarian, nor Greek, but Christ is all in all."[72]

On the other hand, one cannot deny the existence, especially in the later period under discussion, of some communication between Islam and Christianity on the level of spiritual practice and piety. It has been pointed out that a startling similarity exists between the Moslem *dhikr*—the invocation of the name of God connected with breathing—and the practices of the Byzantine hesychasts.[73] Byzantine monasticism continued to flourish in Palestine and on Mount Sinai, while pilgrims continually visited the Holy Land. All this implies the existence of contacts that were other than polemical.

Yet, as we look at the over-all picture of the relations between the two religious worlds, we see that essentially they remained impenetrable by each other. Among all the historical consequences of the Arab conquest of the Middle East, one seems to me to be the *most important*: for *ages* Byzantine Christianity was kept on the defensive. Islam not only obliged the Christians to live in a tiny enclosed world which concentrated on the liturgical cult, it also made them feel that such an existence was a normal one. The old Byzantine instinct for conservatism, which is both the main force and the principal weakness of Eastern Christianity, became the last refuge which could ensure its survival in the face of Islam.

[72]Ed. by A. Papadopoulos-Kerameus, Ἀνάλεκτα Ἱεροσολυμιτικῆς Σταχυολογίας 1, pp. 405-420.

[73]Cf., for example, L. Gardet, "Un problème de mystique comparée," *Revue Thomiste* 56 (1956), pp. 197-200.

2

The Liturgy: A Lead to the Mind of Byzantium

Secular historians study Christianity as a purely historical phenomenon, and history implies variation and change. A Christian approach to history does not deny the reality of change, but it presupposes that God—who transcends history and is not, of course, determined by its laws—also manifests Himself through historical events, which then acquire a normative and, therefore, supra-historical significance. Thus all Christians recognize—or at least should recognize—that in the *historical* event of the incarnation, a decisive act of God has taken place. But the event involved also an historical and cultural milieu, which itself acquired a normative character. God manifested Himself at a given moment in history as the Jewish Messiah, and the recognition of the historical Jesus as savior of all humanity is impossible without accepting also the Biblical Hebrew context of His life and message.

While the incarnation occurred once and for all, and nothing can be added to its saving fulness, the result of Christ's death and resurrection was the establishment of a community—the Church (ἐκκλησία)—and the "wild branch" of the Gentiles (Rom. 11:17) could then grow out of the original "roots." Thus, between the apostolic community and the Church of later times there is also a normative continuity: the unity of Tradition, which implies consistency of belief and experience.

For our own contemporary Orthodox Church, Christian Byzantium is the inevitable historical link with the original apostolic community. Since the sixth century, Constantinople has been the unquestionable center of Christian Orthodoxy in the East, and, after the schism between East and West, it acquired primacy in Orthodoxy as a whole. These were *de facto* historical developments which make it impossible for us to think of Orthodox continuity and consistency in history without referring to Byzantium. Other Christian traditions, Eastern and Western, have also a great wealth of Christian culture, which produced rich fruits of holiness, but—at least in the Orthodox view—Byzantium maintained that doctrinal integrity, that authenticity, which today makes our Orthodoxy Orthodox.

It is clear that the liturgy played a central part in maintaining that identity of the Church. Byzantium knew many heretical patriarchs and emperors and was the scene of many pseudo-councils. No human institution, taken in isolation from the whole body of the Church, could pretend to infallibility. But the liturgical tradition always remained the central expression of the life of the Body, a witness to its permanence and integrity. Such is one of the most essential aspects of the Byzantine inheritance which we now share.

But, in recognizing the continuity, we would be blind not to see the challenge of our secular society and of the great changes which have occurred in our world since Byzantium fell in 1453. In order to face these challenges, a thorough and critical look at the Byzantine tradition is imperative. Neither blind conservatism nor radical change can be seen as adequate responses, and both would be unfaithful to the mind of Christian tradition, as Byzantium itself knew it. Sometimes the best way to kill a tradition is to follow the externals without truly understanding the contents. Living tradition involves that kind of change and adaptability which preserves its continuous relevance; otherwise the Church becomes a museum of pomposity and ritualism, quite acceptable in the framework of a pluralistic and basically superficial society but actually unfaithful to Orthodoxy itself. Thus, in order to be practically helpful, our historical research should

seek out the meaning and purpose of the Byzantine liturgical
tradition, discover its permanent theological dimension and
provide for a pattern of discernment between what is truly
essential and what is historically relative.

My own brief remarks will be limited to two historical
issues: the place of the liturgy in the religious outlook and
experience of Byzantium; and the liturgy considered as a tool
of Byzantine cultural, religious and, to some degree, political
expansion and influence in the Middle East and throughout
Eastern Europe. Indeed, the role of the liturgy as a major—
or perhaps *the* major—means through which Byzantine civilization was, on the one hand, maintained in the face of Islamic
domination in the Middle East and, on the other hand, transmitted to the barbarians in the north and northwest could
become the topic of separate studies which, so far, have not
been approached in a broad historical perspective.

1.

It is well known that, since the capital of the empire was
moved to the New Rome, the church of Constantinople began
to build up a very eclectic theological and liturgical tradition.
Before becoming itself an independent intellectual center, it
welcomed talents and ideas from everywhere. From Alexandria it adopted the system of the computation of the date of
Easter. From Antioch came several of its most distinguished
leaders (including St. John Chrysostom, Nestorius and, in
the sixth century, Romanus the Melode) bringing Antiochian
liturgical traditions to the capital. The arguments of the christological debates of the fifth and sixth centuries were primarily
conceived in Syria and Egypt; Constantinople tried only to
preserve and synthesize the valuable elements of the two
trends. However, even the autocratic power of Justinian was
not able to impose (except briefly, and essentially by force)
this Orthodox synthesis upon Nestorians and Monophysites;
the Nestorians fled and survived in Zoroastrian Persia, whereas the unreconciled Monophysites were soon cut off from the
empire by the Islamic conquest.

The resulting permanent schisms and the new political and cultural situation that prevailed in the seventh century put an end to the period of pluralism and interrelation of several major centers in the Christian East. Confronting Islam and facing new barbarian invasions, Byzantium entered a period of relative isolation and defensive self-affirmation. It is at this time that Byzantine Orthodoxy became practically identified with the Byzantine liturgy. No formal decree of liturgical centralization and uniformity was ever issued, but *de facto* the liturgy of the "Great Church" of Constantinople became the only acceptable standard of churchmanship. Even the Roman church, though respected as orthodox and accepted in its honorary primacy, was criticized for its departures from Byzantine standards.

The most significant and also the best-known expression of this new sense of self-sufficiency is found in the canons of the Synod in Trullo, which condemn the Armenian church for not mixing water into the eucharistic wine (canon 32); enforce as universally obligatory the Byzantine practice of not celebrating the eucharist during Lent except on Saturdays, Sundays and Annunciation day (canon 52); and condemn the fasting practices of Rome and Armenia (canons 55-56) as well as the ancient Christian tradition of offering honey and milk during the eucharist (canon 57). The council also set up regulations on iconography in accordance with patterns and theological ideas prevailing in Byzantium (canon 82).

If considered together with the numerous other disciplinary decrees of the Trullan council, these canons faithfully reflect the rigid and self-assured posture adopted by the Byzantine church on the eve of the period when, after an iconoclastic crisis, it entered a time of spectacular missionary expansion. To the newly converted Slavs and to other nations which remained for centuries in the religious and cultural orbit of Byzantium, the liturgy and practices of the Great Church were presented as untouchable, and converts were generally encouraged to maintain literal and rigid compliance with every detail.

Of course, self-reliance and rigidity were not accepted as absolute principles, and historical changes were inevitable. For example, in the eighth and ninth centuries, the Byzantine church adopted a large body of hymnography written by St. John of Damascus and Cosmas of Maiuma, who lived in Arab-occupied Palestine. As late as the thirteenth and fourteenth centuries, the Typikon of St. Sabbas in Palestine gradually replaced the earlier practices connected with the Great Church and the Studius monastery. Furthermore, the more enlightened leaders of the church of Constantinople were fully aware that liturgical and disciplinary pluralism was a legitimate and ancient fact in the life of the Church. Most significant in this respect is the case of Patriarch Photius. Since Pope Nicholas I had challenged his elevation to the patriarchate on the basis of norms proper to the Roman church, Photius answered by a definition of legitimate pluralism as seen from Byzantium. He wrote to Nicholas in 861: "Everybody must preserve what was defined by common ecumenical decisions, but a particular opinion of a church father or a definition issued by a local council can be followed by some and ignored by others. Thus, some people customarily shave their beards; others reject this practice through local conciliar decrees. Thus, as far as we are concerned, we consider it reprehensible to fast on Saturdays, except once a year (on Holy Saturday), while others fast on other Saturdays as well. Thus, tradition avoids disputes by making practice prevail over the rule. In Rome, there are no priests legitimately married, while our tradition permits men, once married, to be elevated to the priesthood." Here Photius refers to the legislation of the Synod in Trullo, consciously defining it in terms of a local council whose decrees are obligatory only in the East—a moderate point of view, which was soon replaced with a more rigid and formal claim by Byzantine churchmen that the Trullan council was ecumenical and that the West condemns itself by violating its decrees. The conclusion of Photius' letter to Nicholas defines a general principle: "When the faith remains inviolate, common and catholic decisions are also safe; a sensible man respects the practices and laws of others; he considers that it is neither wrong to observe them nor illegal to violate them."[1]

---

[1] *Ep.* 2, PG 102, cols. 604-605D.

However, five years later, in 867, the same Patriarch Photius, in his encyclical letter to the Eastern patriarchs, blasts the same Pope Nicholas for condoning the introduction of Latin liturgical and disciplinary practices in Bulgaria.[2] Indeed, the Byzantine patriarch considered Bulgaria as belonging to his jurisdiction and therefore fully subject to the decrees of the Trullan council. Thus, the attitudes of Photius in 861 and 867 are contradictory only in appearance. They reflect the conviction, shared by all medieval Byzantines, that the integrity of the Byzantine liturgical and disciplinary traditions expressed the Christian faith in its most legitimate and most authentic form and that, therefore, this tradition was absolutely obligatory within the limits of the Byzantine realm itself which, according to Photius, included Bulgaria. But the Byzantines also knew very well of the existence of other traditions and, as Photius did in 861, recognized in principle their legitimacy. There were always those among them who condemned an indiscriminate rejection of the Latin practices by some of their compatriots. After the final schism of 1054, Patriarch Peter of Antioch objected to the attacks by Michael Cerularius against Latin customs and considered the *Filioque* issue as the only serious obstacle to church union.[3] Similarly, Theophylact of Ohrid (d. *ca.* 1108) formally rejected the ritual accusations against the Latins. He wrote: "Unless one ignores ecclesiastical history, one will not use such arguments; church unity is threatened only by those practices which have a doctrinal implication."[4] Even in the late period, when negotiations were permanently on the political agenda of the threatened Byzantine Empire, it was universally recognized in Byzantium that a united church would retain liturgical pluralism. This was admitted also in the more conservative Byzantine circles, which included Mark Eugenicus, at Florence. Nicholas Cabasilas, while arguing in favor of the Eastern tradition of calling the power of the Holy Spirit upon the eucharistic gifts after the words of institution (*epiclesis*), invoked the authority of the Latin liturgical tradition itself

[2]*Ibid.,* cols. 733-736.
[3]PG 120, cols. 812-813A.
[4]PG 126, col. 245B.

in favor of his point of view, implicitly recognizing its legitimacy.[5]

However, even if recognized in principle, liturgical pluralism, known to the early church, was never approved of in practice. Through the centuries, the Byzantines identified more and more their basic religious and cultural experience with the liturgy of the Great Church in Constantinople. This became an essential aspect of Byzantine Orthodoxy and was due to many factors, which certainly included a mystagogical approach to the liturgy, as a visible and symbolic manifestation of an eternal and heavenly order. This conception, inherited from Neoplatonism through the mediation of Pseudo-Dionysius, implied that variety, as well as historical change, was part of the *fallen* order of things and that the divine presence always implied uniformity and immutability. This mentality was never codified into dogma or canonical legislation, but it reflected a basic aspect of the Byzantine religious and social ethos. Historical change and pluralism were not denied in principle, but avoided in conscious practice.

However, it would be a mistake to believe that references to a Neoplatonic world-view alone can explain the liturgical conservatism of the Byzantines. One should also remember an even more important factor: the Byzantine church had never defined its own doctrinal authority in terms which would be institutionally and juridically immutable. Always concerned with maintaining truth against heresy, it did not possess a clear and automatic criterion of what Christian orthodoxy was supposed to be. Of course, it recognized the authority of ecumenical councils, convoked by the emperor and composed of bishops of the entire *oikoumene*. But the Byzantines also knew that many councils which were called together in accordance with accepted norms subsequently proved to be "pseudo-councils"; that many emperors proved in fact to be heretics, and therefore *tyrannoi;* that patriarchs of Constantinople, as well as those of other Eastern sees, gladly followed the doctrines of Monophysitism, Mono-

[5]*A Commentary on the Divine Liturgy,* tr. J. M. Hussey and P. A. McNulty (New York, 1977), pp. 76-79.

theletism or Iconoclasm and that, therefore, for all his prestige and authority, the ecumenical patriarch could certainly not pretend to infallibility. So, in the absence of an ultimate institutional security—which they rejected in the person of the Roman pope—the Orthodox Byzantines looked for signs and spiritual authority in the person of individual saints. One of the greatest among them, St. Maximus the Confessor, was once confronted with the fact that all the patriarchs were condemning him. He was asked what would be his attitude if the Roman church itself approved Monotheletism; and he answered by a reference to Galatians 1:8: "The Holy Spirit anathematizes even angels, if they utter teaching contrary to the [true] kerygma."[6] The idea of the Holy Spirit alone being the ultimate criterion of truth was also strongly upheld in the context of monastic spirituality, where the authority of charismatic leaders was often upheld and even—at least implicitly—opposed to the magisterium of bishops. The case of Symeon the New Theologian is particularly obvious in this respect. In the midst of conflicts with ecclesiastical authorities, he accused them of having received "election and ordination only from men," implying that the *divine* election is not necessarily connected with formal priestly ministry.[7] Also, in 1340, the hesychasts of Mount Athos published their famous *Tomos Haghioretikos,* which directly appealed to the spiritual authority of the monks in defining theological truth.[8] Examples of similar attitudes could easily degenerate into an anti-hierarchical, sectarian or "Messalian" direction whenever the given monastic milieu was not fully committed to a sacramental, or liturgical, understanding of the Church. In fact, the dividing line between Orthodox and "Messalian" spirituality lay precisely in the role of the liturgy. The prophetic or charismatic role of the Orthodox monks was seen as legitimate only in the context of sacramental liturgical communion, which itself presupposed the existence of an institutional hier-

[6]*Acta Maximi,* PG 90, col. 121C.

[7]Cf. for example, *Syméon le Nouveau Théologien, Catéchèses,* ed. B. Krivochéine and J. Paramelle (Sources Chrétiennes 113; Paris, 1965), p. 150.

[8]Ed. V. S. Pseutoga, in P. Chrestou, Γρηγορίου τοῦ Παλαμᾶ Συγγράμματα 2 (Thessaloniki, 1966), pp. 563-578.

archy. "Celebrating the liturgy to the pure, holy and immaculate Trinity," writes Symeon, "is great and awesome and above all glory, enlightenment, command, authority, wealth, power and every kingdom."[9] The text and order of the eucharistic liturgy was also an authority invoked by Maximus the Confessor against the claim made by his Monothelite judges, that the emperor had priestly authority and could therefore define dogma. Rejecting the claim, Maximus answered: "During the holy anaphora at the holy altar, the emperors are mentioned with the laity, after bishops, deacons and every sacred order; the deacon says: 'And the lay people who fell asleep in the faith—Constantine, Constans and the others.' Similarly he commemorates the living emperors after all the sacred orders."[10]

References to similar texts could easily be multiplied, but it is the acceptance of the liturgy and sacramental experience as a criterion of spiritual authority that is important for us now. There is no doubt that in the Byzantine church the liturgical tradition, the liturgical texts and the continuous liturgical activities in which the entire society participated were seen as an essential witness of continuity and integrity. This approach to liturgy and sacraments distinguished Orthodox monastic charismatics from their Messalian counterparts, and also from Western Latin attitudes. Whereas the gradual development in the West of a juridically authoritarian papacy led to an understanding of liturgical rites as external signs placed at the Church's disposal and easily modified and regulated by church authority, Eastern Christianity visualized the liturgy as an independent authoritative source and criterion of faith and ethics. Admittedly this difference was never formalized and, perhaps, never consciously understood by either side, but, seen in historical perspective, it sheds light upon an important aspect of Byzantine civilization.

[9]Hymn 19, ed. J. Koder (Sources Chrétiennes 156; Paris, 1969) 20, 4.
[10]Acta Maximi, PG 90, col. 117CD.

2.

The second historical issue which I wish to consider is the role of the Byzantine liturgy in the survival and spread of Byzantine Christian civilization throughout the Middle East, the Balkans and Eastern Europe. In spite of radically new political and social conditions, the liturgy was maintained in areas conquered by the Muslims. Because Islam was basically tolerant of a ghetto-like survival of Christianity in its midst, Greek, Syriac, Georgian and other communities were not only able to survive in the Middle East but even to show some creativity, which eventually contribute to the development of the Byzantine liturgical tradition as a whole. Thus, we have mentioned before the works of the Palestinian poets in the eighth century (John of Damascus, Cosmas of Maiuma) and the adoption in Byzantium itself, after the twelfth century, of the *Typikon* of St. Sabbas of Palestine. However, the very fact of the survival for more than a millennium in the Islamic world of Orthodox Christians known as "the emperor's people" (μελχῖται) is, in itself, an extraordinary historical fact. And there is no doubt that for these people, the liturgical celebration was the main cultural channel which tied them to Byzantine civilization. The liturgy was lived as a "trip" to the Kingdom of God, and this divine Kingdom, throughout the centuries, had a Byzantine shape and appearance. Neither its Byzantine forms nor its words were ever changed. John of Damascus, when he composed his hymns, was a conquered subject of the Arab Muslim caliph, but he also confessed his uttermost loyalty to Byzantium and never failed to pray to Mary the Theotokos to put "the people of the Ishmaelites under the feet of the Orthodox emperor."[11]

Of course, the role of the liturgy did not consist only in maintaining the spirit of "Byzance après Byzance" in the minds of Christians in the Middle East. It served as practically the only available source of knowledge about Christian scriptures and the doctrines of Christianity. It was the means of a unique aesthetic, intellectual, musical, poetic and visual enjoy-

[11]*Octoechos*, Sunday Matins, Tone 8, canon 2, ode 9, Theotokion.

ment. Its extraordinary richness, both in value and variety, made it a substitute for schooling and sermon-listening. Of course, much of its theological content was hardly understood by the majority, but its external forms and expressions gave an appealing sense of initiation into a transcendent and inexhaustible mystery. Also, the liturgy undoubtedly contributed to the preservation of the Greek language in areas where that language was used; and, in areas where the liturgy was used in translation, it maintained the sense of belonging to a wider, universal, Christian tradition.

However, it was outside the Muslim-occupied areas and throughout Eastern Europe that the liturgy served as the major vehicle of Byzantine cultural expansion. Without engaging once more in a description of Cyrillo-Methodian mission to the Slavs, I must recall here the primarily liturgical purpose and function of that mission. In describing the initial activities of the two brothers of Thessalonica in Moravia, the author of the Life of Constantine-Cyril indicates that Constantine "taught" his Moravian disciples "the whole ecclesiastical office—matins, the hours, vespers, compline and the liturgy."[12] Translations of Scripture were in the form of lectionaries and aimed at fulfilling a liturgical function. In a poetic preamble to one such lectionary, which began (as was always the case in the Byzantine tradition) with the Gospel of John, a poet (who may have been Constantine-Cyril himself) proclaimed the "Cyrillo-Methodian" philosophy of translation:

I am the Prologue of the Holy Gospels:
As the prophets prophesied of old—
"Christ comes to gather the nations and tongues,
Since He is the light of the world . . ."
In offering my prayer to God,
I had rather speak five words
That all the brethren will understand
Than ten thousand words which are incomprehensible.[13]

[12]*Vita Constantini* 15, 2, ed. F. Grivec and F. Tomsic, in *Constantinus et Methodius Thessalonicenses, Fontes* (Zagreb, 1960), p. 131.
[13]Tr. R. Jacobson, "St. Constantine's Prologue to the Gospel," *St. Vladimir's Theological Quarterly* 7 (1963), pp. 15-18.

Of course, the idea of the Prologue and the principle of using the vernacular in the liturgy was not a Byzantine or a "Cyrillo-Methodian" monopoly. Dimitri Obolensky reminds us that the same idea was promoted by a contemporary, King Alfred of England, who also promoted the idea of putting "books which are more needful for all men to know into the language which we can all understand,"[14] but it remains true that the Byzantine church took for granted the principle of linguistic pluralism. This pluralism was also endorsed by liturgical texts, particularly the hymnography of Pentecost day, which were used by Constantine and Methodius in their polemics in Venice and Moravia against the "heresy of the three languages."[15] Of course, the Byzantines were not always fully consistent with the principle. One can recall the often-quoted derogatory remarks of Greek Archbishop Theophylact of Ohrid about his Bulgarian flock, which he describes as "monsters" and as "unclean barbarian slaves who smell of sheepskin."[16] Such texts reflect the snobbishness which often prevailed in Byzantine humanistic and aristocratic circles, but they do not imply formal renunciation of the principle of liturgical translation. The same Theophylact is the author of a Life of St. Clement of Ohrid, a disciple of Cyril and Methodius and a great promoter of their task of "acculturation" in Slavic Macedonia.

It would not be an exaggeration to affirm simply that Byzantine Christian civilization was passed on to the Slavs primarily through the liturgy and only secondarily through the translation of other texts, legal, theological and scientific. This fact is most evident in the case of the Russians. The famous accounts of Vladimir's conversion in the *Primary Chronicle* are mostly concerned with the external forms of worship and disciplinary matters: the worship of the Muslims is seen as abominable; that of the Germans as "lacking beauty"; and that of the Greeks, in St. Sophia, as having

---

[14]*The Byzantine Commonwealth* (London, 1971), p. 335.

[15]According to the *Vita Constantini*, this "heresy" was held by Frankish clergy who maintained that Christians could legitimately worship in three languages only: Hebrew, Greek and Latin, the languages of the superscription on Christ's cross.

[16]*Epist.*, PG 126, col. 508, 308-309.

transported the Russians up to the very heavens. Furthermore, both in the *Chronicle* and in the numerous polemical writings directed against the Latins and available to the Russians, anti-Latin arguments connected with the liturgy are notably prominent, particularly the issue of the "azymes," the unleavened bread used in the eucharist by Western Christians. There is no doubt that in the great mass of anti-Latin polemical writings which came to Russia from Byzantium, the liturgical arguments were more easily understood than those which concerned fine points of theology. The Russians learned very well the lesson that the liturgy is the very expression of the faith, a precious and unchangeable treasure. They were also aware that they had received that liturgy in a complete and written form, and that literal faithfulness to the Greek original was essential.

Whatever problems this attitude would eventually cause— particularly in Muscovy—it is unquestionable that, of all the confessional families of medieval Christendom, Byzantine Orthodoxy was the only one which *de facto* combined a rather strict practice of liturgical uniformity with the principle of unlimited translations of the same liturgical texts into the vernacular languages of various nations. The Latin West, less insistent upon ritual uniformity, remained linguistically monolithic until our own generation, whereas the other non-Byzantine Eastern rites have always been roughly limited by the culture of a single ethnic group (Armenian, Coptic, Syrian, Ethiopian, *etc.*). The case of Georgia is, of course, special; its national liturgical tradition, originally connected with Antioch, was eventually replaced by the Byzantine in Georgian translation. The cultural and religious attraction of Byzantium was apparently irresistible to those nations which, like the Georgians, remained in the fold of Chalcedonian Orthodoxy and thus belonged to the Byzantine "commonwealth." But this irresistibility did not imply linguistic and cultural absorption, because linguistic pluralism was always admitted in principle and practiced not only in areas remote from Constantinople but also in highly visible ecclesiastical centers close to the capital, such as Mount Athos.

So, the liturgy was undoubtedly a truly essential factor

not only in the everyday life of Byzantine society but also in the way in which Byzantine Christian civilization was preserved and transmitted throughout the Middle East and Eastern Europe. It was also an expression of unity in faith and in political world view, and this expression was more than purely symbolic. Not only did it imply the daily commemoration of the patriarch by the various metropolitans of the see of Constantinople but the name of the Byzantine emperor was also becoming known through its mention in the liturgy. The well-known letter of Patriarch Anthony to Grand Prince Basil I of Moscow, written in 1393 and imploring the commemoration of the Byzantine emperor in Russia,[17] illustrates the use made of the liturgy by Byzantine ecclesiastical diplomats to maintain Byzantine political ideology in Muscovy. Clearly, in the last decades of the empire, this was the last tool which was left at their disposal. However, even then that tool remained powerful.

The purpose of this brief essay is only to stress the importance of the liturgy as a source for the understanding of Byzantine civilization and thus to justify the importance of the topic not only for professional liturgiologists and theologians, but also for historians of art, literature, society and political theory. It is, I believe, unnecessary to stress its centrality for those of us who are involved in implanting Orthodox Christianity in America. Indeed, our use of the Byzantine tradition can succeed only if we understand the mind and central inspiration of that tradition without idolizing it.

[17]Ed. F. Miklosich and J. Müller, *Acta Patriarchatus Constantinopolitani* 2 (Vienna, 1862), pp. 188-192.

3

Society and Culture in the Fourteenth Century: Religious Problems*

It is always difficult, in studying any branch of medieval civilization, to single out those problems which can be defined as properly "religious," for religion was, in every medieval society, a necessary and accepted aspect of every intellectual and social concern. This is particulary true in Byzantium in the fourteenth century. The issues implied on the one hand by the so-called "Palamite" controversy and, on the other hand, by the debates between "Latinophrones" and anti-unionists involved the very basis of Byzantine Christian civilization and its future.

While the empire in the fourteenth century was reduced to only a shadow of itself, the Church, as an institution, had never exercised so much influence both inside and outside of the imperial frontiers. This was particularly true of monasticism. Mount Athos, traditionally endowed and administered by the emperors, was now placed in the patriarchal jurisdiction by a chrysobull of Andronicus II (1312).[1] The exact significance of this measure is difficult to evaluate, but it may have contributed to the alliance between monastic circles and the church hierarchy—rather unusual in previous centuries—and, in fact, to a take-over, after 1347, of the high church

---

*Paper originally presented at the XIV° Congrès International d'Études Byzantines, Bucharest, 1971, and published in the proceedings of that congress (1974).

[1]Ph. Meyer, Die Haupturkunden für die Geschichte der Athoskloster (Leipzig, 1894), pp. 190-194.

administration by an entirely monastic personnel, with disciples of Palamas on the patriarchal throne (Isidore, 1347-1349; Callistus I, 1350-1354, 1355-1363; Philotheus, 1354-1355, 1364-1376; Macarius, 1376-1379; Nilus, 1380-1388, etc.).

With the further disintegration of the state, this monastic take-over will have even greater significance because of the relative growth of the partriarchate's importance. As George Ostrogorsky points out, "the patriarchate of Constantinople remained the center of the Orthodox world, with subordinate metropolitan sees and archbishoprics in the territory of Asia Minor and the Balkans, now lost to Byzantium, as well as in the Caucasus, Russia and Lithuania. The Church remained the most stable element in the Byzantine Empire."[2] Geographically and morally, the patriarchate had certainly a greater impact on society than the imperial throne, and this impact inevitably carried with it economic and political consequences.

Emperor Michael VIII (1259-1282) was the last imperial figure who tried to deal with religious problems in a "caesaropapistic" manner (whatever that term means in a Byzantine context). The collapse of the union of Lyons, which he had tried to impose by force upon a hostile majority of churchmen, and the restoration in the diptychs of the name of Patriarch Arsenius (1312),[3] who had challenged Michael's authority, were the signs of a new power acquired by the Church, now ruled mainly by the monastic party, a power that the emperors were too weak to challenge seriously.

Under different circumstances, John Cantacuzenus, with his "political acumen" which made him "head and shoulders above all his contemporaries" as a political leader,[4] would perhaps have succeeded in reestablishing the kind of relations between Church and state which existed in the past. He seems to have seriously tried, at the beginning of his political career, as *megas domesticus* of Andronicus III (1328-1341),

[2]*History of the Byzantine State,* tr. J. Hussey (rev. ed., New Brunswick, N.J., 1969), p. 487.

[3]V. Laurent, "Les grandes crises religieuses à Byzance. La fin du schisme arsénite," in *Académie Roumaine, Bulletin de la section historique* 26 (1945), pp. 61-89.

[4]G. Ostrogorsky, *op. cit.,* p. 503.

to restore the power of the state deeply shaken by the civil wars between the two Andronici. But Cantacuzenus' own political base, as the most prominent representative and spokesman of landed aristocracy,[5] would not allow a lasting restoration of a strong central power. His attempts in this direction were short-lived. For example, he certainly promoted the appointment, in 1334, of a priest of the palace, John Calecas, as patriarch.[6] This appointment may have been aiming at a limitation of monastic influences. The patronage he gave to the Calabrian "philosopher" Barlaam, after his arrival in Constantinople around 1330,[7] is another indication that the monastic zealots were far from being as powerful under Andronicus III and Cantacuzenus as they were under Andronicus II and Patriarch Athanasius. Not only was Barlaam entrusted with the mission to negotiate with Dominican theologians in 1333, but he headed the Byzantine embassy to Avignon in 1339, after having been admitted to present his personal program of church union before the patriarchal synod.[8] All this suggests that the official apparatus of the Church was again, for a brief period, under the control of the government, as it had been under Michael VIII.

However, the new crisis of 1341 showed that there was no real return to the past. The Patriarch John Calecas himself began to use ecclesiastical prestige to challenge the authority of the *megas domesticus* immediately after the death of An-

[5]Cf. the monograph by G. Weiss, "Joannes Kantakuzenus—Aristokrat, Staatsmann, Kaiser und Monch," in *Gesellschaftsentwicklung von Byzance in 14. Jahrhundert* (Wiesbaden, 1969).

[6]Ἰερεὺς τοῦ βασιλικοῦ κλήρου, Gregoras, *Historia* X, 7, 3, PG 148, cols. 696D-698A.

[7]Gregoras, *Historia* XI, 10, Bonn ed., p. 555; Palamas confirms that Andronicus II, his government and the church officials were well disposed towards Barlaam: ὁ Βαρλαὰμ πανταχόθεν ἔχων τὸ δύνασθαι καὶ γὰρ τῇ ἐκκλησίᾳ μέγας ἐδόκει καὶ τῇ πολιτείᾳ καὶ παρὰ τοῦ βασιλέως καὶ τῶν ἐν τέλει πολλῆς ἐτύγχανε τῆς ὑποδοχῆς, ed. A. Moutsoukas, in Γρηγορίου τοῦ Παλαμᾶ Συγγράμματα 2 (Thessaloniki, 1966), pp. 501-502.

[8]G. V. Giannelli, "Un progetto di Barlaam per l'unione delle chiese," in *Miscellanea G. Mercati* (Studi e testi 123, Vatican, 1946), p. 185-201; J. Meyendorff, "Un mauvais théologien de l'unité au XVIe siècle: Barlaam le Calabraise," in *1054-1954: L'Église et les églises* II (Chevetogne, 1954), pp. 47-64.

dronicus III, and to claim political power for himself.[9] In the civil war which followed, John Cantacuzenus could win only by engineering an alliance between his friends, the aristocratic landowners, and the monastic party. Thus, Palamite ecclesiastical zealots became the real arbiters of the conflict. The tempting but simplistic theory according to which the alliance between Cantacuzenus and the monks was essentially promoted by their common economic interests, *i.e.,* the preservation of land property, cannot be substantiated, although it may serve to explain individual cases of political collaboration between monks and aristocrats. In fact, the Cantacuzenist party was socially "mobile,"[10] and the monks' most frequent preaching was against mistreatment of the poor, usury and excessive wealth.[11] They could not be the representatives of a single political ideology. Cantacuzenus secured political victory by adopting, as his own, the theological position and the religious "zeal" of the monastic party, but perhaps the whole style of his government would have followed another direction if he had not been pushed into an alliance with the hesychasts against Patriarch John Calecas and the government of Ann of Savoy in 1341-1347.

Once on the imperial throne, Cantacuzenus tried again to rule the affairs of the Church in the old Byzantine imperial manner: he chose Isidore for the patriarchate in 1347,[12] deposed Callistus in 1353 and appointed Philotheus in order to secure the crowning of his son Matthew.[13] His choices, however, were limited to the representatives of the Palamite

---

[9]The *Tomos* of 1347, a major pro-Cantacuzenist source, presents Calecas as the main architect of the *coup d'état* which toppled the authority of Cantacuzenus in October 1341 (ed. J. Meyendorff, in *Vizantoloshki Institut, Zbornik Radova* 8, 1 = Mélanges G. Ostrogorsky 1), p. 217, lines 141-144.

[10]Cf. particularly G. Weiss, *op. cit.,* pp. 54-60.

[11]For Gregory Palamas particularly, see our *Introduction à l'étude de Grégoire Palamas* (Paris, 1959), p. 396-397; Palamas' sermon against usury: *Hom.* 45, ed. S. Oikonomos (Athens, 1851), p. 45-49; a similar sermon by Nicholas Cabasilas in PG 150, col. 728-750; other examples quoted in G. Prokhorov, "Isikhazm i obshchestvennaia mysl' v vostochnoi Europe v XIV-m veke," in *Akademiia Nauk SSSR, Trudy otdela drevne-russkoi literatury* 21 (1968), pp. 98-99.

[12]Antipalamite tome, PG 150, col. 881 AB.

[13]Cantacuzenus, *Historia* IV, 37, Bonn ed., III, p. 275.

monastic party, which had secured Cantacuzenus' triumph
and whose doctrinal position was endorsed by the Councils
of 1347 and 1351. His own writings in theology clearly prove
that his commitment to the cause of the hesychasts was fully
sincere. Thus, he had acquired a great personal authority in
church affairs and was able to keep it even after his retirement
(1354). His prestige did not depend any longer on political
power. In 1367, the papal legate Paul, in the presence of a
large assembly presided by the reigning Emperor John V,
compares Cantacuzenus—now the monk Joasaph—to a roasting
spit (σουβλίον), able to turn the entire Greek Church
around himself.[14] The characteristic answer of Cantacuzenus
is that, in matters of faith, the emperor has no power and
that only an ecumenical council, convened in freedom, can
tackle the problem of ecclesiastical union.[15]

Thus, imperial authority did not mean full control in
matters of religion. The empire had practically ceased to exist.
But the Church was keeping its influence on the people—in
Constantinople, in much of Eastern Europe and the remaining
imperial territories, and also in occupied Asia Minor. It was
maintaining an administrative structure, which was able to
influence decisively the policies of the great prince of Moscow,
of the Lithuanian state and even the kings of Poland and
Hungary. It was in a position to initiate, or to block securely
negotiations with Rome. No wonder that the particular religious ideology which controlled the Church was a critical
factor in the destiny of Byzantine civilization as a whole.

This is why the victory of the Palamites in 1347 and 1351
is of such capital importance. Within the limits of this brief
essay, we will discuss the implications of this victory in three
basic areas of fourteenth-century Byzantine civilization.

1. Palamism and "Humanism"

The term "humanism" has been vastly misused in connection with Byzantine civilization. If its meaning designate

[14]J. Meyendorff, "Projets de concile oecuménique en 1367," *Dumbarton
Oaks Papers* 14 (1961), p. 174.
[15]*Ibid.*

primarily a phenomenon such as the Italian Renaissance, it is hardly applicable to the Byzantine tradition of secular scholarship, as exemplified by Photius, Psellus, Theodore Metochites and so many others. All of them remained fundamentally faithful to the main principles of a conservative medieval civilization and to church dogma. Those who like John Italus went beyond these strict boundaries suffered formal condemnations. As a result, interest in secular knowledge, particularly in ancient Greek philosophy, were *de facto* and *de jure* limited to copying of manuscripts, to artificial imitation of ancient authors in poetry and prose, and to the teaching of Aristotelian logic in schools. Platonic and Neoplatonic authors were considered particularly dangerous for Orthodoxy and only a few isolated intellectuals ventured to express direct interest in their ideas. For the mass of the Byzantines, the solemn anathemas of the *Synodikon,* repeated every year, served as a permanent and serious warning: "To those who study Hellenic sciences and do not take them as tools of instruction only, but follow their futile theories and accept the latter as true . . . anathema."[16]

These obvious limitations of Byzantine "humanism" were still insufficient to prevent a significant segment of society— especially the monks—to look with hostility upon those who expressed interest in ancient Greek philosophy. The original controversy between Palamas and the Barlaam, the Calabrian "philosopher," involved this issue as well: for Palamas, Greek philosophy presents "the deceiving appearance of true wisdom" (σοφίας ἀληθινῆς ἀπατηλὸν εἴδωλον).[17] He compares Greek philosophers to snakes, whose flesh is "useful" only if "one kills them, and dissects them, and uses them with discernment as a remedy agains their own bites."[18] Barlaam, on the contrary, refers to the Neoplatonists and to

[16]Τοῖς τὰ ἑλληνικὰ διεξιοῦσι μαθήματα καὶ μὴ διὰ παίδευσιν μόνον ταῦτα παιδευομένοις, ἀλλὰ καὶ δόξαις αὐτῶν ταῖς ματαίαις ἑπομένοις . . . ἀνάθεμα, *Synodikon,* ed. J. Gouillard, in *Travaux et mémoires* 2 (Paris: Centre de recherche d'histoire de civilization byzantines, 1967), p. 56.

[17]*Triads* I, 1, 17, ed. J. Meyendorff, *Gregoire Palamas. Défense des saints hésychastes* (Spicilegium Sacrum Lovaniense 30, Louvain, 1959), p. 49.

[18]*Ibid.,* I, 1, 11, p. 35.

Plato himself, recognizing them as authorities for his concept of knowledge of God.[19]

The debate on "secular wisdom" (ἡ θύραθεν σοφία) did not last very long, not because the difference between Palamas and Barlaam was, on this point, superficial and "external,"[20] but because Barlaam left for Italy, while later anti-Palamites ceased their attacks on the mystical spirituality of the hesychasts and limited the controversy to the theological issue of the distinction between "essence" and "energy" in God. The victory of the monastic party in 1347-1351 simply implied the reaffirmation of a "watchdog policy" of the Church against possible resurgence of "secular humanism." This partially explains the pro-Western—in fact pro-Italian—tendencies of several prominent Byzantine "humanists" after 1351. Even when the debate was not technically concerned with the usefulness of Plato and Aristotle in Christian theological thinking, it is clear that, for the hesychasts, the authentic, "natural" man—and therefore the whole complex of human faculties of knowledge—is the man "in Christ," potentially transfigured and "deified" through participation in Christ's "body."[21] For them, secular philosophy could, at best, still be useful in the understanding of creation, but not for the knowledge of God, in which was found the ultimate meaning of human existence. This basic position of Palamas, which largely corresponded to the tradition of the Greek fathers, especially to the thought of Maximus the Confessor, did not, however, mean that the religious zealots had included in their program of action any systematic struggle against the Hellenic heritage of Byzantine civilization. There were times, especially during the reign of Andronicus II, of intellectual peace between the monks and the "humanists."

[19]See especially the Second Letter to Palamas, in G. Schirò, *Barlaam Calabro epistole* (Palermo, 1954), pp. 298-299.

[20]This is the opinion of G. Schirò, "Gregorio Palama e la scienza profana," in *Le Millénaire du Mont Athos, 963-1963: Études et Mélanges* 2 (Chévetogne, 1965), pp. 95-96.

[21]See our discussion on Palamite theology in *Introduction à l'étude de Grégoire Palamas* (Paris, 1959), p. 223-256; Eng. tr. *A Study of Gregory Palamas* (London, 1965), pp. 157-184. Cf. also D. Staniloae, *Viata si invatatura sfantului Grigorie Palama* (Sibiu, 1938), pp. 89 ff.

Theodore Metochites, Grand Logothete and *mesazon* of Andronicus II, is justly considered as the main precursor and in fact the founder of Byzantine "humanism" in the fourteenth century. As such he has recently attracted the attention of several scholars.[22] He was the teacher of Nicephorus Gregoras,[23] probably the most eminent anti-Palamite after 1347. There is no evidence, however, that Metochites himself was, at any time, in any conflict with the monks. Quite to the contrary, Gregory Palamas, writing against Gregoras in 1356-1358, remembers that, when he was seventeen (*i.e.*, around 1313), Metochites had praised his knowledge of Aristotle.[24] The episode is also reported in the Encomion of Palamas by Patriarch Philotheus, writing around 1368.[25] Obviously, the personality and the scholarship of Metochites remained highly respected in Palamite circles, which implies that the ecclesiastical zealots, who took over the Byzantine church with the help of Cantacuzenus, were actually not opposed to "secular wisdom" as such, but only to the theological position on the knowledge of God adopted, in the name of that "wisdom," by Barlaam and Gregoras.

A similar conclusion can be drawn from the fact that the Palamites of the fourteenth century expressed respect for such authorities at Patriarch Gregory of Cyprus (1283-1289), clearly a "humanist" by temperament and formation, because he sustained the notion of "eternal manifestation" of the Spirit from the Son, *i.e.*, the doctrine of "uncreated energies" defended by Palamas.[26] Similarly, Palamas refers to early

[22]Cf. particularly H.-G. Beck, *Theodoros Metochites. Die Krise des byzantinischen Weltbildes in 14. Jahrhundert* (München, 1952); H. Hunger, "Theodoros Metochites als Vorlaufer des Humanismus in Byzanz," *Byzantinische Zeitschrift* 55 (1952), pp. 4-19; I. Sevcenko, *Études sur la polémique entre Théodore Métochite et Nicéphore Choummos. La vie intellectuelle et politique à Byzance sous les premiers Paléologues* (Bruxelles, 1962).

[23]See mainly R. Guilland, *Essai sur Nicéphore Grégoras* (Paris, 1926), pp. 7-8.

[24]The treatises of Palamas against Gregoras are still unedited: the text referring to the meeting between Metochites and the young Gregory Palamas is quoted from the *Codex Coislinianus* 100, fol. 236, in J. Meyendorff, *Introduction*, p. 47 n. 15; on the date of the treatises against Gregoras, see *Introduction*, p. 379.

[25]PG 151, col. 559D-560A.

[26]Cf. praises to Gregory of Cyprus by Philotheus, *Against Gregoras* VI,

teachers of "pure prayer" and the psychosomatic invocation of the name of Jesus; in his lists we find the name of Theoleptus of Philadelphia, together with that of Patriarch Athanasius I.[27] If the austere monk Athanasius can indeed be considered a model for the ecclesiastical zealots of the fourteenth century and was certainly nothing of a "humanist,"[28] Theoleptus of Philadelphia had been an adversary of both Gregory of Cyprus and Athanasius, and is closely connected with the Choumnos family, one of the pillars of anti-Palamism between 1341 and 1347.[29]

What these facts show is that the religious controversies of the fourteenth century should not be considered as a direct continuation of the disputes which divided the Byzantine church at the end of the thirteenth, *i.e.*, the issues of union or the Arsenite schism. The problem of "humanism" was not on the agenda during the first two Palaeologans. It only appeared as an issue briefly in the dispute between Barlaam and Palamas (1337-1341), and only because of Barlaam's attacks on monastic spirituality. The victory of the Palamites meant that

PG 151, col. 915CD; by Joseph Calothetus, another Palamite theologian, in his Life of Athanasius I, Gregory's successor on the patriarchal throne, ed. by Athanasius, in Θρακικά 13 (1940), p. 87; the antipalamite Acindynus considers Gregory of Cyprus as a pro-Latin heretic (quotation in J. Meyendorff, *Introduction*, p. 29).

[27]*Triads* I, 2, 12, *ed. cit.*, p. 99; II, 2, 3, p. 323.

[28]His biographer Theoctistus mentions the fact that he received little general instruction (Life of Athanasius, ed. A. Papadopoulos-Kerameus, "Zhitia dvukh vselenskikh patriarkhov," in *Sankt-Peterburg Universitet, Istoriko-Filologichesky Fakultet, Zapiski* (1905), p. 26; cf. also Gregoras, *Historia* VI, 5, Bonn ed. I, p. 180. On Athanasius, see R. Guilland, "La correspondance inédite d'Athanase, patriarche de Constantinople," in *Mélanges Charles Diehl* I (1930), pp. 121-140; also M. Banescu, "Le patriarche Athanase I et Andronic II Paléologue, état religieux, politique et social de l'Empire," in *Académie roumaine. Bulletin de la section historique* 23 (1942) pp. 1-28. A large part of the correspondence between Athanasius and Andronicus II is ed. and tr. by Alice Mary Talbot (Dumbarton Oaks Texts 3, Washington, D.C., 1975).

[29]On Theoleptus, see Nicephorus Chumnus, Encomion on Theoleptus, in Boissonade, *Anecdota graeca* V (Paris, 1883), pp. 201-213; also S. Salaville, "Deux documents inédits sur les discussions religieuses byzantines entre 1275 et 1310," *Revue des Études Byzantines* 5 (1947), pp. 116-136. (Several other articles on Theoleptus by S. Salaville are referred to in our *Introduction*, p. 31, n. 23). See also V. Laurent, "Une princesse au cloitre; Irène Eulogie Choumnos Paléologine," *Echos d'Orient* 29 (1930), pp. 29-60; cf. our *Introduction*, pp. 125-26.

an independent "humanism" had now lost its chance in Byzantium. No new anathemas against "secular wisdom" were
added to the *Synodikon*, but eminent representatives of "humanism"—Barlaam, Nicephorus, Gregoras, Demetrius Cydones—were mentioned by name, as enemies of the Church
and of Orthodoxy.[30]

At different times, the question of the relationship between
the emergence and development of hesychasm in the Byzantine world has been related to the new "humanist" trends in
the Palaeologan artistic "renaissance," both in Byzantium itself and in the Slavic countries.[31] Fruitful in itself, this
hypothesis can only be used with caution. For example, the
fact, established above, that hesychasts and humanists lived
in relative peace in the early years of the fourteenth century
must be taken into consideration. The church of the Chora,
i.e., the most remarkable Constantinopolitan monument of the
"renaissance," was redecorated precisely during that period,
under the sponsorship of Theodore Metochites, the real father
of "secular humanism" in the fourteenth century.[32] There
cannot be any doubt, however, that the so-called "second
South Slavic influence in Russia" (fourteenth-fifteenth century) was largely penetrated with hesychastic literature and
ideas, and may have expressed a definite universalist ideology
of the Byzantine ecclesiastical zealots. But even there, the
hesychasts did not exercise absolute monopoly: the metropolitan of Russia, Theognostus (1328-1353), was a friend
of Nicephorus Gregoras and an anti-Palamite.[33] On the other

[30]*Synodikon,* ed. J. Gouillard, pp. 81-87.

[31]Cf. M. M. Vasic, "L'hésychasme dans l'Église et l'art des Serbes du
Moyen Age," in *Recueil Uspenskij* I (Paris, 1930), pp. 110-123; also N. K.
Goleizovsky, "Poslanie ikonopistsu i otgoloski isikhazma v russkoi zhivopisi
na rubezhe XV-XVI vv.," *Vizantiiskii Vremennik* 26 (1965), pp. 219-238;
"Isikhazm i russkaia zhivopis VIV-XV vv.," *Vizantiiskii Vremennik* 29
(1968), pp. 196-210.

[32]See the remarkable publication of the late P. Underwood, *The Kariye
Djami* (Bollingen Series 70, New York, 1966), 3 vols. A fourth volume
contains a discussion of the religious and cultural background of Kariye,
including an article by the present author.

[33]Gregoras, *Historia* XXVI, 47-48, Bonn ed. III, pp. 113-115. G. Prokhorov
has tried to show that this information of Gregoras concerning the anti-
Palamism of Theognostus cannot be true, but his arguments are not fully conclusive: "Isikhazm i obshchestvennaia mysl' v vostochnoi Europe v XIV-m

hand, hesychast spirituality may have had quite a different impact on art in the Slavic countries and in Byzantium. There is no evidence, for example, that any major figure of Byzantine hesychasm—Athanasius I, Palamas, the patriarchs of the late fourteenth century—manifested any peculiar interest for art. There is even reason to believe that their monastic austerity was not favorable to expensive decoration of churches. In Russia, however, the Great Lavra of the Trinity, founded by St. Sergius, was indeed the center of a remarkable revival in fresco painting, as it was also one of the major channels of Byzantine cultural and religious influence in Muscovite Russia.

2. Meeting the West

The problem of religious union with Rome stood at the center of Byzantine politics throughout the fourteenth century, but a deeper intellectual and cultural encounter was also happening, and this was indeed a new development. As is well known, of all the Palaeologan emperors, Andronicus II was the only one who never entered into union negotiations with Rome after his solemn rejection of the union of Lyons at the Council of Blachernae in 1285.

It is only under Andronicus III, certainly not without the active participation of the Grand Domesticus John Cantacuzenus, that new initiatives were taken to restore relations with the papacy. The most active role was then played, as we have seen above, by Barlaam the Calabrian (discussions of 1333, embassy to Avignon in 1339).[34] In 1347, at the end of the civil war, Cantacuzenus—now reigning emperor—sends John Sigerus to Avignon with a proposal of holding an ecumenical council of union.[35] Twenty years later, at a time when, officially, he was nothing else than the "monk Joasaph" but

veke," in *Akademia Nauk SSSR. Trudy otdela drevne-russkoi literatury* 23 (1968), pp. 104-105.

[34]Cf. C. Gianelli, "Un progetto," pp. 157-208; J. Meyendorff, "Un mauvais théologien," pp. 47-64.

[35]Cantacuzenus, *Historia* IV, 9, Bonn ed. III, pp. 58-60; cf. J. Gay, *Le pape Clément VI et les affaires d'Orient* (Paris, 1904), pp. 94-118.

while, in fact, he was continuing to exercise a decisive influence in both political and ecclesiastical affairs, Cantacuzenus again promoted the idea of a council before the papal legate, Paul.[36]

Until the great conciliar crisis in the West, the idea of the council found no support in Rome, but it is quite important to remember that it had been systematically advanced by Cantacuzenus and officially supported by the Palamite Patriarch Philotheus and his synod, who exorted his colleague, the archbishop of Ohrid, to cooperate with the project[37] and appointed a delegation which was to meet Pope Urban V at Viterbo.[38]

For all Byzantines, the question of ecclesiastical union was primarily a matter of political urgency and implied the hope for a Western crusade against the Turks. The difference which separated the Palamites from the "Latinophrones" concerned methods and priorities, not the very idea of church union. On the one hand, the Palamites envisaged no ecclesiastical union without a free solution of theological issues at a council, because, as Cantacuzenus said to Paul, "the faith cannot be forced" (ἀναγκαστὴ ἡ πίστις οὐκ ἔστιν)[39]; on the other hand, the "mystical theology" which the Councils of 1341 and 1351 had formulated implied an absolute primacy of the religious knowledge over politics and even over national interest. It is in order to secure a free and authentic dialogue on theology that Cantacuzenus, supported by the hesychast patriarchs, tried persistently to organize an ecumenical council with the Latins. Actually, it is his project which will be finally realized in the fifteenth century, in Ferrara-Florence, without achieving, however, the union of

---

[36]J. Meyendorff, "Projects de concile oecuménique en 1367; un dialogue inédit entre Jean Cantacuzène et le légat Paul," *Dumbarton Oaks Papers* 14 (1960), p. 149-177; on Cantacuzenus' activities after his abdication see also L. Maksimovic, "Politicka Uloga Iovana Kantakuzina pose abdikacije (1354-1383)," in *Vizantoloshki Institut, Zbornik Radova* 9 (Belgrade, 1966), pp. 121-193.

[37]Ed. F. Miklosich and J. Müller, *Acta Patriarchatus Constantinopolitani* 1 (Vienna, 1860), pp. 491-493.

[38]On these negotiations, see mainly O. Halecki, *Un empereur de Byzance à Rome* (Warsaw, 1930), pp. 163-165.

[39]*Dialexis* 16, ed. J. Meyendorff, "Projets," p. 174, lines 198-199.

minds which was, according to Cantacuzenus, a condition for a true ecclesiastical union.

The openness of Cantacuzenus and his friends to a "dialogue" with the West is also illustrated by the sponsorship of translations from Latin into Greek of major Western theological sources. The personalities of the two brothers Prochorus and Demetrius Cydones are well known for their translations of Latin theological authors, particularly of Aquinas' *Summae,* and of major texts by Augustine and Anselm. Cantacuzenus himself used Demetrius' translation of the *Refutation of the Qurran* by the Florentine Dominican Ricaldus de Monte Croce (1309) as a sourcebook for his own writings against Islam.[40] A similar knowledge of and respect for Western Latin sources—rather unusual in Byzantium—is found in Nicholas Cabasilas' *Explanation of the Divine liturgy*: Cabasilas, in his polemics against the Latin doctrine of eucharistic consecration through the "words of institution," finds arguments in the Latin liturgical tradition itself and, like Cantacuzenus, quotes his texts very accurately.[41]

Nicholas Cabasilas and Demetrius Cydones were both members of the aristocratic and intellectual circle of Cantacuzenus' friends. But while Cabasilas remained in the ex-emperor's close *entourage* after 1347, endorsing his religious policies, Cydones became the chief advisor and the main architect of John Palaeologus' personal conversion to the Latin church in 1369.

The religious evolution of Demetrius Cydones was determined by his discovery of Thomism as a philosophical system. As he himself clearly states in his writings, he suddenly discovered that the Latin West was not a barbarian land of "darkness," as Byzantine humanists since the time of Photius thought it to be, but a new dynamic civilization, where ancient

---

[40]Τῆς τάξεως τῶν πρεδικατόρων ἤτοι τῶν κηρύκων 'Ρικάλδος, *Contra Mahometem Oratio* I, 4, PG, 154 col. 601C; the text of Demetrius' translation is published in PG 154, cols. 1037-1052.

[41]Chapters 29-30, ed, Périchon (Sources chrétiennes 4 bis, Paris, 1967), pp. 179-199; Eng. tr. by J. M. Hussey and P. A. McNulty (London, 1960), pp. 71-79; on the Greek translations of Latin theology in the fourteenth century, see St. Papadopoulos 'Ελληνικαὶ μεταφράσεις Θωμιστικῶν ἔργων. Φιλοθωμισταὶ καὶ ἀντιθωμισταὶ ἐν Βυζαντίῳ (Athens, 1967).

Greek philosophy was prized more than in Byzantium itself. He then began to castigate his compatriots for considering that in the whole universe there are only "Greeks" and "barbarians," that the latter are no better than "asses" or "cattle," that Latins, in particular, are never able to rise intellectually above the requirements of the military or merchant professions, while in fact so many Latin scholars were dedicated to the study of Plato and Aristotle.[42] "Because [the Byzantines] did not care for their own [Greek] wisdom," he continues, "they considered [Latin] reasonings as being Latin inventions"; in fact, if only one took the trouble of unveiling the meaning of the Latin books, hidden by a foreign tongue, one would find that "they show great thirst for walking in the labyrinths of Aristotle and Plato, for which our people never showed interest."[43] In other word, for Cydones, Thomas Aquinas, and certainly also the Italian Renaissance, were more "Greek" than Byzantium, especially since the latter has been taken over by the hesychasts! Neither papal Rome nor imperial Constantinople are for Cydones the highest criterion of wisdom, but ancient Greece. And who can blame him for discovering that the classical Hellenic heritage was better kept in the universities of the Latin West than among the religious zealots of Mount Athos?

Thus, the new "opening to the West," so characteristic for the religious and intellectual life of Byzantium, leads to a polarization of minds between those who, like Cantacuzenus and the hesychasts, were ready to negotiate ecclesiastical union, but only through serious theological debate, and those, like Cydones, for whom theological issues ranked very low in the order of priorities, but who were discovering for themselves and for Hellenic civilization a new and brilliant future in the framework of the Western Renaissance.

---

[42]*Apologia* I, in G. Mercati, *Notizie di Procoro e Demetrio Cidone* (Studi e testi 56, Città del Vaticano, 1931), p. 365, lines 77-84.

[43]*Ibid.*, p. 366, lines 91-96.

3. Influence in Eastern Europe

Since the attempts at union with the West were failing one after the other, Byzantium, in its policy of survival, had to rely on the prestige which it still possessed throughout Eastern Europe. This prestige was essentially based on the jurisdictional and moral power of the patriarch of Constantinople, controlled, since 1346, by the Palamite "religious zealots."

Always faithful to the imperial idea of a universal Christian state,[44] but placing the interest of the Church and the integrity of Orthodoxy, as defined by the councils of 1341, 1347 and 1351, ahead of all other considerations,[45] including the interests of "Hellenism" and the political schemes of John Palaeologus, the hesychast patriarchs tried to foster the direct administrative power of the patriarchate wherever that was possible, and to maintain its moral prestige and authority wherever direct jurisdiction could not be maintained anymore. The remarkable flexibility and skill of Byzantine ecclesiastical diplomacy has been shown by D. Obolensky in connection with the alternation of Greek and Russian metropolitans on the see of "Kiev and all Russia" during the fourteenth century.[46] But there are other illustrations of the same.

In the Balkans, Bulgaria and Serbia had taken the opportunity of the empire's collapse in 1204 to reestablish their political and ecclesiastical independence with Rome's help. In the fourteenth century, however, the influence of the hesychast

[44]As late as 1393, Patriarch Anthony rebuffs the great prince of Moscow Vassili Dmitrievich, who had asked for the permission to drop the name of the emperor from liturgical commemorations in the Russian church. "The emperor," he wrote, "is the emperor of the Romans, that is of all Christians" (βασιλεὺς καὶ αὐτοκράτωρ ῾Ρωμαίων πάντων δηλαδὴ τῶν χριστιανῶν); ed. Miklosich and Müller 2, p. 190.

[45]Cf. especially G. Prokhorov, "Publitsistika Ioanna Kantakuzina, 1367-1371," *Vizantiiskii Vremennik* (1968), pp. 323-324.

[46]"Byzantium, Kiev and Moscow: A Study in Ecclesiastical Relations," *Dumbarton Oaks Papers* 11 (1957), pp. 23-78. A text of Nicephorus Gregoras (*Historia* XXXVII) incorrectly reproduced in the Bonn corpus but found integrally in V. Parisot, *Livre XXXVII de l'Histoire Romaine de Nicéphore Gregoras* (Paris, 1851), p. 68, affirms that a formal agreement existed on the issue between Byzantium and the Russian principalities.

monasticism, which went across linguistic, national and political boundaries, was able to reestablish a new sense of Orthodox unity and thus to limit the impact of Western influence. One of the main leaders of the Athonite hesychasm, Gregory of Sinai, settled on Bulgarian territories, in Paroria, and his disciples, the Bulgarian patriarch Euthymius and St. Theodosius of Trnovo, led the intellectual revival in Bulgaria under Tsar John Alexander.[47] Another disciple of Gregory of Sinai, Callistus, twice patriarch of Constantinople (1350-1354, 1355-1363), kept in close touch with his Bulgarian friends, while showing less tolerance towards the Serbs, whose pugnacious leader, Emperor Stephen Dushan, had elevated the archbishopric of Pec to the rank of patriarchate in 1346. However, Callistus' competitor and successor, Philotheus, was to settle the dispute and recognize the Serbian patriarchate in 1375.[48] It is certainly the friendship and cooperation of Callistus with the Bulgarians which allowed him to establish, on their northern borders and in an area where Bulgarian bishops so far had exercised jurisdiction, a new metropolitanate: that of Οὐγγροβλαχία with residence at Arges, transferring to the new see the former metropolitan of Vicina, Hyacinthus. The new see was to be in the direct jurisdiction of Constantinople.[49] Established at the formal request of the *voivode* Alexander Basarab, the metropolitanate was to protect the area against Roman Catholicism, sponsored by Hungary.[50] Characteristic of the independent policy of the patriarchate, this move was taken in 1359 at the time of constant pro-

[47]The basic sources for Byzantine-Bulgarian relations during this period are still the books of P. Syrku, *K istorii ispravlenia knig v Bolgarii v XIV veke, I. Vremia i zhizn' patriarkha Evfimia Ternovskago* (St. Petersburg, 1898), and K. Radchenko, *Religioznoe i literaturnoe dvizhenie v Bolgarii v epokhu pered turetskim zavoevaniem* (Kiev, 1893).

[48]Cf. M. Lascaris, "Le patriarcat de Pec a-t-il été reconnu par l'Église de Constantinople en 1375?," in *Mélanges Charles Diehl I* (Paris, 1930), pp. 171-178; V. Laurent, "L'archevêque de Pec et le titre de patriarche après l'union de 1375," *Balcania* 7, 2 (Bucharest, 1944), pp. 303-310.

[49]Ἵνα τελῇ τὸ ἀπὸ τοῦδε καὶ εἰς τὸ ἑξῆς . . . ἡ εἰρημένη πᾶσα Οὐγγροβλαχία ὑπὸ τὴν καθ' ἡμᾶς ἁγιωτάτην τοῦ Θεοῦ μεγάλην ἐκκλησίαν, ed. Miklosich and Müller 1, p. 385.

[50]Δέχεσθαι τὴν εὐσέβειαν καὶ ἀποτρέπεσθαι τάς τε παρασυναγωγὰς καὶ τὰ ἔκφυλα καὶ ἀλλότρια δόγματα: Miklosich and Müller 1, p. 336.

Western attempts by the reigning emperor John V Palaeologus. It will have a lasting significance for the future cultural and political identity of Wallachia, with its destiny clearly distinct from that of its Slavic neighbors.

We know much less about the exact significance of the patriarchate's action in distant Caucasus, but documents show that the Byzantine Church continued to exercise administrative control over the metropolitanate of Alania, on the northern border of the independent church of Georgia. Patriarch John Calecas had divided the metropolitanate by appointing a separate "metropolitan of Soteropolis," but his act was rescinded under Isidore, in 1347. After having been divided again under Callistus, in July 1356, Alania was finally united once more by Philotheus in 1364.[51] These various acts, certainly connected with internal political events in Alania, constitute an exact parallel to the policy of the same patriarchs, and of Cantacuzenus, in Russia. In both areas, John Calecas and Callistus promoted decentralization, while Philotheus and Cantacuzenus favored creation of a strong ecclesiastical power, itself dependent upon Constantinople.

The territory of ancient "Kievan Rus" was divided in the fourteenth century between the Golden Horde, the grand duchy of Lithuania and the kingdom of Poland. The church, however, remained administratively united under a single "metropolitan of Kiev and all Russia," appointed from Constantinople and often receiving direct instructions from Byzantium about the best way of managing a metropolitanate "carrying great power and controlling myriads of Christians."[52] Naturally all three powers wanted to use the Church in their own struggle for supremacy, and Byzantine ecclesiastical diplomacy had to play a complicated game of checks and balances in order to retain a unified church organization, independent of petty politics of local princes, maintaining its religious mission under the Mongol occupation and preserv-

[51]Ed Miklosich and Müller 1, pp. 258-260, 356-363, 477-478.

[52]Τὴν ἁγιωτάτην μητρόπολιν Κιέβου καὶ πάσης 'Ρωσίας πολλὴν καὶ μεγάλην τὴν ἐπικράτειαν ἔχουσαν καὶ χριστωνύμῳ κατὰ μυριάδας εὐθυνομένην λαῷ: Philotheus, Act of Consecration of Alexis (1354), Miklosich and Müller 1, p. 336.

ing its identity in the face of Poland's Roman Catholic zeal. Its tools were administrative skill, cultural influence and religious authority. The effectiveness of the tools was often weakened by internal struggles, such as the civil war of 1341-1347 and the deposition of Cantacuzenus in 1354, during which the warring Greek parties were not insensible to lavish bribes distributed by Lithuanian or Muscovite agents.

Except for brief periods under John Calecas (1334-1347) and Callistus (1353), the monastic party of Byzantium supported the policies of the grand duke of Moscow, an ally and a vassal of the Mongols, against rival claims of Lithuania and the pretenses of Poland to establish a separate metropolitanate in Galicia. In 1308, under Patriarch Athanasius I, Metropolitan Peter, a Galician by birth, was allowed (or instructed) to take up residence in Moscow, under Mongol occupation, while keeping the title of "Kiev and all Russia." Similarly, his successor, the Greek Theognostus (1328-1353), adopted the same pro-Muscovite and pro-Mongol attitude. A separate metropolitanate of Galicia, created by John Calecas under Polish pressure, was suppressed in 1347 under Patriarch Isidore, as we learn from a letter of Emperor John Cantacuzenus to Theognostus.[53] The pro-Muscovite policy of Cantacuzenus was, however, challenged by the powerful grand duke of Lithuania, Olgerd (1341-1380), who obtained the consecration of a separate metropolitan, Theodoret, by the Bulgarian patriarch of Trnovo (1352) and later, in 1355, the appointment of "Roman, metropolitan of Lithuania," by Callistus.[54] The eventual take-over of Byzantine ecclesiastical policies by the team Cantacuzenus-Philotheus annulled these gains of Olgerd and reestablished Byzantine support for the Muscovite candidate, Alexis, appointed "metropolitan of Kiev and all Russia" on June 30, 1354, i.e., before the election of Roman.[55] Roman, who died in 1362, was to have no successor. Led by Orthodox princes, who, although vassals of the

[53]Miklosich and Müller 1, pp. 261-263.

[54]Numerous documents on these episodes are examined in J. Meyendorff, "Alexis and Roman: A Study in Byzantine-Russian Relations (1352-1354)," *Byzantinoslavica* 28, 2 (1967), pp. 278-288.

[55]Miklosich and Müller 1, pp. 336-340.

Mongols, appeared as a greater security for the church than the Roman Catholic kings of Poland or the pagan prince of Lithuania, the principality of Moscow was also more open to Byzantine cultural and political influence and more receptive to the impact of the monastic revival.[56] Metropolitan Alexis, having received Byzantine support as the only legitimate metropolitan "of all Russia," was also to become regent of the Muscovite principality and, in fact, to lead the struggle against Lithuania.

It is doubtful whether, without the moral prestige of "ecclesiastical legitimacy" bestowed upon them by Byzantium, the Muscovites would have ever been able to resist Olgerd, who succeeded in devastating twice, in 1368 and 1372, the environs of Moscow itself, occupying the greater part of the ancient Russian lands—including Kiev, the old capital—and ruling over an empire which went from the Baltic to the Black Sea, and from the Dniester to Kaluga, supported by the prince of Tver and, at times, by Novgorod. Olgerd was even expressing readiness to become an Orthodox Christian in order to gain the support of the Church. This support was, however, refused by the deliberate policy of Patriarch Philotheus and John Cantacuzenus.

However, after 1370 a shift in Byzantine tactics became discernible. Philotheus realized that continuous warfare between Moscow and Lithuania practically disqualified Alexis from being the metropolitan "of all Russia"; Lithuanian territory was inaccessible to him.[57] The patriarch was obliged to concede the erection of a separate metropolitan of Galicia (1371).[58] In 1375, he appointed a Bulgarian, Cyprian, as

[56]On this, see A. Takhiaos, Ἐπιδράσεις τοῦ ἡσυχασμοῦ εἰς τὴν ἐκκλησιαστικὴν πολιτικὴν ἐν Ῥωσίᾳ 1328-1406 (Thessaloniki, 1962).

[57]In 1370, he reproaches Alexis for not making visitations to Kiev and Lithuania (οὔτε εἰς τὸ Κίεβον ὑπάγεις οὔτ' εἰς τὴν Λητβᾶν, Miklosich and Müller 1, p. 321). The letter is attributed to Callistus in the Miklosich-Müller edition of the Acta; Philotheus' authorship is restored by A. Pavlov, Pamiatniki drevne-russkago Kanonicheskago Prava 1 (Russkaia istoricheskaia Biblioteka 6, St. Petersburg, 1880), appendix, cols. 155-156.

[58]King Casimir the Great, in a stern letter to the Byzantine patriarch, was threatening to "baptise" the Galicians into Roman Catholicism, Miklosich and Müller 1, pp. 577-578.

"metropolitan of Kiev, Lithuania and Little Russia," while Alexis was still alive.[59]

The shift, however, was only tactical and in no way changed the fundamental priorities of Byzantine ecclesiastical politics. Moscow was to remain the center of Russian lands, and Cyprian was instructed to reside there after the death of Alexis (1378), whom he succeeded as "metropolitan of all Russia," thus preserving the administrative unity of the metropolitanate (excluding only Galicia). The tactical change consisted in that the Church now recommended to the Moscovites an alliance with Lithuania and Poland against the Mongols. Presumably, the now powerful Moscovite principality was considered able to withstand the "Western" danger while also liberating itself from the Mongol yoke. This policy was supported by the Russian monastic party, led by the great St. Sergius of Radonezh, with whom Philotheus also corresponded. A powerful party of boiars continued, however, to defend the policy of alliance with the Mongols and even opposed to Cyprian the scandalous candidacy of Mitiaj-Michael as metropolitan.[60] Finally, Cyprian succeeded in occupying his see in Moscow (1379-1382, 1389-1406). His influence contributed to the famous victory of Kulikovo over the Mongols (1380). He travelled freely to Lithuanian territories and even visited Trnovo. By 1397, he found himself at the center of plans for a general alliance of Poland, Hungary and Russia against the Turks.[61] Translator of Byzantine texts and reformer of the liturgy, he was to be, more than anyone, instrumental in promoting the hesychast program in Russia.

Conclusion

A historian has recently used the term "political hesychasm" to designate the remarkable activity of John Cantacu-

[59]Miklosich and Müller 2, p. 14, line 13; 2, p. 120, lines 7-8.

[60]Cf. G. M. Prokhorov, *Provest' o Mitiae-Mikhaile i ee literaturnaia sreda, Avtoreferat* (Leningrad, 1968).

[61]Letters of Patriarch Anthony of Constantinople to Cyprian and to King Jagiello of Poland in Miklosich and Müller 2, pp. 280-285.

zenus and Patriarch Philotheus in the second half of the fourteenth century.[62] There is no doubt, in any case, that the religious and theological debates in Byzantium had much more
than a purely theoretical significance. They contributed little
to the survival of Byzantium as a state (a survival which by
then was quite impossible), but decisively shaped the various
aspects of what Nicholas Iorga has called "Byzance après
Byzance" in the whole of Eastern Europe.

[62]G. Prokhorov, *Isikhazm,* p. 95.

IV
THEOLOGY

1

The Holy Spirit, as God *

In contemporary Western Christian thought, a theology of the Spirit is most frequently expressed in the context of a new search for religious freedom. The Spirit is seen as justifying either institutional change, or a religion of personal experience, or spiritual phenomena known as "pentecostal." Unfortunately, traditional Western systematic theology, medieval or reformed, provides little material or context for an organic and integrated theology of the Spirit. It remains rather speculative as to the identity of the "giver" and, therefore, its interpretation of "gifts" is frequently quite arbitrary. Here perhaps lies one of the reasons for contemporary theological *désarroi.*

In the Christian East, the theology of the Spirit has also found little systematic development. However, some basic points of reference are found in the great trinitarian disputes of the fourth century which lead to the affirmation of the Spirit's *divinity,* as the third *person* of the Trinity, and also in the interpretation of human salvation and ultimate destiny in terms of *deification.* These points of reference are therefore of central importance for the Orthodox interpretation of both scriptural and traditional data on the Holy Spirit, as they are expressed in the liturgy of the Church, the experience of the saints, and the life of the Christian community.

In short compass, it would obviously be impossible for me to attempt a truly systematic presentation of pneumatology. I

*Originally published in *The Holy Spirit,* ed. D. Kirkpatrick (Nashville, Tenn.: Tidings, 1974), pp. 76-89.

will limit myself to the basic trinitarian and anthropological frames of reference which lead to my understanding of the Spirit as God, and then draw some theological implications for our own concerns today.

1. The trinitarian dimension

It has been often noted that East and West differ in their approach to the mystery of the divine Trinity. The West takes for granted God's unity and approaches his "trinity" as a matter of speculation, while the East starts with a living experience of the *three* and then moves to affirm their equal divinity and, therefore, their unity. Thus the Greek Cappadocian fathers of the fourth century were accused of tritheism because "the groundwork of (their) thought lay in the triplicity of equal hypostases (persons), and the identity of the divine *ousia* (substance) came second in order of prominence to their minds."[1]

This difference of approach to the trinitarian mystery is not a philosophical one. It is based on a fundamental interpretation of the New Testament by the Greek fathers who understood the Christian faith itself as primarily a revelation of divine *persons*. The Christian faith for them is first of all an answer to Jesus' question, "Whom say ye that I am? . . . The Son of the living God" (Matthew 16:15-16). The authority and effectiveness of Jesus' actions, as well as of His teachings, depend upon His personal identity. Only God Himself can be the *Savior*, only God overcomes death and forgives sins, only God can communicate divine life to humankind. And the same approach is valid for their interpretation of Jesus' sending of "another" comforter from the Father—the Spirit. The primarily personal revelation of God is discovered by the early Greek fathers not only in the classic trinitarian formula—the baptismal formula of Matthew 28:19, or the three gifts personally qualified in II Corinthians 13:14 ("the grace of our Lord Jesus Christ, and the love of God the Father, and the communion [κοινωνία]

---

[1]G. L. Prestige, *God in Patristic Thought* (London, 1952), pp. 242-43.

of the Holy Spirit") but also in the Spirit speaking personally to Philip (Acts 8:29), to Peter (Acts 10:19; 11:12), to
the church of Antioch (Acts 13:12), to the apostolic council
of Jerusalem ("it seemed good to the Holy Spirit and to us"
—Acts 15:25). The Spirit is understood here as a presence
distinct from that of Jesus but possessing the same divine
sovereignty.

It is therefore understandable that the insistence by the
Cappadocian fathers on this personal (hypostatic) distinctiveness could lead them to a trinitarian system in which their
enemies saw tritheism. They were ready to run that risk in
order to preserve the biblical understanding of a living and
acting God, fully independent from the impersonal idealism
of Greek philosophy. Even the Nicaean formulation of "consubstantiality" was long suspect in the East—and not only
among the Arians—of being both unbiblical and too philosophical. It was finally accepted, but only in combination with
the traditional (Origenistic) reaffirmation of the three distinct
hypostases in God.

The struggle against Arius, who accepted the distinction
but not the substantial co-equality and co-sovereignty of the
divine persons, was about the nature of salvation. This is
particularly evident in the writing of Athanasius. It immediately and necessarily involved not only the person of Jesus
Christ, but also that of the Spirit through whom the Son of
God became man in the bosom of Mary, and through whom
also, until the parousia, He is present in His body, the Church.
It is in writings by Athanasius—his *Letters to Serapion*—that
one finds the first elaborate patristic argument defending the
divinity of the Spirit. It is the same soteriological approach
that one finds in the other major fourth-century treatise on
the same subject: the *De Spiritu Sancto* of St. Basil of Caesarea. Both Athanasius and Basil consider the saving activity
of the Spirit accessible to the Christian experience, as being
necessarily effected by God Himself. Since the *personal* character of the Spirit is taken for granted, the evidence of the
Spirit's divinity is there to see.

The divine identity of the "comforter" is, therefore, a
basic coordinate of the Christian idea of salvation. It is re-

flected not only in the theological tradition of the Christian East but also, very prominently, in its liturgy. A prayer addressed personally to the Spirit, "O heavenly King," is the initial act of every liturgical action in the Orthodox Church. The sacraments and, more particularly, the sacrament of the Christian *koinonia* itself, *i.e.,* the eucharist, culminate in an invocation of the Spirit. Hymnology, especially that of the feast of Pentecost, proclaims the same relationship between the Spirit's act and His divine identity:

> The Spirit bestows all things: it appoints prophets; it consecrates priests; it gives wisdom to the simple; it turned fishermen into theologians; it gathers together the whole assembly of the Church. O Comforter, consubstantial and co-reigning with the Father and the Son, glory to Thee.

> We have seen the true light; we have received the heavenly Spirit; we have found the true faith, worshipping the undivided Trinity, who has saved us.

In the text of the Nicaean Creed, in fact the creed adopted at the Council of Constantinople in 381, the divine identity of the Spirit was defined in terms of His "procession from the Father." This definition is in accordance with the theology of the Cappadocian fathers who saw in the *person* of God the Father the very "origin of the Godhead." It is precisely as God that the Spirit "proceeds from the Father" directly, while creatures are not direct products from the Father but come into being through the operation and mediation of the Logos. Thus, the proclamation of the Spirit's "procession from the Father" is equivalent to the proclamation of His pre-eternal divinity.

At this point, it is easy to discern the difference of approach to the mystery of the Trinity between the Greek fathers of the fourth century and the Latin West. In trying to define a doctrine of salvation, the Latin West became preoccupied with the issue of justification by faith, its relation to human "works" and produced systems explaining the very process of salvation, *e.g.,* the Anselmian doctrine of satisfaction. The personal divine identity of Christ and the Spirit, though an intellectual necessity—"only God Himself can fully satisfy divine justice"—became in fact a peripheral issue rather than a matter of direct Christian experience, grounded in the Gospel itself and providing the *starting point* of all theology. This development was itself based upon a doctrine of God which tended to relativize the *personal,* or trinitarian life of God, and approach Him first as one single essence, while considering the persons as internal "relations." There is no doubt that this approach to God, popularized by St. Augustine, is, to a degree, responsible for the fact that so many Christians today are practically deists. Venerating God as a single "heavenly Father," they tend to view trinitarianism as a mere speculation. In such a context, there is no real place for a theology of the Holy Spirit except in terms of "gifts" unrelated to the internal life of God.

These obvious differences of perspective between East and West constitute the background of the famous controversy on *Filioque.* As is well known, the "Nicaean" Creed, which was adopted as a solemn confession of faith by the universal Church at its ecumenical councils of the fourth century, was interpolated locally in Spain (sixth or seventh century). The interpolated text was adopted throughout Carolingian Europe (eighth through ninth centuries) and, in spite of strong objections by contemporary Roman popes, it was transformed into a tool of anti-Greek polemics by Charlemagne. The interpolation consisted in an insertion of the words "and from the Son" (Latin: *Filioque*) in the text of the creed, so that the paragraph which originally affirmed the procession of the Spirit "from the Father" (simply quoting John 15:26), now read: "(I believe) in the Holy Spirit, Lord, Giver of Life, who proceeds from the Father and the Son." Eventually, under German pressure, the church of Rome itself accepted the interpolation in spite of violent reactions by Greek theologians, particularly Photius (ninth century), who were not objecting to the idea that the gifts of the Spirit—in the "economy" of the incarnation—were granted through Christ, *i.e.,* through the Son, but against the Augustinian reduction of the hypostatic, personal life of the three divine persons to mere "relations." Photius considered the Latin understanding of God as "modalistic" ("Sabellian" or "semi-Sabellian").

Contemporary Orthodox theologians, particularly Karsavin and Lossky, have expressed the opinion that the *Filioque* dispute is at the very root of ecclesiological differences between East and West. In Western "papal" ecclesiology the presence of the Spirit, *i.e.,* a divine presence which restores and enhances a person's *free* response to God, is fully subordinated to the ecclesiastical institution, based upon a "vicar" of Christ. Whether or not one accepts this scheme, which may appear as somehow artificial, it is certainly true that essentialistic deism hardly allows for any real theology of the Spirit as an active, personal and guiding presence in the church community and in the personal life of the Christian. The "gifts of the Spirit" tend to be understood within the framework of individual or group psychology, for which there can be no ecclesiological or theological framework.

In any case, in order to understand the Orthodox approach to pneumatology, one has to start with the divinity of the Spirit as that was established in the great anti-Arian controversies of the early church. Then one must accept a trinitarian theology which presupposes that the personal identity of the Spirit is understood absolutely, together, of course, with the doctrine of consubstantiality, preserving the essential unity of the Godhead.

2. The anthropological dimension

As we have noticed in the first part of this essay, the main patristic argument for the divinity of Christ and the Spirit was soteriological, because salvation itself was as "deification" *(theosis)*. Obviously only God can "deify." The argument is exemplified in the famous formulae found in almost identical words in Irenaeus ("The Word became man, so that men could become God," *Adversus haereses* V, *praef.*), and in Athanasius ("He was made man that we might be made God," *De Incarnatione* 54), which are applicable to both the "economy" of the Son and to that of the Spirit.

The patristic idea of deification was sometimes identified as pantheistic. It was assumed that it suppressed the necessary distinction and distance between God and creation, and that it reflected a spirituality which suppressed the integrity of the *humanum*. However, most contemporary patristic scholars would disagree with such an evaluation. The very word deification *(theosis)* was used previously by Greek philosophers in a non-biblical and non-Christian context, but its use by the Greek fathers and in the entire Orthodox tradition was based on the theology of the "image of God" within personality, and its various equivalents, *i.e.*, upon a *theocentric* idea of humanity which cannot be adequately expressed in Western categories of "nature" and "grace."

Using a terminology very closely connected with St. Paul's, Irenaeus considers an individual to be "composed of a body taken from the earth, and a soul which receives the Spirit from God" *(Adversus haereses* III, 22, 2). "If the Spirit is wanting to the soul," he continues, "man is being left carnal, shall be an imperfect being, possessing indeed the image of God in his formation, but not receiving the similitude through the Spirit" *(ibid.* V, 9, 1). Not only is the Holy Spirit, paradoxically, considered as a component of true humanity, but Irenaeus also very specifically connects the Spirit with the "similitude." He interprets the similitude both as distinct from the "image" and as the perfection of the individual, granted through the Spirit, provided one presents a free response to God's calling and presence. The individual is not a static and "closed" being. One is given the free task of perfecting oneself, and the role of the Spirit is to "seal" and direct one's ascent to God, so that this ascent may be in conformity with the divine, unending, limitless aim which God has set as one's destiny. The Spirit is not the bestower of "supernatural" gifts —additions to an otherwise "natural" human existence. He not only grants forgiveness and justification, he makes one become fully human.

This theocentric anthropology, so clearly expressed already in Irenaeus (second century), will always be taken for granted by Greek patristic writers. The term "deification," which does not yet appear as such in Irenaeus, will later become standard; it will designate "communion" with God. That communion is one's destiny since the individual's creation is according to God's "image and likeness." That has been made impossible, however, because of sin and death which "reigned" (Romans 5:14) over humanity until the coming of Christ, but it is now made accessible again by the power of the Spirit sent by Christ from the Father. It will find ultimate fulfillment in the age to come.

This basic and central role of the Spirit in defining what the individual is, and how one participates in the saving act of God in Christ, not only presupposes the divinity of the Spirit as third person of the Trinity, but also has direct implications for spirituality and ecclesiology.

Since "deification" is not only a free gift of the Spirit, but also requires one's cooperation, it is inevitably a dynamic process. It implies graduation and stages of communion with God. It implies a religion of *personal experience.* The monastic literature of the Christian East is particularly rich in its understanding and description of the various degrees of spiritual progress. One of the classics of Eastern monastic spirituality, written by St. John, abbot of Sinai (seventh century), even bears the title of *Ladder of Divine Ascent.* It is a systematic, spiritual and psychological analysis of one's road to the direct vision of God.

This monastic spirituality inevitably had close Neoplatonic parallels. The risk of transforming Christianity into a dematerializing and depersonalizing escapism was a very real one. However, the most prominent leaders of Eastern monasticism succeeded in providing an antidote to the "platonizing" temptation. This antidote was found in a biblical theology of the body and in sacramentalism. The condition and basis for an authentic Christian experience was seen in baptism and the eucharistic communion. The point is made with particular clarity in the writings of an anonymous fourth-century writer who uses the pseudonym of "St. Macarius." It is interesting that his insistence on defining the Christian faith in terms of *personal* experience of the Holy Spirit, and the explicitly biblical character of his spirituality, endeared him to John

Wesley, who translated his writings into English.[2] "Macarius" also ranks among the most popular spiritual writers of the East and is noteworthy for his persistence in defining the Christian experience in both sacramental and pneumatological terms.

> By analogy of faith, the divine Spirit, our Advocate, who was sent to the apostles and through them drawn down upon the only true Church of God at the moment of baptism, this Spirit in various manifold ways accompanies every man who comes to baptism in faith.[3]

> When God created Adam He did not give him bodily wings like the birds, but prepared for him in advance the wings of the Holy Spirit—the wings He desires to give him in the resurrection—to lift him up and carry him wherever the Spirit wishes. (*Hom.* 5, 11).

> It is possible to taste in Christianity the grace of God: Taste and seen that the Lord is sweet (Psalm 34:8). This tasting is the dynamic power of the Spirit manifesting itself in full certitude in the heart. The sons of light, ministers of the New Covenant in the Holy Spirit, have nothing to learn from men; they are "taught by God" (John 6:45). Grace itself engraves the laws of the Spirit on their hearts . . . (*Hom.* 15, 20).

The references to a conscious "certitude" of communion with the Spirit and the quotation from John 6:45 on the immediacy of the Spirit's teaching are very characteristic, not only for Macarius, but for the entire tradition of Eastern spirituality. St. Symeon the New Theologian (eleventh century) will be one of the most explicit spokesmen of this "prophetism of holiness." Tasting, experiencing God in the

---

[2]J. Wesley, *A Christian Library* 1 (Bristol, 1749). On Wesley's admiration for Macarius, see A. Outler, ed., *John Wesley* (New York, 1964), p. 9 n.26, and pp. 274-75.

[3]*Epistula Magna*, ed. W. Jaeger, *Two Rediscovered Works of Ancient Christian Literature: Gregory of Nyssa and Macarius* (Leiden, 1954), p. 236.

Spirit, as light, as joy, as truth, is the personal goal of each Christian. This experience is *accessible* to one in this world as an anticipation of the Kingdom to come. Each Christian, therefore, has access to the fullness of revelation and knowledge. One does not have to "learn from men." One enjoys the gift of the Spirit which was given through baptism.

Whether one labels this understanding of the Christian gospel "mystical" (the Christian East is often called "mystical" but the word is misleading in its Western connotations) or "eschatological," it is clear that it has important *ecclesiological* implications.

It is a fact that the Orthodox East, while recognizing the teaching responsibility of the ordained ministry, particularly bishops, also admits the *saints* as authoritative witnesses of truth. Historical examples of doctrinal conflicts between bishops, on the one hand, and popular opinion, frequently led by monks, on the other, are quite numerous. The solitary struggle of St. Maximus the Confessor, a simple monk, against an almost universally recognized "Monothelite" establishment (seventh century) is the best known. The episcopal ministry implies teaching responsibility, but all forms of institutional *infallibility* are formally excluded. The priestly and prophetic functions are both necessary to the Church. Both are maintained by the same Spirit. The Spirit created the apostolic ministry at Pentecost. The Spirit maintains the Church through history and also grants gifts to the entire people of God, to the saints and prophets, those living witnesses of God's presence in the world.

The mystery of the Church consists precisely in that its various ministries find an ultimate unity in *the Spirit, as God*, in whom all contradictions and tensions are resolved, particularly the tension between freedom and authority. Christian freedom is not reducible to a freedom of choice between good and evil, or between various alternatives of earthly behavior. It is, first of all, the possibility to be *fully human, i.e.*, to be in full possession of one's life and one's potentials, to be liberated from the powers of mortality and evil. Now, as we have seen in the theological anthropology of St. Irenaeus— also shared by the later patristic tradition—to be fully human means to be in communion with God, or to have fully restored in oneself the third and highest component of humanity, the presence of the Holy Spirit. This is why Gregory of Nyssa (fourth century) identified the "image of God" in one with *freedom*. In fact, he is in full agreement with Irenaeus on this point, since "where the Spirit of the Lord is, there is freedom" (II Corinthians 3:17).

However, the freedom given to one by "the Spirit of God" is not a freedom for anarchy. It is precisely when discussing the gifts of the Spirit that St. Paul also warns: "Let all things be done decently and in order" (I Corinthians 14:40). The Spirit is the source of freedom and the principle of order in the Church. The same Spirit inspires the prophets and guarantees the effectiveness and permanence of sacramental ministry. Thus, the Montanists who believed that the Church was to be led by prophets, ultimately became a sect. But, on the other hand, a human institution which becomes an end in itself and claims infallibility is nothing but the demonic temptation described by Dostoevsky in his "Legend of the Grand Inquisitor."

The true, "catholic" tradition of Christianity is the one where institutional and charismatic leadership are able *to recognize in each other the same Spirit*. This mutual recognition and authentication is not simple coexistence or simply a "creative tension," as between the divided powers of a democratic society. It is a common belonging and a joint communion with the Spirit as God. Clearly, throughout history there were conflicts between priests and prophets. It is noteworthy, also, that the Orthodox East never lost the sense of their distinctiveness. For example, the monastic communities and their leaders have traditionally been recognized as having a non-institutional, but a real authority in the Church at large. The numerous challenges presented by monks to contemporary church establishments during the early Christian and Byzantine periods, as well as the witness of the "holy elders" *(startsy)* in nineteenth-century Russia, to cite a more recent example, are all signs of a continuous recognition in Eastern Christendom of a charismatic leadership. That leadership at no time challenges the episcopal authority founded in the

sacramental nature of the Church. Neither the gift of episcopal ministry nor that of charismatic leadership, if authentic,
is a created or humanly devised gift. They are founded in
one's participation in the same divine Spirit granted to the
Church at Pentecost, distributed in baptism, and always working at the "building-up" of the Body of Christ.

Conclusion

If the divinity of the Spirit is the very foundation of
trinitarian theology and also of the Christian understanding
of salvation, there are other particularities in His existence
which remain largely undeveloped in theological books but
which appear both in Scripture and in the life of the Church.
The "Spirit of God moved upon the face of the waters"
(Genesis 1:2) at the very inception of creation.[4] The Word,
however, was the one *by whom* all things were made (John
1:3). The Word (not the Spirit) "became flesh," yet it is
because the Holy Spirit came upon Mary (Luke 1:35), which
heralded the beginning of a "new creation." And it is again
the Spirit who makes Christ present in the midst of His disciples until He comes again. Every baptism is "sealed" by
the Spirit, who is also invoked at the celebration of the eucharist "to make" the bread and wine the body and blood of
Christ.[5] The saints also, while they practice the permanent
"Jesus prayer," define their life as a "collection of the Spirit."[6]

All these forms of the Spirit's presence and action follow
the same pattern. The Spirit is inseparable from the Son, both
preceding Him and completing or "sealing" the Son's action.
But the Spirit never calls persons to Himself, but to the Son,
the God-man, the New Adam, the only one in whom the
"hypostatic union" took place—the full union of God and
humanity. The role of the Spirit in salvation (and also in the

---

[4]The identification of the "Spirit of God" with the "Holy Spirit" is widespread in patristic exegesis.

[5]Cf. text of the "epiclesis" in the liturgy of St. John Chrysostom.

[6]This was particularly the case of the celebrated St. Seraphim of Sarov (d.
1833).

internal life of God?) is "kenotic"; it is always directed to the Other. This "kenoticism" leads modern theologians to discern, in the Spirit, the feminine aspect of the "image of God" in personhood.[7] Provided one avoids anthropomorphism and unhealthy gnostic speculation, one can find here the true theological basis for the image of motherhood, also applied to the Church as temple of the Spirit, or to Mary as the mother of the New Adam, head of the Body.

Thus, authentic pneumatology is always both trinitarian and "churchly." Without this foundation, the theological justifications of the "gifts of the Spirit" risk becoming nothing more than rationalizations for passing fads.

[7]Would this be supported by the fact that the Hebrew word for "spirit" (*ruah*) is feminine?

2

The "Defense of the Holy Hesychasts" by St. Gregory Palamas

A major spiritual and intellectual figure of Orthodox Byzantium, Gregory Palamas—monk, archbishop and eminent theologian—dedicated most of his active life to theological argument centered upon one basic truth: the living God is accessible to personal experience because He shared His own life with humanity.

Both his contemporaries and later generations have regarded the nine treatises composed by Palamas in 1338-1341 and entitled *For the Defense of those who practice Sacred Quietude* (Ὑπὲρ τῶν ἱερῶς ἡσυχαζόντων) as the most important of all his writings. Since they were published in three groups of three books to refute first the oral teaching, then the written polemics of the Calabrian philosopher Barlaam, they are frequently referred to as the *Triads*. The Greek term *hesychia* ("quietude") is found in monastic literature since the fourth century to designate the mode of life chosen by hermits, dedicated to contemplation and constant prayer. Such monks were also known for centuries as *hesychasts*. Barlaam had denied the legitimacy of their spiritual methods and their claims to experience divine presence. Palamas stood up to defend them, and his *Triads* introduce the reader into the very substance of the religious experience of the Christian East.

1. The hesychast tradition

Solitary life in the Egyptian or the Palestinian deserts was the original form of Christian monasticism. Already in the fourth century it was adopted by St. Anthony, who, according to his biographer St. Athanasius the Great, was the founder of the monastic movement and became the model of all later anchorites. The appearance of cenobitic monasticism with St. Pachomius, who in Egypt founded the first disciplined communities of monks, did not prevent further development of eremitism and the coexistence, throughout the Christian East, of both cenobites and anchorites throughout the early Christian centuries and the Middle Ages.

The term "hesychast" (ἡσυχαστὴς) was used to designate a "hermit" or anchorite from the very beginnings of monastic history. It appears in the writings of Evagrius[1] (fourth century), of St. Gregory of Nyssa[2] and in imperial legislation referring to monastic status.[3]

Among the early teachers of monastic spirituality, Evagrius Ponticus formulated better than any other that fundamental doctrine on prayer which will inspire the hesychasts in all later centuries. According to Evagrius, prayer is "the highest act of the mind," the activity "appropriate to the dignity of the mind," an "ascent of the mind to God." "The state of prayer," he wrote, "can be aptly described as a habitual state of imperturbable calm. It marches to the heights of intelligible reality the mind which loves wisdom and which is truly spiritualized by the most intense love."[4]

According to Evagrius, a permanent "prayer of the mind" or "mental prayer" (νοερὰ προσευχή) is the goal, the content and the justification of hesychastic, eremitic life. He sees it as "natural" to the human mind. In prayer, man becomes truly himself by reestablishing the right and "natural" relationship with God.[5]

[1]*Rer. mon.*, PG 40, col. 1253B.
[2]*In psalm.*, PG 44, col. 456C.
[3]Justinian, *Nov.* 5, 3; ed. R. Schoell and G. Kroll, p. 32.
[4]Evagrius, *The Praktikos: Chapters on Prayer*, tr. by J. E. Bamberger (Spencer, Mass.: Cistercian Publications, 1970), pp. 63, 69.
[5]On Evagrius and his influence, see particularly I. Hausherr, "L'hésychasme,

Modern historical scholarship has shown that the doctrine on prayer found in Evagrius was, in fact, an expression of a peculiar Origenistic metaphysics, based on Neoplatonism, which conceived the "mind" as naturally divine and as having originally existed without matter, so that the present material world is nothing but a consequence of the Fall.[6] Actually, Evagrius was even formally condemned by the ecumenical council of 553 because of his Origenism. Nevertheless, his writings on prayer remained extremely popular and were often circulating under pseudonyms, particularly that of St. Nilus of Sinai. This does not mean, however, that their readers shared the author's metaphysical presuppositions. In the mainstream of the Eastern spiritual tradition, the mental prayer of Evagrius began to be understood and practiced in the context of a christocentric spirituality. The "mind" ceased to be opposed to matter, because Christian monasticism fully accepted the implications of the incarnation. Thus, the "mental prayer" addressed by Evagrius to the Deity, which he understood in a Neoplatonic and spiritualized sense, became the "prayer of Jesus."

In the late fourth century, this evolution of hesychast spirituality in the direction of christocentrism was greatly influenced by the writings of an unknown author who used the pseudonym of St. Macarius the Great. The writings of Pseudo-Macarius, very often quoted by Palamas, are rather different from the Neoplatonic intellectualism of Evagrius. The center of human consciousness and of divine presence in man is seen as occurring not in the "mind" but in the "heart." On this point, Macarius uses a vocabulary closer to the language of the Psalms (and of Jewish anthropology in general) than of Neoplatonism.[7] "It is possible to taste in Christianity the grace of God," he writes, "and see that the Lord is sweet

étude de spiritualité," *Orientalia Christiana Periodica* 22 (1956), pp. 5-40 (with reference to earlier and important studies by the same author).

[6]On this, see particularly A. Guillaumont, *Les 'Kephalaia Gnostica' d'Evagre le Pontique et l'histoire de l'origénisme chez les Syriens* (Paris, 1962).

[7]On the role of the "heart" in early Christian spirituality, see particularly A. Guillaumont, "Le coeur chez les spirituels grecs à l'époque ancienne," in the article "Cor et cordis affectus," *Dictionnaire de spiritualité* 14-15 (Paris, 1952), cols. 2281-2288.

(Ps. 34:9). This tasting is the dynamic power of the Spirit manifesting itself in full certitude in the heart. The sons of light, ministers of the New Covenant in the Holy Spirit, have nothing to learn from men; they are 'taught by God' (Is. 54:13, Jn. 6:45). Grace itself engraves the laws of the Spirit on their hearts . . . In fact, the heart is master and king of the whole bodily organism, and when grace takes possession of the pasture-land of the heart, it rules over all its members and all its thought; for it is in the heart that the mind dwells, and there dwell all the soul's thoughts; it finds all its goods in the heart. That is why grace penetrates all the members of the body."[8]

In Macarius, the goal of prayer is not the disincarnation of the mind but a tranfiguration of the entire person—soul and body—through the presence of the incarnate God, who is accessible to the conscious "certitude of the heart."

Side by side with great monastic personalities and communities which remained firmly in the framework of Orthodox Christianity, early Christian monasticism also witnessed the appearance of sectarian groups. Some forces of monastic spirituality consciously opposed personal religious experience to the sacramental and hierarchical structure of the Church. Of particular significance in this respect was the so-called "Messalian" movement, which denied the necessity of baptism and other sacraments, rejected the need for social responsibility and recognized only charismatic leadership, as distinct from the teaching and pastoral ministry of bishops and priests. Throughout the Middle Ages the Messalians, also known as "Euchites" or "Bogomils" or, in the West, "Cathars," also promoted dualistic conceptions rooted in Manichaeism. The attempts of some modern scholars to interpret the writings of Pseudo-Macarius himself as a Messalian document seem unconvincing to this author.[9]

---

[8]*Hom.* 15, 20, PG 34, col. 589AB; ed. Dörries (Berlin, 1969), p. 139.

[9]On the Messalian interpretation of Macarius, see particularly H. Dörries, *Die Überlieferung des messalianischen Makarius-Schriften* (Leipzig, 1941); on a different view, J. Meyendorff, "Messalianism or Anti-Messalianism? A Fresh Look at the 'Macarian' Problem," in *Kyriakon. Festschrift Johannes Quasten,* ed. P. Granfield and J. J. Jungmann (Münster-Westf., 1974), pp. 585-90.

It remains, however, that the problem of a possible connection between Messalianism and some branches of hesychasm is not new. In particular, Barlaam the Calabrian himself accused the Byzantine hesychasts, his contemporaries, of being Messalians. It seems, in fact, that he envisaged any claim of real and conscious experience of God as a form of Messalianism. Palamas had no difficulty in showing that Orthodox hesychasts shared neither the anti-sacramentalism of the Messalians nor their particular pretention to see the very essence of God with their material eyes. He did not deny, however, that on the popular level some contact between the Messalians and the Orthodox monastic milieu was very possible. We will see below that he may have been personally involved in such contacts himself.

In any case, the historical significance and influence of the writings of Pseudo-Macarius was not in promoting heretical Messalianism but in reorienting the mystical tradition of the Evagrian type towards a more christocentric and sacramental understanding of prayer. Thus, the great teachers of the "Jesus prayer" or "prayer of the heart" in the following centuries were men like St. Diadochus of Photice (fifth century) and St. John Climacus (580-650), who generally maintained the hesychast tradition in the biblical and incarnational context proper to the Greek patristic thought.[10] For them, prayer was basically a simple though difficult discipline of "keeping one's mind in the heart," of "placing" there the name of Jesus—since the name of God is identified with the presence of the divine person Himself—or of "attaching the name of Jesus to one's breath" (St. John Climacus). The Jesus prayer also took the form of a constant mental repetition of a brief sentence such as "Lord Jesus Christ, Son of God, have mercy upon me, a sinner."

The spirituality centered upon the Jesus prayer, which

[10]The most famous and influential collection of writings concerned with the hesychast prayer tradition is the *Philokalia* published by St. Nicodemus the Haghiorite in 1782. The publication of a full English translation is in progress, *The Philokalia* 1, tr. and ed. G.E.H. Palmer, P. Sherrard, K. Ware (London: Faber and Faber, 1979). For a short survey of the hesychast tradition before Palamas, see J. Meyendorff, *St. Gregory Palamas and Orthodox Spirituality* (Crestwood, N.Y.: St. Vladimir's Seminary Press, 1974), pp. 7-71.

originated in eremitic monasticism, became a constant practice not only in cenobitic monasteries but also among the laity. Its simplicity and directness pointed to the essential content of the Christian faith and led to that personal experience of God without which—according to St. Symeon the New Theologian (949-1022)—there is no true Christianity.

In the late thirteenth century, some written "methods" of the Jesus Prayer also propose a breathing technique aimed at attaching prayer to a constant physiological element of human life: the act of inhaling air. The exact meaning of this technique, which has been compared to *yoga,* was often misunderstood, perhaps by some of its unsophisticated practitioners and, in any case, by Barlaam, who attacked it violently. This explains one of the major themes of the *Triads* of Palamas, which aimed at defining the role of the human body in prayer and, consequently, in a christocentric conception of human life in its wholeness.

2. The life of Palamas

Born in 1296 in Constantinople, of a noble family close to the court of Emperor Andronicus II, Gregory lost his father at the age of seven but continued his education at imperial expense.[11] The usual Byzantine curriculum included a thorough study of the *Logics* of Aristotle, and the young Gregory excelled in it. At the age of twenty, however, he decided to adopt the monastic life and persuaded all the other living members of his family—mother, two brothers and two sisters —to follow his example.

On Mount Athos, he joined the community of the oldest and the remotest of all the Athonite monasteries, the "Great Lavra" of St. Athanasius. He also spent some time as a hermit at the *skete* of Glossia, also on Athos. Around 1325, Turkish raids on the Athonite peninsula obliged many monks to leave

---

[11]The biography of Gregory Palamas is known to us primarily through an *Encomion* composed by his friend and disciple, Philotheus Coccinus, Patriarch of Constantinople; text in PG 151, cols. 551-656. For a complete account, see J. Meyendorff, *A Study of Gregory Palamas* (second ed., London and New York, 1974), pp. 28-113.

the Holy Mountain. Gregory and some friends found refuge in Thessalonica, where they formed a spiritual circle based on prayer and established connections in the city. Writers hostile to Palamas associate some of his activities during that period with the "Bogomil" or "Messalian" sectarians mentioned earlier. It will be shown later that Palamas very clearly rejected the doctrinal views of the sectarians.

Palamas' own Orthodox commitment is further demonstrated by the fact of his ordination to the priesthood, at the canonical age of thirty (1326). Together with a few other monks, he then lived in a hermitage near Berrhoia, following the pattern of "hesychast" life inherited from earlier centuries. Each week, for five days, he practiced the ideally uninterrupted "prayer of Jesus" in his hermitage, rejoining his community on Saturday and Sunday for eucharistic and human fellowship with the brethren. By 1331, Gregory returned to Mount Athos, where he followed the same mode of life at the hermitage of St. Sabbas, near his original monastery, the Lavra. Having acquired some prestige in the Athonite community, Gregory began to publish writings of hagiography and spirituality. In 1335-1336, he became for a brief period abbot of the monastery of Esphigmenou. Soon, however, he was drawn into the arena of theological controversy, ecclesiastical strife and political turmoil which was to dominate the rest of his life, without changing anything of his spiritual commitments and theological persuasion.

The debate between Palamas and the Greek Italian "philosopher," Barlaam the Calabrian, began as a debate on theological method. Both men were engaged in discussing the problem of the Latin addition of the *Filioque*—"the Holy Spirit who proceeds from the Father *and the Son*"—to the original text of the creed. However, for Barlaam, who, like Palamas, defended the Greek view, the issue was one of dialectic proof on the basis of scriptural or patristic statements, since no direct knowledge of God and of the relations between the persons of the divine Trinity was accessible to the human mind. Palamas, on the contrary, approached theology not only as a conceptual exercise based on "revealed premises" but also, and primarily, as an expression of true Christian experience.

Using the same technical Aristotelian terms as his opponent, Palamas insisted that theological discourse concerning the Trinity could reach *apodictic* (and not only *dialectic*) conclusions, *i.e.*, it could lead to *truth itself.* The character of this discussion has led some historians to establish a parallel with the controversies between nominalists and realists in the contemporary Latin West, even if the context and character of the two debates are clearly different.

Barlaam resented the challenge presented to him by monks, whom he saw as intellectually unqualified fanatics. When he attempted to learn more about the hesychast methods of prayer—the basis of the "experience" to which they were always referring—he was shocked even more profoundly, particularly by the claim that the human body, and not only the mind, could be transfigured by divine light and contribute to the knowledge of God. It is this discussion which led not only to the writing of the *Triads* by Palamas, but also to the involvement of both Church and society in the debate.

In June and August 1341, two successive councils held in Constantinople rebuked Barlaam, who left Byzantium and ended his days in Italy. However, just as his defense of the hesychasts seemed to have triumphed, Palamas became deeply entangled in the consequences of the civil war which followed the sudden death of Emperor Andronicus III (1341). The most important political personality of the court, the Grand Domesticus John Cantacuzenus—a supporter of intellectuals who originally patronized Barlaam but eventually sided with the monks—was dismissed by a regency which included Patriarch John Calecas. Palamas, seen as a friend and supporter of Cantacuzenus, was condemned and imprisoned, whereas the patriarch gave support to his theological adversaries, particularly Gregory Acindynus, who objected not to the basic hesychastic spirituality, as did Barlaam, but to the theological formulations espoused by Palamas. If God was absolutely transcendent, but also could be "experienced" and "seen" as an uncreated and real Presence, one had to speak both of a totally transcendent divine "essence" and of uncreated but revealed "energies." It is this famous distinction which Acindynus refused to admit. For him God was identical with His essence, and a vision of God, if it was to be admitted as a possibility, was a vision either of that divine essence itself or else of its *created* manifestations. No real distinctions were conceivable in the uncreated being of God Himself.

The civil war ended with the victory of Cantacuzenus in 1347 and with his crowning as co-emperor, sharing power with the legitimate heir, John V Palaeologus. In 1347 and, particularly, 1351, new councils endorsed the theology of Palamas against the objections of the philosopher and historian Nicephorus Gregoras, who supported the views of Acindynus. In 1347, Gregory Palamas was elected archbishop of Thessalonica. His monastic friends and disciples—Isidore, Callistus and Philotheus Coccinus—successively occupied the patriarchal throne. The victory of hesychasm, as expressed not only in monastic spirituality but also in the theology of Palamas, influenced Eastern Orthodoxy as whole, in Byzantium and throughout Eastern Europe. A generation of spiritual zealots came to positions of leadership and contributed greatly to the survival of Orthodox Christianity during the hard years of Ottoman rule in the Middle East. The spiritual legacy of hesychasm was also transmitted to Russia.

In 1354-55, Gregory Palamas spent a year in Asia Minor as prisoner of the Turks, who had intercepted his boat as he was travelling between Thessalonica and the capital.[12] Ransomed by the Serbs, he returned to his episcopal see, where he died on November 14, 1359.[13]

In 1368, a decision of the synod of Constantinople, presided over by Patriarch Philotheus, proclaimed Gregory Palamas as a saint. His relics are venerated to this day at the cathedral of Thessalonica.

---

[12]On this episode, the most recent study is by A. Philippidis-Brat, "La captivité de Palamas chez les Turcs: dossier et commentaire," *Travaux et mémoires* 7 (Paris: Centre de recherche d'histoire et civilisation byzantines, 1979), pp. 109-221.

[13]Cf. however an attempt to date the death of Palamas as early as 1357 in H. V. Beyer, "Eine Chronologie der Lebensgeschichte des Nikephoros Gregoras," *Jahrbuch der Österreichischen Byzantinistik* 27 (Wien, 1978), pp. 150-153.

3. The Triads for the Defense of the Holy Hesychasts

In spite of the fact that the *Triads* were written as a polemical work directed against the positions of Barlaam the Calabrian in his controversy with the hesychast monks, they represent a major witness to the content and meaning of Christian experience. The author never speaks of that experience as being individually his own. He is certainly not a representative of any form of esoteric mysticism. Quite to the contrary, his intention is to formulate an objective theological foundation justifying his brothers, the hesychast monks, in their understanding of prayer and in the pursuit of their avowed goal, the deification or *theosis* of man in Christ. The main concern of Palamas is to affirm that this goal is not reserved to isolated "mystics" but is, in fact, identical with the Christian faith itself and therefore offered to all the members of the Church, in virtue of their baptism. It is also his contention that the entire Greek patristic tradition can be seen as an affirmation of the goal of *theosis*.

In a detailed introduction to my edition of the original Greek text of the *Triads,* I attempted to describe the circumstances and the chronology of the first encounters between Palamas and Barlaam.[14] Their correspondence began in early 1337, as we saw earlier, and was initially concerned with the problem of the "apodictic" or "dialectic" knowledge of God. The logic of the debate soon led Barlaam to criticize the very notion of "spiritual knowledge" affirmed by the monks and to attack with particular virulence their method of prayer, which implied the participation of the *body* in the continuous practice of the Jesus prayer and, consequently, in the very reality of communion with God. Some of the writings of the Calabrian philosopher used derogatory terms: the monks were

[14]Ed. J. Meyendorff, *Gregoire Palamas. Défense des saints hésychastes. Introduction, texte critique, tradition et notes* (second ed., Louvain, 1973), I, pp. I-L; cf. also the series of my earlier studies reprinted in *Byzantine Hesychasm: Historical, Theological and Social Problems* (London: Variorum Reprints, 1974). For an updated discussion of the chronology, see Robert E. Sinkewicz, "A New Interpretation of the First Episode in the Controversy between Barlaam the Calabrian and Gregory Palamas," *Journal of Theological Studies* (1980), pp. 489-500.

"people-having-their-soul-in-their-navel" (ὀμφαλόψυχοι)
because, following the instructions of authors like Nicephorus
the Hesychast, they disciplined their attention by lowering
their eyes "towards the center of their bodies" and thus concentrated on prayer. Barlaam also affirmed that secular education or "acquisition of wisdom" was a condition for a true
knowledge of God.

Palamas began writing his first *Triad for the Defense of
the Holy Hesychasts* on the basis of his own face-to-face discussions with Barlaam and also of some oral accounts of the
philosopher's views. However, the name of Barlaam is not
yet mentioned in the first *Triad*. Faced with this indirect re-
buttal, Barlaam softened some of his more extreme criticisms
(suppressing allusions to navel-watching, *etc.*) and published
a three-part treatise: *On the Acquisition of Wisdom, On
Prayer* and *On the Light of Knowledge.* The second *Triad* of
Palamas—written during a trip of Barlaam to Avignon in 1339,
where he unsuccessfully negotiated church union with Pope
Benedict XII—is a formal refutation of these treatises.

Upon his return to Constantinople, faced with the now
public polemical exchange with a respected leader of Athonite
monasticism, Barlaam published a new treatise, entitled
Against the Messalians, openly accusing his opponents of
preaching the doctrine of a formally condemned sect. As we
have seen earlier, the Messalians or "Bogomils" claimed to
contemplate, through prayer, the very essence of God with
their material eyes. This provided Palamas with the topic of
his last *Triad,* where the argument concentrates upon the distinction in God between "essence" and "energy." Disclaiming
any Messalian influence but maintaining the full reality of
communion with God Himself and not only with "created
grace," Palamas develops his doctrine of the uncreated divine
energies.

The debate ends with the endorsement given to Palamas
first by the whole monastic community of Mount Athos (the
so-called *Tomos Haghioretikos*) and then by the Council of
Constantinople in 1341 and the emigration of Barlaam to
Italy in the same year.

It can be safely said that the true message of Byzantine

medieval hesychasm and the essential meaning of what is now generally called "Palamism" is fully expressed in the *Triads*. In the course of his later life, Gregory was confronted with major political difficulties and was faced with the opposition of Acindynus and Gregoras. He wrote profusely in the form of theological letters or lengthy treatises.[15] His theology acquired greater—almost scholastic—rigidity, but no substantially new dimension was added to the vision already found in the *Triads*. However, it is not possible to acquire a full understanding of Gregory Palamas, as a person and as a churchman, without reading also his 61 preserved sermons, delivered when he served as archbishop of Thessalonica. Here he appears not as a polemicist or a theologian playing with concepts but as an accessible pastor, concerned with the spiritual and social welfare of his simple flock. This aspect of his personality is certainly as revealing of his authentically Christian experience as his theological arguments against Barlaam, Acindynus or Nicephorus Gregoras.

4. Philosophy and Salvation

One of the most striking characteristics of Byzantine medieval Christianity is its concern with the role of ancient Greek philosophical categories in the formulation of Christian theology and spirituality.[16] In fact, unlike their Latin contemporaries who "discovered" Greek philosophy—in Latin translations from the Arabic—in the twelfth century, the Byzantines had never forgotten Plato and Aristotle, who represented their own Greek cultural past and were always accessible to them in the original Greek text. But at the same

---

[15]The complete edition of the theological writings of Palamas is in the process of completion by P. Chrestou (cf. Παλαμᾶ Συγγράμματα, Thessaloniki, vol. 1, 1962; vol. 2, 1966; vol. 3, 1970).

[16]There is an abundance of recent publications on this subject by authors adopting different and sometimes contradictory points of view; see for example I. P. Medvedev, *Vizantiisky Gumanizm* 14-15, 20 (Leningrad, 1976); G. Podskalsky, *Theologie und Philosophie in Byzanz* (München, 1977). For a general objective and accessible presentation, see particularly D. M. Nicol, *Church and Society in the Last Centuries of Byzantium. The Birkbeck Lectures, 1977* (New York: Cambridge University Press, 1979).

time, they always recognized that this past was a "pagan" past. Thus, the ancient Greek heritage could still be useful in such fields as logic, physics or medicine (hence the inclusion of Aristotle in the standard Byzantine educational curriculum followed by Palamas in his youth), but not in religion. Metaphysical and religious truths could validly originate only in the Christian revelation. This is the reason why Plato and the Neoplatonists were always looked upon with suspicion in conservative—and particularly monastic—circles of the Byzantine church. Indeed, in any form of Platonic thought, no understanding of reality was possible without metaphysical, *i.e.,* in fact theological, presuppositions.

It is not astonishing, therefore, to find out that every year on the first Sunday of Lent—also known as the "Sunday of Orthodoxy"—all Byzantine Orthodox churches resounded with formal and repeated anathemas against "those who follow the foolish opinions of the Hellenic disciplines" and particularly against those "who considered the ideas of Plato as truly existing" or who believe (with Aristotle) in the eternity of matter.[17] These anathemas were first issued in the eleventh century on the occasion of the condemnation of the philosopher John Italus, but their inclusion in the liturgical *Synodikon* of the Sunday of Orthodoxy gave them permanent significance.

Clearly, however, Greek philosophical concepts were inseparable from many aspects and formulations of the patristic tradition which was the common model and authority for all Byzantines. The repeated clashes between "humanists" who tended to minimize the prohibitions against "Hellenic wisdom" and those theologians, predominantly monastic, who insisted upon the incompatibility between "Athens" and "Jerusalem" (to use the old expression of Tertullian) could not solve the issue in a definitive way. Similarly, in the controversy between Barlaam and Palamas, both sides acknowledged the authority of the Christian revelation and, on the other hand, admitted that ancient philosophers possessed a

---

[17]J. Gouillard, "Le Synodikon de l'Orthodoxie. Edition et commentaire," *Travaux et mémoires* 2 (Paris: Centre de recherche d'histoire et de civilisation byzantines, 1967), p. 59; also Τριώδιον (Athens: ed. Phos, 1958), p. 160.

certain natural ability to reach not only created but also divine truths. What, then, separated them and made the debate appear to be essentially a debate on the relation between ancient philosophy and the Christian experience?

On the one hand, the different backgrounds and intellectual formation of Palamas and Barlaam led them to assign to Greek philosophy a different *degree* of authority. Barlaam's contacts with Western thought and his involvement in the "humanist" milieu in Byzantium were leading him to an enthusiastic endorsement of Aristotle and Neoplatonic authors as the essential criteria of Christian thought. "I cannot conceive that God has not illuminated them in a certain manner, and feel that they must surpass the multitude of mankind."[18] Palamas, on the contrary, preferred to approach the ancient Greek philosophical tradition as requiring a baptismal rebirth —a death and a resurrection—as a condition for its integration into the tradition of the Church: This is the meaning of his image of serpents being killed and dissected before providing materials used in helpful drugs.[19]

However, beyond this difference of taste and method one discovers a deeper and more serious conflict between the two men. Barlaam launches against the monks the somewhat superficial accusation of "ignorance," which appears at the very outset of the debate. He also contends that "God is only knowable through the mediation of His creatures."[20] Of course, Barlaam may be misrepresented by Palamas when he is accused of teaching that knowledge of God is possible *only* through creatures. The Calabrian philosopher does believe also in an illumination of the mind which leads to a vision of the divine Being. He is familiar with—and admires— the writings of Pseudo-Dionysius and of St. Maximus the Confessor, where a direct vision of God and deification are seen as the goal of Christian life. It remains, nevertheless, that a certain "knowledge of beings" (γνῶσις τῶν ὄντων) is, for Barlam, a *condition* for illumination, and it is this

---

[18]First letter to Palamas, ed. G. Schirò, in *Barlaam Calabro epistole greche i primordi episodici e dottrinari delle lotte esicaste* (Palermo, 1954), p. 262.

[19]*Triads* I, 1, 20.

[20]*Triads* I, 1, quest.

which led to his conflict with the monks and which is unacceptable to Palamas. If "knowledge," identified with secular education, is necessary to know God, what is the meaning of Matt. 11:25 ("You have hidden these things from the wise and prudent and have revealed them to babes") or of the references, so frequent in Palamas,[21] to Rom. 1 or I Cor. 1-2 which speak of the "wisdom of this age" being "put to shame"?

In Palamas there is no denigration of the "knowledge of beings" and, therefore, no obscurantism. Furthermore, his own understanding of illumination in Christ implies that the mind, transfigured by grace, opens up also to a knowledge of creatures. Neither is there, in Palamism, a systematic opposition to secular learning. Not only is Palamas himself clearly indebted to his training in Aristotelian logics, but also his disciple and biographer, Philotheus Coccinus, always embellishes his writings with references to authors of antiquity. Furthermore, the triumph of Palamism in the Byzantine church, completed in 1351, did not interrupt the development of secular humanism, which produced on the eve of Byzantium's fall such figures as Gemisthus Pletho and Bessarion.[22]

The debate between Barlaam and the hesychasts can probably be best understood in the light of their different interpretations of what St. Maximus the Confessor used to call "natural contemplation" (φυσικὴ θεωρία), or the new state of created being in Christ. Barlaam—and also the medieval Latin tradition—tends to understand this created *habitus* as a condition for and not a consequence of illumination by grace. Palamas, on the contrary, proclaims the overwhelming novelty of the Kingdom of God revealed in Christ, and the gratuitous

---

[21]See, for example, *Triads* I, 1, 14-15; I, 1, 13, *etc.*

[22]Some art historians have attempted to connect the victory of Palamism with a decay of the so-called "Palaeologan renaissance" in Byzantine art. However, the very concept of "renaissance," when applied to Byzantine society, can only have a very relative significance. Social and cultural rather than theological factors should be used to explain its "decay." See J. Meyendorff, "Spiritual Trends in Byzantium in the late Thirteenth and early Fourteenth Centuries," in P. Underwood, *The Kariye Djami* 4 (Princeton, N.J., 1975), pp. 93-106; also *Byzantium and the Rise of Russia* (New York: Cambridge University Press, 1981), pp. 138-144.

character of the divine and saving acts of God. Hence, for him, vision of God cannot depend upon human "knowledge." Of course, in Greek patristic terminology, and particularly in St. Maximus, "nature" presupposes divine presence in man, *i.e.,* "grace." No opposition between "nature" and "grace" is therefore possible.[23] But salvation itself begins by a divine act providing direct knowledge of God which restores "nature" to its original state and also allows for a truly "natural" contemplation of God through His creatures. Palamas always remains basically faithful to the thought of St. Maximus who, together with Pseudo-Dionysius, is the patristic author most frequently quoted in the *Triads.*

5. Knowledge beyond knowledge

The philosopher Barlaam's debate with Palamas on the subject of Greek philosophy and its relevance to Christian thought had inevitably to confront the nature of Christian experience itself, which was described by Palamas as being *beyond nature.* Barlaam, on the contrary, seems to have clung to the Aristotelian approach which defines all human knowledge as being based on perception *by the senses;* while he admits the possibility of a positive illumination of the mind transcending the senses, this remains within "the nature of the mind." Of course, Barlaam also knew the apophatic or "negative" theology of the Greek fathers and particularly Pseudo-Dionysius. According to him, this theology maintained the limitations of the human mind, whose knowledge of God could only be symbolic or relative. Indeed, the meaning of negative theology consists precisely in saying only what *God is not,* not what *He is.*[24] In the *Triads* Palamas argues, on the

[23]On the positions of St. Maximus on this point, see particularly L. Thunberg, *Microcosm and Mediator. The Theological Anthropology of Maximus the Confessor* (Lund, 1965), pp. 327-330.

[24]Cf. my analysis of Barlaam's thought in "Un mauvais théologien de l'unité," in *L'Église et les églises* 2 (Chevetogne, 1955), pp. 47-64 (reprinted in *Byzantine Hesychasm,* London: Variorum, 1974); for a more positive evaluation of Barlaam, see G. Podskalsky, *Theologie und Philosophie in Byzanz* (München, 1977), pp. 124-157.

other hand, that "God is not only beyond knowing but also beyond unknowing."

Both protagonists clearly agreed on the central role of the *via negativa* in Christian theology, as an expression of God's transcendence. The writings of the fathers—and particularly Dionysius—emphasized, as the starting point of any Christian discourse about God, the affirmation that God is not any of the creatures and that therefore the created mind which "knows" only creatures can only conceive God by the method of exclusion. The most frequently repeated liturgical prayers, familiar to all, were using the same apophatic approach to God: "Thou art God ineffable, invisible, incomprehensible," proclaimed the preface of the eucharistic canon of the liturgy of St. John Chrysostom celebrated in all the churches. According to the fathers, this transcendence of God was experienced by Moses when he entered the cloud on the top of Mount Sinai and there perceived the presence of God in the darkness of unknowing.

However, the major point made by Palamas in his *Triads* is precisely that the darkness of the cloud surrounding God is not an empty darkness. While eliminating all perceptions of the senses or of the mind, it nevertheless places man before a Presence revealed to a transfigured mind and a purified body. Thus, divine "unknowability does not mean agnosticism, or refusal to know God" but is a preliminary step for "a change of heart and mind enabling us to attain to the contemplation of the reality which reveals itself to us as it raises us to God."[25] In other words, true knowledge of God implies a transfiguration of man by the Spirit of God, and the negations of "apophatic" theology signify only the inability of reaching God without such a transfiguration by the Spirit.

This approach to the issue of the experience of God implies, in Palamas, both a basic anthropological presupposition and a theological principle.

The anthropological presupposition is that man is capable of *transcending his own nature,* that, being created according to the image of God, he possesses "an organ of vision" which

[25]V. Lossky, *The Mystical Theology of the Eastern Church* (Crestwood, N.Y.: St. Vladimir's Seminary Press, 1976), p. 43.

is "neither the senses nor the intellect." He is admitted to "true vision" when he "ceases to see." And one clearly discovers—in connection with the christological views of Palamas —that this capacity of transcending oneself is always understood personalistically: The person (or *hypostasis*), in virtue of its freedom (which *is* the image of God, according to St. Gregory of Nyssa) possess an *openness,* a capacity *to love* the other and particularly, therefore, to love God and to know Him in love.

The theological principle presupposed by Palamas is that God, even when He communicates Himself to the purified body and mind, *remains transcendent* in His essence. In this, Palamas follows St. Gregory of Nyssa, who spoke of mystical experience in terms of an experience of divine inexhaustibility and used the term *tension* (*epektasis*) to describe it. Communion with God never becomes exhaustion or saturation but implies the revelation that *greater things* are always to come. The model of the Song of Songs inspires the mystics to describe union with God as a limitless ascent "from glory to glory" similar to a perfect form of erotic love in which true joy is, at the same time, fulfillment and further expectation.

Thus, apophatic theology is much more than a simple dialectical device to ascertain the transcendence of God in terms of human logic. It also describes a state beyond the conceptual process, where God reveals Himself positively to the "spiritual senses," without losing anything of His transcendence, as "light," as "source of deification," while remaining "more-than-God" and "more-than-Principle." This is what leads Palamas to his distinction between the ultimately transcendent and unknowable essence of God on the one hand and, on the other, the deifying and uncreated energies through which man enters in communion with the Unknowable.

6. The transfigured body

Throughout the centuries, Christian spirituality has often been influenced by Platonic terminology and ideas, which tended to describe the fallen state of man in terms of an opposition between spirit and matter. For Origen and Evagrius, the ultimate goal of prayer and contemplation is for the mind to become "free from all matter."[26] This spiritualistic and intellectual trend in spirituality was familiar to Barlaam, who, on the other hand, had no taste for the more sacramental and more biblical anthropology connected with the writings of Pseudo-Macarius. He was even less able to appreciate the spiritual methods or exercises which appear in texts of the late thirteenth century (although they are certainly more ancient in origin) and which aim at reestablishing the unity of spirit and body, as a single psychosomatic organism, in the act of prayer.

Two of such methods, very similar in content, are formally referred to by Palamas in the *Triads*.[27] The first, by an unknown author, is attributed to St. Symeon the New Theologian.[28] The second is by the hesychast Nicephorus, an Italian who became a monk on Mount Athos during the reign of Michael VIII Palaeologus (1259-1282).[29] As one can see from the following excerpt from Nicephorus, they describe a breathing discipline aimed at acquiring permanent "vigilance" in prayer and presupposing that the *heart* is the vital center of psychosomatic life.

> You know that we breathe our breath in and out only because of our heart . . . so, as I have said, sit down, recollect your mind, draw it—I am speaking of your mind—in your nostrils; that is the path the breath takes to reach the heart. Drive it, force it to go down to your heart with the air you are breathing in. When it is there, you will see the joy that follows: you will have nothing to regret. As a man who has been away from home for a long time cannot restrain his joy at seeing his wife and children again, so the spirit over-

[26]Evagrius Ponticus, *Praktikos* 119; tr. J. E. Bamberger (see n.4 above), p. 75.

[27]*Triads* I, 2, 12 and II, 2, 2; ed. J. Meyendorff, pp. 99, 320-324.

[28]Published by I. Hausherr in "La méthode d'oraison hesychaste," *Orientalia Christiana Periodica* 9. 2 (1927).

[29]PG 147, cols. 945-966.

flows with joy and unspeakable delights when it is united again to the soul.

Next you must know that as long as your spirit abides there, you must not remain silent nor idle. Have no other occupation or meditation than the cry of: "Lord Jesus Christ, Son of God, have mercy on me!" Under no circumstances give yourself any rest. This practice protects your spirit from wandering and makes it impregnable and inaccessible to the suggestions of the enemy and lifts it up every day in love and desire for God.[30]

We do not know for sure whether Barlaam met hesychasts who applied this rather simple breathing technique literally or whether he witnessed naive or superstitious abuses. In any case, his stand against the practice was unambiguous. He called the monks *omphalopsychoi*—"people-whose-soul-is-in-their-navel"—and protested the very principle that the body can or should participate in "pure prayer."

The reaction of Palamas—as reflected in *Triads* I, 2 and II, 2, which represent the most direct and self-explanatory sections of his work—is to refer to the human body as the natural "temple of the Holy Spirit which is in us" (I Cor. 6:19). He is unconcerned with the various physiological views about the location of the mind, whether in the brain or the heart, but tends to prefer the Macarian concept of the heart as the main "instrument" of the Spirit. His biblical references all point to the actions of God upon and through the material and fleshly side of man, as well as through the soul, and in opposition to the Platonic dualism between spirit and matter. His implications are also sacramental: Baptism and eucharistic communion sanctify the whole man. Why not also accept and encourage the participation of the body in prayer?

As we have seen in connection with the treatment of apophatic theology by Palamas, God transcends creatures as such, not the human body or mind in particular. Thus, His revela-

[30]Tr. in J. Meyendorff, *St. Gregory Palamas and Orthodox Spirituality* (Crestwood, N.Y.: St. Vladimir's Seminary Press, 1974), pp. 59-60.

tion of His presence and of His sanctifying Spirit touches both the spiritual and the physical sides of man. Without this presence and this sanctification no real communion with God is possible.

7. The uncreated glory of Christ

In his theological defense of hesychasm, Palamas is particularly concerned to avoid one possible misunderstanding: the identification of the Christian experience with either intellectual knowledge or any form of physical or mystical—but *natural*—vision. As we have seen earlier, he does not deny the relative achievements of Greek philosophy, and he defends the participation of natural human functions, such as the body or the "heart," in perceiving divine Presence. However, the Presence itself is not the simple result of "natural" efforts, whether intellectual or ascetical, but is the gift of personal divine communion or deification (*theosis*) which transcends the creaturely level of human life. It is "uncreated" because it is the self-giving God Himself. It is a "hypostatic" light, "seen spiritually by the saints," which "exists not symbolically only, as do manifestations produced by fortuitous events," but is "an illumination immaterial and divine, a grace invisibly seen and ignorantly known. What it is, they do not pretend to know (*Triads* II, 3, 8).

In the context of this affirmation of God's real manifestation to creatures, Palamas, following Maximus the Confessor and John of Damascus, refers to the New Testament accounts and references to the transfiguration of Christ on the mount (Math. 17:1-9; Mk. 9:2-9; Lk. 9:28-36; II Pet. 1:17-21). And since the mount of transfiguration is traditionally identified with Mount Tabor, the whole debate between Barlaam and Palamas is frequently referred to as the controversy on the "Taboric light." Indeed, in Greek patristic tradition since Origen and St. Gregory of Nyssa, the vision of God is always defined as a luminous vision, probably because the central biblical (and particularly Johannine) theme of "light" and "darkness" was also familiar to Neoplatonists and could easily serve as a convenient theological model. However, one of the major concerns of Palamas is to draw a sharp distinction between any form of light-experience outside of the Christian revelation, and the real vision of God as Light which appeared to the disciples on the mount of transfiguration and which, in Christ, has become accessible to the members of His Body, the Church. Indeed, true "deification" became possible only when, according to the expression of St. Athanasius, "God became man in order that man might become God in Him."[31] Consequently, according to Palamas, a radical change in the relationship between God and man intervened with the incarnation, which leaves all other experiences and discoveries—either in the Old Testament or among the Greeks —as mere shadows of the realities to come. He writes: "Deification would have belonged to all nations even before [Christ] came if it naturally pertains to the rational soul, just as today it would belong to everyone irrespective of faith or piety" (*Triads* III, 1, 30).

This does not imply, however, that Palamas understands deification in Augustinian terms, implying a strict opposition between "nature" and "grace." As has been shown by many modern historians, Greek patristic anthropology is "theocentric." At his creation, man was endowed with some "divine characteristics," in that he is God's image and likeness. According to St. Maximus the Confessor, these characteristics are "being" and "eternity" (which God possesses by nature but which He also gives to man).[32] Earlier, St. Irenaeus of Lyons identified the "spirit" naturally belonging to man with the Holy Spirit.[33] Consequently, man is not fully man unless he is in communion with God: He is "open upwards" and destined to share God's fellowship.[34] However, because God remains absolutely transcendent in His essence, man's communion with Him has no limit. It never reaches an End, which would be a dead end. God is both transcendent and inex-

[31]*Ad Adelphium* 4, PG 26, col. 1077A.
[32]*Chapters on Love* 3, 25, PG 90, col. 1024BC.
[33]Cf. for example *Adv. Haer.* V, 6, 1.
[34]More references and discussion in J. Meyendorff, *Byzantine Theology. Historical Trends and Doctrinal Themes* (second ed., New York, 1979), pp. 138-150.

haustible. Man's communion with Him can never be "closed" through exhaustion. This is the transcendence which Palamas defends and sees as the most central, the most positive and the most essential aspect not only of hesychasm, as a tradition of monastic spirituality, but also of the Christian faith as such: In Christ, man enters into communion not with "the God of the philosophers and the savants" but with the one who in human language can only be called "more-than-God" (*Triads* III, 1, 31).

Hypostatically, "personally," the Logos—second person of the Trinity—by assuming the fullness of humanity, became, in His Body, the source or locus of deification. Being "deified" means "being in Him," *i.e.,* participant of His Body, which is penetrated (by virtue of the "communication of properties" in the hypostatic union)[35] with divine life or "energy." Eucharistic communion in the deified humanity of Christ, in the form of Bread and Wine, has precisely this meaning. Here is an often quoted passage of Palamas on this crucial issue:

> Since the Son of God, in His incomparable love for man, not only united His divine hypostasis with our nature, by clothing Himself in a living body and a soul gifted with intelligence . . . but also united Himself . . . with the human hypostases themselves, in mingling Himself with each of the faithful by communion with His holy body, and since He becomes one single body with us (cf. Eph. 3:6) and makes us a temple of the undivided Divinity, for in the very body of Christ dwelleth the fullness of the Godhead bodily (Col. 2:9), how should He not illuminate those who commune worthily with the divine ray of His body which is within us, lightening their souls, as He illumined the very bodies of the disciples on Mount Tabor? For, on the day of the transfiguration, that body, source of the light of grace, was not yet united with our bodies; it illuminated from outside those who worthily ap-

---

[35]For the principles and terminology of post-Chalcedonian Christology, see J. Meyendorff, *Christ in Eastern Christian Thought* (New York, 1975), particularly the chapter on St. Maximus, pp. 131-151.

proached it, and sent the illumination into the soul by the intermediary of the physical eyes. But now, since it is mingled with us and exists in us, it illuminates the soul from within.[36]

It is precisely because Palamas understands illumination in the framework of Orthodox christology that he insists on the *uncreated* character of divine light. This uncreated light is the very divinity of Christ shining through His humanity. If Christ is truly God, this light is authentically divine. The same christological framework makes it inevitable to distinguish between the transcendent essence or nature of God and His energies. Indeed, in Christ, the two natures—so precisely defined at Chalcedon as both "unseparable" and "unconfused"—remain distinct. Therefore, deification or communion between divinity and humanity does not imply a confusion of essences or natures. It remains nevertheless *real* communion between the Uncreated and His creature, and real deification—not by essence but by *energy*. The humanity of Christ, "enhypostasized" by the Logos, is penetrated with divine energy, and Christ's body becomes the source of divine light and deification. It is "theurgic," *i.e.,* it communicates divine life to those who are "in Christ" and participate in the uncreated energies active in it.

Another aspect of the Christian experience particularly important in monastic spirituality as described by Palamas is its eschatological character. The reference to II Peter 1, where the episode of the transfiguration of Christ is interpreted as "confirming the prophetic word" appears repeatedly in the *Triads* (cf. II, 3, 18). It places hesychast spirituality in the context of the biblical notion of "prophecy," which in the Old Testament implied an anticipated vision of the Messianic age realized in Christ, and which still remains in the New Testament as an experience by "the saints" of the age to come.[37] However, whereas the Old Testament prophets per-

---

[36]*Triads* I, 3, 38; ed. J. Meyendorff, p. 193; cf. tr. and commentary in *A Study of Gregory Palamas,* pp. 150 ff.

[37]This theme is particularly emphasized in the Tome of the Holy Mountain, a document drafted by Palamas and signed in 1340 by representatives of the

ceived only a symbolic anticipation of the Kingdom, the New Testament Church, founded on sacramental communion and "life in Christ," offers a participation in the very reality of the divine life. Granted to all the baptised, this participation is personal and conscious: It happens in the "heart" of the saints.

8. Essence and energies of God

The distinction in God between "essence" and "energy"— that focal point of Palamite theology—is nothing but a way of saying that the transcendent God remains transcendent even as He also communicates Himself to humanity.

The distinction, which was officially endorsed by the Orthodox Church at a series of councils in the fourteenth century, has later been a topic of debate and controversy. It is obviously impossible to present here all the elements of the debate.[38] I will limit myself to a few simple remarks which will allow the reader to understand better an affirmation which appears repeatedly in the *Triads* and is more specifically developed in texts of *Triad* III.

Having initially attacked the hesychast monks for their claim to possess a real experience and vision of God—which he himself tended to consider as either mystical illumination of the mind, or a symbol, or an aberration—Barlaam the Calabrian, facing oral and written rebukes, published a book entitled *Against the Messalians*. By identifying the monks as

monasteries of Mount Athos in support of his theology (text in PG 150, col. 1225-1236; cf. J. Meyendorff, *A Study of Gregory Palamas,* pp. 48-49, 193-196).

[38]Earlier in this century, the distinction was fiercely criticized by the French Assumptionists S. Guichardan and M. Jugie, primarily in the name of the notion of simplicity of God as defined in Latin scholastic thought. For my own presentation of the issue, see *A Study of Gregory Palamas,* pp. 202-227. For the abundant bibliography which appeared since then, see D. Stiernon, "Bulletin sur le palamisme," *Revue des études byzantines* 30 (1972), pp. 231-337. But the debate continues. See, for example, the critical articles on "Palamism" by J. Ph. Houdret, J. M. Garrigues, J. S. Nadal and M.-J. Le Guillou published in *Istina,* 1974, No. 3; and responses by A. de Halleux, "Palamisme et Tradition," *Irénikon* 48 (1975), pp. 479-493, and by Orthodox authors (G. Barrois and Ch. Yannaras) in *St. Vladimir's Theological Quarterly* 19. 4 (1975).

Messalians—a condemned charismatic sect—he was accusing them of pretending "to contemplate the essence of God with their physical eyes." It was, therefore, inevitable for Palamas to recall the apophatic theology of the Greek fathers, which affirmed the absolute transcendence of the divine essence, inaccessible to the angels themselves.

However, for Palamas, this transcendent essence of God would become a philosophical abstraction if it did not possess "power," *i.e.,* "the faculties of knowing, of prescience, of creating" (*Triads* III, 2, 5). In other words, the God of Palamas is a living God, ultimately indescribable in the categories of essentialist Greek philosophy. He says as much himself, referring to the revelation of the divine name to Moses on Mount Sinai: "When God was conversing with Moses," writes Palamas, "He did not say, 'I am the essence,' but 'I am the One Who Is' (Ex. 3:14). Thus, it is not the One Who Is who derives from the essence, but essence which derives from Him, for it is He who contains all being in Himself" *Triads* III, 3, 11).

The real communion, the fellowship and—we can almost say—the familiarity with the "One Who Is" is, for Palamas, the very content of the Christian experience, made possible because the One Who Is became man. It is this familiarity and immediate communion with God that was at stake, according to Palamas in his debate with Barlaam. For Barlaam, God was identical with His essence, and there was no real possibility for man to be in communion with divine essence. "Illumination," conceived as a created state, was however accessible, but through a mediation of the angelic hierarchies. On this point, Barlaam was undoubtedly referring to the famous writings of Pseudo-Dionysius the Areopagite, who viewed God-man relationships as a scale of mediations, the "celestial" and the "ecclesiastical" hierarchies, a Christian version of the Neoplatonic world system. Palamas rejected this approach with indignation. Of course, he respected the writings of Pseudo-Dionysius, whom he counted among the greatest fathers of the Church, but, as we have shown elsewhere, he took the "hierarchies" of Dionysius as describing the relationships between God and man as they existed in the

Old Testament, when God spoke only "through angels" (Heb. 2:2).[39] After the coming of Christ, however, God enters into immediate communion with humanity. "Did He not deign to make His dwelling in man," asks Palamas, "to appear to him and speak to him without intermediary, so that man should be not only pious, but sanctified and purified in advance in soul and body by keeping the divine commandments, and so be transformed into a vehicle worthy to receive the all-powerful Spirit?" (*Triads* III, 3, 5).

So, communion with God in Christ is real and immediate. It is not pantheistic absorption into the Divine, however. Man, being "in God" or rather "in Christ," preserves his full humanity, his freedom (he is required to "keep the commandments"); and he participates in a process which knows no end, because God, in His transcendent essence, is always "above" any given experience of Him. But man's communion is not with "created grace" only, but with God Himself. This is the meaning of the doctrine of the "uncreated energies" which, as we have seen earlier, is rooted in the christological doctrine of "hypostatic union" as it was formulated in the East after Chalcedon, particularly by St. Maximus the Confessor.

The doctrine of the energies was defined with ever greater refinement in the later writings of Palamas, particularly those which he directed against Gregory Acindynus in 1342-1347. But in order to understand these conceptual and frequently polemical definitions, the initial freshness of his debate with Barlaam, as it is found in the *Triads,* is always to be remembered, as the necessary context of Palamite theology. The only concern of Palamas was to affirm simultaneously the transcendence of God and His immanence in the free gift of communion in the body of Christ. This concern could not be fully expressed in philosophical or conceptual terms. In maintaining it, Palamas is neither an innovator nor a blind conservative; but as an authentic spokesman for the Greek patristic

[39]"Notes sur l'influence dionysienne on Orient," in *Studia Patristica* 2 (Texte und Untersuchungen 64; Berlin, 1957), pp. 547-552.

tradition, he never lost sense of the tension and the polarity between Greek thought and the Christian gospel. It is this sense which opposes him to his theological critics, old and new.

V

AUTHORITY
AND STRUCTURE IN
THE CHURCH

1

St. Basil, the Church, and Charismatic Leadership*

Early Christian monasticism was a spontaneous and popular movement. A great number of men and women, following the example of a few leaders, adopted various forms of monastic life without preliminary planning or formal training. In the fourth century, Egypt, Palestine, Syria and Eastern Asia Minor saw the emergence of the movement, and its impact upon the life of the Christian Church at large soon turned out to be a real challenge: spiritual, ecclesiological and theological.

Historically, it is easy to find models for Christian monasticism in pre-Christian Judaism, or in some Stoic or Neoplatonic trends, but it is in Christianity that monks assumed a truly central spiritual role, particularly in the East. Inevitably, this raised problems of Christian institutional structure, Christian spirituality and Christian theology. The fact that no Christian leader responsibly opposed the monastic movement in principle indicates that monasticism was unanimously accepted as reflecting some basic aspects of the Christian faith itself. But, at the same time, deviations and exaggerations of the monastic ideals in some groups soon became apparent and controversial. It became inevitable to raise issues of norms and discipline. The very existence of a definite category of Christians practicing a distinct way of life and setting up their

*Originally published under the title "St. Basil, Messalianism and Byzantine Christianity" in *St. Vladimir's Theological Quarterly* 24 (1980), pp. 219-234.

own organizations parallel to the existing ecclesial community inevitably involved church unity itself.

All the major leaders of the Christian Church in the third and, particularly, the fourth centuries had to face the problem. Some intellectuals, like Origen and Evagrius, attempted to build up a philosophical and theological system which would serve as a foundation for monastic spirituality and life-style. Others, like St. Athanasius of Alexandria in his *Life of St. Anthony,* created the image of a monastic saint—the ὅσιος of Byzantine hagiology—which eventually was accepted, together with the older image of the martyr, as a pattern and an ideal for future generations. But no one better than St. Basil of Caesarea understood the challenge of monasticism to the Church as a whole and attempted to understand the phenomenon in the framework of Christian theology and ecclesiology, so that monasticism could be accepted and integrated in a wholesome vision of Christianity.

In this paper, my goal is not to describe again in detail the teaching of St. Basil on monastic asceticism. Several excellent scholars have done so rather exhaustively. The problem which interests me particularly is one which really belongs to the history of Eastern Christianity in general. It is the problem of spiritual leadership in doctrinal and disciplinary matters, which has been so often claimed and exercised—either individually or collectively—by representatives of monasticism. It is a fact that, throughout the Byzantine period, there is an abundance of historical examples showing monks challenging the authority of bishops (and, indeed, emperors), defending either Chalcedonian Orthodoxy or, on the contrary, Monophysitism, standing for the veneration of icons, opposing compromises in the field of morals or ecclesiastical discipline and often, breaking communion with established ecclesiastical authority in the name of what they considered to be the truth. Furthermore, Byzantine monastic authors, like Symeon the New Theologian in the early eleventh century or the hesychasts of the fourteenth, affirm the inherent charismatic authority of monastic leadership on theological grounds. This trend in the history of Byzantine Christianity is usually associated with the influence of the writings of Pseudo-Macarius, and Pseudo-Macarius is, in turn, identified as representing the thought of the so-called Messalians, a charistmatic sect opposing church order and sacraments which had wide ramifications in the late medieval period. As a result, the contemplative monasticism symbolized by Macarius, which has become the actual mainstream of Eastern Christian spirituality, is often suspect of crypto-Messalianism, anti-intellectualism and char-'ismatic fanaticism. Is this suspicion justified?

It appears to me that St. Basil and his writings on the monastic ideal must be brought into the debate, not only because, throughout the centuries, his authority was unquestioned in all circles of Byzantine monasticism, but also because he himself was directly in touch with those early forms of ascetic and spiritual life where Messalianism found its roots: the circle of Eustathius of Sebaste, whose influence upon the 'thought of Basil himself is recognized by students of the period.[1]

1. St. Basil, the Eustathians and the Church

At the time when St. Basil committed himself to the ideals of Christian monasticism (*ca.* 358), the monastic movement was already flourishing in Eastern Asia Minor. Not only could 'Basil immediately join an existing milieu of ascetics, but for over a decade he considered himself a disciple and a close friend of Eustathius, an eminent spiritual leader who, like Basil himself, was eventually elevated to the episcopate and had become, around 856, the metropolitan of Sebaste, in Roman Armenia, a province adjacent to Cappadocia.

The relationship which exists between the teachings of

[1]Cf. particularly F. Loofs, *Eustathius von Sebaste und die Chronologie der Basilius-Briefe. Eine patristische Studie* (Halle, 1898); D. Amand, *L'ascèse monastique de Saint Basile: Essai historique* (Maredsous, 1948), pp. 52-61; and several studies by J. Gribomont: "Le Monachisme au IVe siècle en Asie Mineure: de Gangres au Messalianisme," *Studia Patristica* 2 (Texte und Untersuchungen 64; Berlin, 1957), pp. 400-415; "Eustathe de Sébaste," *Dictionnaire d' histoire et de géographie ecclésiastiques* 16 (Paris, 1967), cols. 26-33; "St. Basile et le monachisme enthousiaste," *Irénikon* 62 (1980), pp. 123-144.

Eustathius and the ascetical doctrine of St. Basil is of crucial importance for our theme. Since no writings of Eustathius survive, the positions of his group can be ascertained primarily on the basis of the canons of the Council of Gangra, which was held around 340 A.D. and issued statements condemning some ascetical doctrines of the "Eustathians." These doctrines included the formal rejection of marriage and family life (canons 1, 9, 10, 14, 15, 16) and, therefore, of married priesthood (canon 4), the establishment of separate monastic communities independent of bishops and priests (canons 5, 6, 7, 8, 11), and a practice of fasting which neglected established criteria such as the celebration of the Lord's day. Also the Eustathians never ate meat (canons 2, 18, 19).

Basil, who was a friend of Eustathius until 373, *i.e.,* long after the Council of Gangra, does not seem to have formally recognized the validity of the Gangra decrees. This is, of course, quite understandable, because the bishops gathered in Gangra under the presidency of the notorius Eusebius of Nicomedia, the most prominent among the court bishops supporting Arianism in the last years of the reign of Constantine, were Arians. Eustathius, on the contrary belonged to the group of moderate homoiousians and, around 367, formally endorsed the Orthodox faith of Nicaea. Eustathius and Basil were thus in doctrinal agreement and belonged to the same ecclesiastical party. The long friendship between the two men was also based on their common dedication to the ideals of monasticism. Their eventual quarrel (after 373) was connected with Eustathius' refusal to recognize the consubstantiality of the Spirit with the Father and the Son.

One cannot be fully sure whether Eustathius himself personally shared the extreme asceticism condemned at Gangra, or whether those errors belonged only to some of the overzealous members of his circle. The second alternative seems more probable. Eustathius eventually became a metropolitan, which implied formal recognition of established church practices and a disavowal of ascetic extremism. Thus one learns from Epiphanius the story of an extreme "Eustathian," the presbyter Aërius, who refused to fulfill the assignment given to him by his metropolitan, to head a hospice at Sebaste.

Eventually Aërius, who, like other extremists, considered social work as unnecessary, broke with Eustathius in the name of extreme asceticism.[2]

But it is unquestionable that not only Eustathius but also his friend Basil belonged to the monastic milieu which was condemned at Gangra, even if he did not share the extremism of some. This clearly appears in the *Asceticons* of St. Basil. Without condemning marriage, Basil formally recommends a freely accepted separation if one of the parties decides to enter the ascetic life.[3] Contrary to Gangra, which forbids monasteries to accept runaway slaves (canon 3), he prefers the risk of social disobedience and its consequences,[4] as he also does in connection with the taxes owed to the state: the monk is ultimately free of all social obligations.[5] Actually, the relationship of the Basilian and the Eustathian ideals of monasticism goes even deeper than these examples of ethical behavior. This deeper unity of inspiration has been recently described by Paul Fedwick[6] and it has a great bearing upon the question which occupies us in this paper.

Basil, and probably Eustathius, was promoting monasticism not as a separate order, not even as a particular category of Christians, but as an ideal for "complete" or "perfect" Christians (τέλειοι χριστιανοί) constituting the community of the Church. In the *Asceticons,* when St. Basil speaks of community, he does not mean a monastery, but the Church itself. All the historians of monasticism have identified Basil as a strong and articulate adversary of individualism, of eremitism understood as a personal exploit, and as an advocate of the cenobium or "common life." Monastic leaders of East and West, like St. Theodore of Studius and St. Benedict of Nursia, have found inspiration in his emphasis on love

[2]Epiphanius, *Panarion,* 75; ed. K. Holl, III (Leipzig, 1933), pp. 333-340.

[3]*Great Asceticon* (or "Longer Rule"), 12; PG 31, col. 948C-949A; tr. by W. K. L. Clarke, *The Ascetic Works of Saint Basil* (London: SPCK, 1925), p. 173.

[4]*Ibid.,* 11; col. 948AC; tr. pp. 172-173.

[5]*Ibid.,* 8; col. 936D; tr. p. 167. These and other parallelisms between the doctrines condemned at Gangra and the teachings of St. Basil are discussed in J. Gribomont, "Le monachisme," pp. 405-406.

[6]*The Church and the Charisma of Leadership in Basil of Caesarea* (Toronto, 1979). See particularly pp. 12ff, 156-160.

and community. Indeed, Basil always repeats that no man is individually self-sufficient; that all men need neighbors to rebuke them for their faults; that solitary life is not propitious to acts of charity without which there is no Christianity; that the gifts of the Spirit themselves are always received with the others and for the others. All these precepts became essential to cenobitic monasticism. And yet Basil himself did not create or promote separate monastic communities, as St. Pachomius, the real father of the cenobites, was doing in Egypt. The entire emphasis of his teaching was on the building-up of the entire body of the Church. In his conception, those who strive to become "perfect Christians" by remaining celibate, by obeying their leaders, by engaging in works of charity, should not separate themselves from the community of the Church, but only from worldly goods, thus setting an example for all. They are strictly forbidden to hold separate eucharistic assemblies, as will be later the case for monastic cenobia, and certainly to abstain from the sacraments for prolonged periods (as the hermits will frequently do, following the example of St. Anthony). Rather, Basil's "perfect Christians" are called to remain in the community, leading what the French sometimes called a *vie dévote*.

The Council of Gangra was probably right in discovering in the circle of Eustathius of Sebaste some extremist trends. These were condemned in the canons. But there is no evidence whatsoever that Basil ever condoned such excesses. Indeed, he never required celibacy or condemned married priesthood or considred that the perfect ascetics are above works of charity. Such requirements would lead to the very opposite of what was his major concern. He never condoned a separate class of ascetics who would break the unity of the Church. Perhaps Basil was even a little naive in believing that this unity could be maintained simply by preserving moderation in ascetic percepts and, on the other hand, in setting up the ascetic ideal as a pattern for all Christians. But this is precisely what he was doing in his *Asceticons,* his letters and his entire ministry. In reading St. Basil, one does not find references to "monks" following a special discipline different from that of other members of the Church. Basil always addresses his fol-

lowers as simply "Christians," while calling them to "perfection."[7] It is only when monasticism really developed into a
distinctive and canonically definable segment of the Christian
community—a development which occurred under the influence
of such monastic legislations as the Rule of Pachomius—that
'Basil's *Asceticons* also began to be read as monastic rules.
His appeals to community life in the Church were then
applied to the monastic community as a separate entity. But
this was not Basil's own intention.

There is every reason to believe that Basil disapproved of
excessive asceticism no less than the fathers of the Council
of Gangra did, but instead of simply condemning such excesses, as they did, he defined 'the ideals of the "Eustathians"
in the framework of an eschatological and pneumatological
conception of the ecclesial community itself.

Of course, some forms of separate ascetic community life
did exist in Basil's time, but Basil viewed such communities
as local "churches." This is shown, in particular, in the use
of the New Testamental term προεστώς to designate the
leader of a "Basilian" brotherhood, a term which in the New
Testament (I Tim. 5:17; cf. also προϊστάμενος: Rom.
12:8, I Thess. 5:12, I Tim. 3:4) designates the "president"
of the eucharistic assembly in a local church.

But this apparent confusion in Basil's writings on the one
hand between the ascetic ideal and Christianity as such, and,
on the other hand, between the sacramental leadership of the
bishop and the charismatic ministry of a monastic community,
raises the more general problem of the nature of the charismata of knowledge, of teaching and of leadership. Indeed,
St. Basil clearly teaches that the gift of knowledge belonging
to the "leader" is also bestowed upon the entire community
of Christians, so that the teacher is responsible before that
community and can be judged "by the very people who are
entrusted to him."[8] When he exhorts the προεστῶτες, as
teachers of the word, to practice what they preach, this is, on
the part of Basil, more than a simple moral exhortation. Together with the other Cappadocian fathers, he always refuses

---

[7]See P. Fedwick, *op. cit.*, p. 165 n. 28.
[8]*Moral Rule* 36; PG 31, col. 844D-845A.

'to distinguish clearly between personal sanctity and the char-'isma of preaching—a distinction which has been so clearly drawn in the West by St. Augustine in his polemics with the Donatists. For Basil—and for the Christian East in general—*theologia* implies personal experience and contemplation. Thus, the paradox and possible tension between institutional and charismatic leadership is not resolved in Basil's understanding of the Church except in his sense of the unity of the 'Church through the eucharist and through the charismata of the Spirit, which are diverse and include, in the one and the 'same body of the Church, the charisma of leadership as well as that of obedience.[9] But there is no clear juridical or canonical definition of the various forms of leadership and various forms of obedience in the church community. What is certain, however, is that Basil opposes the charismaticism of the extreme Eusthathians who, according to the Council of Gangra, despised the *synaxeis* of the Church (canon 5) and held their own assemblies without priests and without the local bishop's authorization (canon 6). He insists that the sacrifice of the eucharist is, in a singular (ἐξαιρέτως) and original way (πρωτοτύπως), the function of priests, although it is also an action of the whole Church.[10]

It is precisely in his remarkable sense of church unity, but not in any formal and canonical definition of clerical leadership or any denial of the charismatic role of ascetics, that 'Basil's ecclesiology is clearly distinct from the incipient Mes-'salianism which was already appearing among the monks of Asia Minor at his time.

2. *Messalianism and the Church*

In later Eastern Christendom, the monastic communities—always popular and finding thousands of followers in all

---

[9]This point is clearly developed in Basil's treatise *On the Holy Spirit*. Cf. particularly chapter 61.

[10]*Small Asceticon*, 265; PG 31, col. 1261D-1264A. I do not agree with J. Gribomont ("Le Monachisme," pp. 406-407) that this particular passage on the priests can in any way be seen as an approval by Basil of the "Eustathian" practices condemned at Gangra.

social groups—were, in virtue of the existing canonical legislation, always submitted to the jurisdiction of local bishops.
No religious orders exempt from that jurisdiction ever developed in the East, as they did in the medieval West. The
thought of St. Basil, with its insistence on the unity of the
Church, certainly contributed to that vision of monasticism as
part of the general body of Christians. But inside monasticism
'there always has been a reaction against the integrating
'trend, as the various "charismatic" movements, usually covered
by the term "Messalianism," clearly show.

It is very difficult and perhaps even impossible to give
a single definition of Messalianism. "Messalians," also known
as "Euchites" or "Enthusiasts" and later designated by the
Slavic term of "Bogomils," periodically appear in various
regions between the fourth century and the end of the Middle
Ages. The Western Cathars or Albigensians were a branch
of the same movement.[11] Furthermore, the contemplative
monks of Mount Athos known as hesychasts were, in the
fourteenth century, accused by their adversaries of actually
being "Messalians" although they formally belonged to the
official Orthodox Church and claimed to adhere rigorously to
its doctrines. Finally, in our own days, several scholars have
identified the writings attributed to one of the founders of
Egyptian monasticism, St. Macarius the Great, as having
been in fact composed by a leader of the Messalian sect in the
late fourth or early fifth century.[12] Thus, since the writings of
Pseudo-Macarius have been extremely popular and influential,
Eastern Christian spirituality as a whole becomes somehow
suspect of "Messalianism" at least in those of its aspects which
'are connected with the idea of "charismatic" or spiritual leadership and with an "experiential" interpretation of the Christian faith. One of the foremost contemporary historians of
Eastern Christian spirituality, Irénée Hausherr, once wrote:

[11]Of the considerable literature on the movement, D. Obolensky's *The
Bogomils* (Cambridge, 1948) remains the most comprehensive.

[12]The most recent monograph on the subject is by H. Dörries, *Die Theologie
des Makarios/Symeon* (Abhl. des Akad. der Wissenschaften in Göttingen,
Phil.-Hist. Kl. 103; Göttingen, 1978).

"The great spiritual heresy of the Christian East is Messalian-ism."[13]

There is, of course, no possibility of discussing this problem here at length. My intention is only to point out St. Basil's spiritual inheritance insofar as it is related to the problem. We have seen earlier that Basil was very closely connected with Eustathius of Sebaste, whose extremist friends (if not Eustathius himself) were condemned in Gangra around 340 A.D. Soon after that council, by the end of the fourth century, the term "Messalianism" was already used to designate the sectarian tendencies among the ascetics. According to two later witnesses, the priest Timothy of Constantinople (sixth century) and St. John of Damascus (eighth century), the "Messalians" were condemned around 390 A.D. at another council in the city of Side in Pamphylia. The council was presided by a close friend and disciple of Basil, Amphilochius of Iconium, and the priest Timothy specifically says that the heretics condemned at Side were not only "Messalians" but also "Eustathians," so that the connection between the two groups can be considered as firmly established.[14]

The doctrines of the Messalians as condemned in Side are described in some detail by Timothy and John of Damascus. They also appear in a contemporary Syrian work, the so-called *Book of Degrees* or *Liber Graduum*.[15]

If one examines carefully this evidence concerning these heretical Eustathians or Messalians of Asia Minor, one immediately discovers where their doctrines differed from the ideals of Basil. First of all, our sources indicate that the Messalians professed Sabellian or docetic doctrines (cf. Timothy 6, 8). But these could have been standard accusations, justified or not, levelled against them on the basis of second-hand evidence and rumors, as frequently happened in procedures

---

[13]"L'erreur fondamentale et la logique du messalianisme," *Orientalia Christiana Periodica* 1 (1935), p. 328.

[14]Cf. more detailed evidence of the connection in J. Gribomont, "Le monachisme," pp. 414-415.

[15]Text in *Patrologia Syriaca* 3 (Paris, 1926). The editor, M. Kmosko, provides the text with an introduction which also contains other texts concerning the Messalians, including particularly the later descriptions by Timothy and John.

against all dissidents. Another frequent accusation is that of dualism, but this is generally rather vague. In any case, it is difficult to establish for sure whether it implied real onto-logical dualism or was simply some standard reference to the dangers of evil presence in man's soul, so frequent in monastic literature. What is quite clear, however, is that the major thrust of the Messalians—which is so different from Basil's thought and would develop throughout the centuries into a variety of fantastic beliefs—was a challenge to the Church as sacramental body. The Messalians considered themselves as a spiritual elite which recognized only that hierarchy which was based on spiritual and ascetic exploits. According to *Liber Graduum*, the Christian community is divided in two distinct groups: the "righteous" and the "perfect." The "righteous" alone are obligated to practice good works, help the poor and, in general, fulfill the commandments of standard Christian morality. The "perfect ones" receive special gifts of the Spirit and, as a consequence, stand above manual labor and good works, and even above fasting and asceticism. They possess what the Messalians called "true love" and the vision of God, which made it superfluous for them to fulfill the external de-mands of ethical commandments. The sacraments themselves are of no use to the "perfect."

Such radical charismatic elitism was clearly a major temp-tation for early monasticism, and the persistence of Messalian-'ism throughout the centuries shows that its appeal remained strong for a long time. But it is also clear in the case of Basil, and probably in that of Eustathius of Sebaste as well, that both leaders opposed charismatic elitism and wanted to inte-grate the monastic zealots into an ecclesial conception of their vocation. This is the real meaning and purpose of Basil's ascetical writings. However, as we have seen earlier, Basil did not deny the very principle of spiritual or charismatic leadership totally, but rather provided it with a legitimate framework in the Church.

It is my conviction also that the writings of the Pseudo-Macarius have basically the same significance and the same 'intent as the *Asceticons* of St. Basil. Clearly their author 'wrote in a style different from Basil's. He was less concerned with external discipline and more with individual spiritual perfection. But, just as Basil, he knew the Messalians well and, sometimes using their writings, was attempting to integrate the positive side of their ideals in a sacramental and ecclesial context.[16] The author of the writings attributed to Macarius is unknown to us, but we know that he most probably lived in Eastern Asia Minor and was Basil's younger contemporary. Not only was he not a Messalian, but he could have belonged to the very circle of Basil's friends. This conclusion is suggested by the close parallelism which exists between the so-called Great Letter of Pseudo-Macarius and the *De instituto christiano* by Basil's own younger brother, Gregory of Nyssa.[17]

One of the greatest achievements of St. Basil, and indeed also of his brother Gregory, was that they succeeded in channelling the monastic movement into the mainstream of Christianity and preserved it from sectarianism. This was both an institutional and a theological achievement to which the unknown author of the "Macarian" writings also contributed much. Whereas Basil's primary message was about the values of community life, both Gregory and Macarius maintained the doctrine of personal communion with God as the very content of Christianity in general and of the monastic ideal in particular. Their approaches were different but not incompatible, as the close connection between some of their writings shows. Both agreed that each human person is destined to union with God and that the Messalians were wrong in limiting the goal of "deification" or *theosis* to the select few. But, at the same time, Gregory and Macarius have in common one idea which became the basis of the Eastern Christian spiritual tradition as a whole: perfection is given by the grace of God

---

[16]I have developed more detailed arguments on this subject in my article "Messalianism or Anti-Messalianism? A fresh look at the 'Macarian' problem," in *Kyriakon. Festschrift Johannes Quasten* 2 (Münster-Westf., 1975), pp. 585-590.

[17]The parallelism was established by Werner Jaeger, *Two Rediscovered Works of Ancient Christian Literature: Gregory of Nyssa and Macarius* (Leiden, 1954). Scholars argue the point whether Macarius was influenced by Gregory (Jaeger) or whether Basil's brother used Macarius as a cource (Gribomont).

only to the degree in which man himself, freely and personally, seeks union with Christ in the Holy Spirit, so that
theology itself is an expression of this personal experience.
To quote Vladimir Lossky, "if the mystical experience is a
personal working out of the content of the common faith,
theology is an expression, for the profit of all, of that which
is experienced by everyone."[18] No institution, no external
authority—not even that of the Church—stands between the
human person and God, although the authenticity of the personal experience is possible only when it is sought out in the
community, on the basis of sacramental belonging to the
Church and, therefore, in union with all the saints of all
times.

For the Messalians, the mystic alone without anyone's
help—and even without membership in the Church, since
baptism is "useless" (John of Damascus 4, 5, 6, 17; Timothy
2, 3, 12)—reaches the knowledge of God "in the fullness of
experience and assurance" (ἐν πάσῃ αἰσθήσει καὶ πλη-
ροφορίᾳ). He then becomes the sole authority for himself
and others, irrespective of any sacramental ministry. Both
the parallelism and the contrast are blatant.

Actually Gregory of Nyssa and Macarius agree with the
Messalian criticism of a magical conception of sacraments.
They both stress the human effort which makes baptism effective in one's personal life: "When one is born from above
(Jn. 3:3) from water and the Spirit," Macarius writes, "one
does not remain for ever in the infancy of spiritual age, but
one professes and grows in a daily fight and effort, using
much patience in the struggle against the adversary."[19] But
baptism—i.e., also the Church—remains the basis and condition of progress: "Since the coming of Christ, men are pro-
gressing through the power of baptism towards the original
stature of Adam and become the masters of demons and
passions."[20]

[18]The Mystical Theology of the Eastern Church (Crestwood, N.Y.: St.
Vladimir's Seminary Press, 1976), p. 8-9.

[19]Macarius, Epistula Magna, ed. W. Jaeger, op. cit., p. 236.

[20]Macarius, Hom. 1, in Neue Homilien des Makarius/Symeon, ed. Kloster-
mann and Berthold (Texte und Untersuchungen 12; Berlin, 1961), p. 3.

Thus towards the extreme ascetics, Gregory and the Pseudo-Macarius are adopting, on the level of personal spirituality and theology, the same moderate, integrating stand as Basil did on the level of behavior and community life. They do not fully resolve the problem of the relationship between divine grace and human freedom. They leave the paradox 'fully real, which certainly explains why they could have been occasionally branded as "semi-Pelagians" by Westerners.

It is, indeed, true that the Messalians were, in a sense, the Pelagians of the East. Exalting ascetic exploits and claiming that charismatic leadership alone is admissible in Christianity, they rejected the objective sacramental grace offered by the Church and challenged the authority of the bishops, whose power they considered as only human. However, whereas Western Christendom stood firmly on Augustinian grounds in affirming the primacy of grace and, eventually, the powers of the hierarchy *ex opere operato,* the East took the risk of leaving the problem partially unsolved. It condemned the Messalians for their rejection of Church and sacraments, but it did not condemn the very principle of a charismatic leadership, remaining alive side by side with the institutional, and did not exclude any member of the Church from the duty to acquire "a fullness of experience and assurance" of the truth through a free and personal effort.

In Byzantium, the Messalian movement continued to exist under a variety of forms and was condemned repeatedly by church councils. But at the same time, inside the Church itself, spiritual leaders, predominantly monastic, were able 'frequently to challenge ecclesiastical (and civil) authorities, to which they never conceded a monopoly on truth and knowledge. St. Maximus the Confessor, a simple monk who was also the greatest Byzantine theologian of the seventh century, was once confronted with the fact that all the patriarchs, including the bishop of Rome (so he was told), had accepted the heresy of Monotheletism: "The Holy Spirit," he answered, "anathematizes even the angels themselves if they affirm a position contrary to the (apostolic) kerygma."[21] Such an atti-

---

[21] *Acta Maximi;* PG 90, col. 121 C.

tude was certainly not limited to individual mystics or hermits, who would be more likely than others to share the Messalian spiritual individualism. The most articulate spokesman for cenobitic monasticism in the eighth and ninth centuries, Theodore of Studius, broke communion with two successive patriarchs, opposing their leniency (or *oikonomia*) towards former iconoclasts and imperial whims.

It is clear, however, that if Byzantine Christianity did not allow bishops to monopolize the spiritual and doctrinal leadership of the Church, this did not imply that any such monopoly belonged to charismatic monks. Examples of monastic 'leaders condemned for heresy or for what we might call charismatic indiscipline are very numerous, and we have seen earlier that the major point made by Basil in his ascetic writing was to make every Christian, including particularly the ascetic, responsible for his teachings and behavior to the entire body of the Church.

Furthermore, the history of the Byzantine church seems to indicate that boundaries between heretical Messalianism and Orthodox monasticism were not always clear. Both were popular movements, spreading among unlearned people, so that at times their forms of behavior were not immediately distinguishable. It seems also that, in the later Byzantine period, some Messalians were deliberately infiltrating the ranks of Orthodox monks in order to propagate their doctrines. In the eleventh century, Anna Comnena reports that a priest of the Blachernae imperial palace was found to be a Messalian.[22] On the other hand, there is no doubt that some Byzantine spiritual writers did not adopt the careful moderation which we saw in St. Basil when they spoke of spiritual leadership. The most notorious of such prophetic spirits was Symeon the New Theologian, probably the greatest of medieval Byzantine mystics (949-1022). The literal meaning of many texts of Symeon seems to affirm that the gift of sacramental priesthood itself depends on the holiness of the candidate, and that a priest who does not personally possess the vision of God

---

[22]*Alexiad* X, 2; ed. B. Leib (Coll. Budé, Paris, 1943), p. 189; Eng. tr. by E.R.A. Sewter (Baltimore, Md: Penguin Books, 1969), p. 295.

and the illumination of the Spirit is an intruder.[23] Symeon also fought for the right of nonordained monks to exercise spiritual direction and hear confessions. In his case, the boundaries between a Messalian and an Orthodox view of the *charismata* of the Spirit become quite thin. But, to judge Symeon, one should once more remember the conscious option taken by Byzantine Christianity not to quench the prophetic spirit. And a prophet Symeon really was. His entire message consists in warning his monastic community of St. Mamas in Constantinople against a formal and ritualistic understanding of the monastic vocation. "I beg you," he addressed them, "let us try, in this life, to see and contemplate [Jesus]. For if we are deemed worthy to see Him sensibly, we shall not see death; death will have no dominion over us (Rom. 6:9)."[24] Actually, Symeon was a priest himself, and his appeals for an experiential faith were always coupled with the most realistic expressions of eucharistic sacramentalism.

Reflecting a similar tradition, in the year 1340 the monks of Mount Athos, led by Gregory Palamas, spoke out for what they saw as true Orthodoxy against the views of Barlaam the Calabrian. They signed a document, known as the *Hagioretic Tome* or "Tome of the Holy Mountain," where they also described the role of those who, in the Church, "have been initiated by experience" (οἱ αὐτῇ τῇ πείρᾳ μεμυημένοι) to the mysteries of the Kingdom of God. These men are those "who, for the sake of an evangelical life, have renounced possessions, human glory and the pleasures of the body," *i.e.*, those who practice the traditional monastic vows of poverty, obedience and celibacy. According to the *Tome,* these men perform a ministry similar to that of the prophets of the Old Testament. Just as the ancient prophets sensed the trinitarian nature of God which was fully revealed only in Christ, so the prophets of the post-Christian era experience

---

[23]Cf. reference in *Syméon le Nouveau Théologien, Traités théologiques et éthiques* I (Sources chrétiennes 22, Paris, 1966), pp. 21-25. On the issue, see also the relevant comments by Joost Van Rossum, "Priesthood and Confession in St. Symeon the New Theologian," *St. Vladimir's Theological Quarterly* 20 (1976), pp. 220-228.

[24]*Cat.* II; ed. B. Krivocheine, *Syméon le Nouveau Théologien, Catéchèses* (Sources chrétiennes 96, Paris, 1963), pp. 421-424.

and announce deification (or *theosis*), the union with God in the age to come. As examples of such new testamental prophets, the *Tome* cites Dionysius, Maximus the Confessor and Macarius, whose disciples the hesychasts of late Byzantium claimed to be. So the "experience" of the saints is seen as an eschatological anticipation of realities which in substance belong to the whole Church.[25] The saints are neither elitist visionaries nor theological innovators but, like the prophets of the Old Testament, they acquire "spiritual senses" which allow them a clearer vision of God and an anticipated experience of things to come. Their prophetic role does not suppress the responsibility of the bishops or the validity of conceptual theological elaborations, but it does possess an authority of its own. The institutional and sacramental authority of the bishops and the spiritual authority of the saints coexist in the catholic Church, and the tensions which occasionally arise between them cannot justify the suppression of either one. The authority of the Church does not suppress the authority of the Spirit, and the spiritual leaders understand their leadership only in the context of the sacramental communion of the Church.

Conclusion

The most solemn and the most official document reflecting the mind of Byzantine Christendom—the so-called *Synodikon of Orthodoxy*—is a sort of expanded liturgical creed used every year on the first Sunday of Lent to commemorate the end of the iconoclastic crisis in 843 and constantly updated since then to reflect the current teachings of the Church. The *Synodikon* contains an expanded and very formal condemnation of the Messalians, who consider that "baptism is simple water, which does not produce remission of sins and does not come from the Spirit, whereas they themselves pretend that they bestow the gifts of the Spirit in their own initiatory rites,

[25]*Hagioretic Tome*; PG 150, cols. 1225-1236; crit. edition by P. Chrestou in Γρηγορίου τοῦ Παλαμᾶ Συγγράμματα II (Thessaloniki, 1966), pp. 567-578.

falsely called monastic habit, during the invocation which they pronounce then." The Messalians are also condemned for saying among other things that "communion with the Body and Blood of our Lord and Savior Jesus Christ is communion with simple bread and wine" and for calling themselves "citizens of Christ's Kingdom" (χριστοπολῖται).[26] But at the same time, the same *Synodikon* also formally endorses the theology of Gregory Palamas, the author of the *Hagioretic Tome,* as being in full accord with Athanasius and Basil, with the two Gregories and John Chrysostom, as well as with Cyril, Maximus and John of Damascus.[27]

What these texts show to us is that Byzantine Christianity did not attempt to resolve, through any conceptual or institutional formula, the paradox of a simultaneous existence in the Christian Church of both sacramental and spiritual leadership. It has never attempted to reduce the Christian faith either to a dependence on institutional authority or to reliance upon a few charismatics. It seems to me that the conscious preservation of the paradox was possible only because the locus of the Christian experience was always seen in the Church as eucharistic community, which always presupposes at the same time a continuity in the apostolic faith through ecclesial discipline and a charismatic event revealed to and accepted by each human person in full freedom, together with the entire community.

It seems to me also that one must admit the existence of this paradox in Eastern Christianity to understand not only the history of monasticism but also the significance of Byzantine opposition to authoritarian concepts of the Church developed in the West during the Middle Ages.

As a churchman, Basil of Caesarea was dedicated to reconciliation on the basis of truth itself, not only words or formulas. As a theologian, he taught his contemporaries to use

[26]J. Gouillard, "Le Synodikon de l'Orthodoxie: Edition et commentaire," *Travaux et mémoires* 2 (Centre de Recherche d'Histoire et Civilisation byzantines: Paris, 1967), p. 69. The text of the *Synodikon* can also be found in any edition of the Greek Triodion, but it has been dropped from the Slavic editions since the eighteenth century.
[27]*Ibid.,* p. 89.

terms and philosophical concepts responsibly. As a teacher of
asceticism and spiritual life, he understood, better than many
in his age, that authority and freedom, obedience to superiors
and personal experience of God, should not be mutually
exclusive. In this sense, Byzantine Christendom and the Orthodox Church has always recognized him as a foremost and
unquestionable father and teacher.

Ecclesiastical Regionalism: Structures of Communion or Cover for Separatism?*

In discussing issues of ecclesiology, the temptation is always great to manipulate concepts and doctrinal definitions while avoiding a critical approach to their application in practice. It is easy, for example, for an Orthodox theologian to describe the ecclesiology of St. Ignatius of Antioch and to construct an apologetic argument in favor of the contemporary Orthodox position concerning Roman primacy. But it is more difficult to analyze ecclesiastical institutions—as they developed in East and West—in their existential role of maintaining the faith, shepherding the faithful and accomplishing the Church's mission in the world. At all times such institutions, whose aim is to express the nature and mission of the Church, had the tendency to develop independently from ecclesiology and to follow their own internal logic. They were conditioned not only by what we call today the "eucharistic ecclesiology" of the early period but also by the practical requirements of the day, so that their original meaning later became almost unrecognizable. Some of these developments may sometimes be seen as both inevitable and desirable, inasmuch as they might have responded to the concrete needs of Christian

*Paper originally delivered at a colloquium on "The ecclesiology of Vatican II: dynamism and perspectives," held at the Istituto per le scienze religiose, Bologna, Italy, April 8-12, 1980, with the subtitle "Issues of dialogue with Roman Catholicism," and published in St. Vladimir's Theological Quarterly 24 (1980), pp. 155-168.

mission in history. But, in that case, the dialogue on Christian unity itself must take history into account; it should be concerned not only with the *content* of the Christian faith and the *validity* of Christian institutions but also with their efficacy in the present and the future.

So, all the dimensions of the Christian faith become necessarily involved in the unity dialogue: Is the Jesus-event a *hapax* event which judges history? Does the apostolic experience—the experience of the original witnesses of Jesus—contain a permanent and unchangeable model for church institutions? Or are some institutions only a product of subsequent history and, therefore, legitimately changeable? Are they, in other words, the guardians of a reality which transcends history, or an expression of history itself?

Most Christians—particularly the Christians involved in ecumenism—will agree that these questions, formulated in this way, are legitimate and basic questions, and that they are particularly relevant in the field of ecclesiology. Orthodox and Catholics are generally ready to go a long way together in facing them. They agree that the apostolic *kerygma* implies basic sacramental and ecclesial structures intrinsic to the very nature of the Church. This is, indeed, the starting point of our dialogue, which has been significantly expanded by Vatican II with the new emphasis in Roman Catholic ecclesiology on the significance of the local church and on conciliarity. In each sacramental community, proclaims the constitution *On the Church,* "Christ is present" and "by virtue of Him, the one, holy, catholic and apostolic Church gathers together" (III, 26).[1] Although episcopal conciliarity as defined in the same constitution of Vatican II is formally and strictly dependent upon communion with Rome and the pope's *plena potestas* —a dimension which clearly presents a major problem for the Orthodox—there is a new readiness on the part of Rome to accept such categories of ecclesiological thought as the concept of "sister churches." The term has been used in correspondence with Constantinople, and various meetings between

[1]*The Documents of Vatican II,* ed. W. M. Abbott, S. J. (New York, 1966), p. 50.

popes and patriarchs have adopted a procedure pointing at a certain parity of functions, not at papal monarchy.

It is clear, therefore, that the issue of regionalism—not only in the sense of the sacramental reality of the "local church" headed by a bishop but also in the sense of regional primacies and synods—is on the agenda of today's ecumenical discussion. The same issue is obviously central in terms of the internal structure of the Roman Catholic Church (*e.g.,* the authority of national and regional synods *vis-à-vis* Rome) and of the Orthodox Church, which is constituted today by a rather loose communion of independent "autocephalous" churches. But the discussion of these issues involves not only abstract problems of ecclesiology, but also issues of practical administration, of age-old habits and mentalities, and of changing requirements in the contemporary world. These historical realities have existed in the past, as they exist today. In the eyes of some, they justify a relativistic approach to ecclesiology. Indeed, if church institutions can be reduced to relative historical phenomena, Christian unity, they say, should rather be understood as a "spiritual" fellowship with a minimum of institutional coordination. A hermeneutical approach to the New Testament stressing institutional and theological pluralism in the early Christian communities is also being used to justify ecclesiological relativism as an acceptable ecumenical methodology.

If, however, one does not accept such an approach, and if one accepts—as Catholics and Orthodox usually do—that the sacramental nature of Christian ecclesiology implies a given and unchangeable structure reflecting the sacramentality, then one is also obliged to approach historical development critically and look for Christian unity consistent with that which is originally and unchangeably given. However, even then one has no right to discard historical development as such, or to deny that church institutions can legitimately be adapted to particular requirements of history.

Thus, historians and theologians have often recognized that the Roman primacy has not reached its contemporary state of development for theological and ecclesiological reasons only. Factors of a historical—and therefore relative—

nature have also played a role in that development. The assumption by the Roman church of the Roman imperial idea in the West, the politics of Italian courts during the Middle Ages and the Renaissance, the Counter-Reformation, the modern challenge of secularism, and many other factors have influenced not only the institution of the papacy but also some of the doctrinal formulations which express it. The problem now is to determine whether these developments were legitimate or not.

In this paper, however, I am not concerned with a critique of western institutional changes but with regionalism in Orthodoxy, which is so often opposed to Roman universalism. Since the East has remained more reluctant than the West to finalize its attitudes through formal dogmatic definitions, I believe that the Orthodox theologian today enjoys full freedom to approach this aspect of the past and the present of his church with a critical eye. Personally, I regret that this freedom is not used more widely, and I believe that unless the Orthodox learn that form of legitimate self-criticism, their claim to preserve apostolic truth will remain ineffective in contemporary ecumenical dialogue.

1. Regional structures in history

It is not necessary to recall in detail the origins and the ecclesiological basis of regional episcopal synods. According to the *Apostolic Tradition* of Hippolytus (I, 2) the consecration of a new bishop required the presence of several bishops for the laying-on of hands. Moreover, the significance of regular synods of bishops in each *province* is well attested in the third century by Cyprian. The particular role of the synod was to preserve doctrinal orthodoxy and disciplinary unity. There is no doubt that, at that time, the Church was already facing the problem of possible conflict between its concern for universal unity and the conviction, frequently expressed by individual bishops in their local churches and by provincial bishops assembled in council, that their responsibility for truth was to God alone and not to some institution outside of their own region. On the one hand, men like Irenaeus, Tertullian and Cyprian were all conscious of the unity of the world episcopate in the confession of the one Christian truth. Unity —which at least in the West included particular respect for "apostolic" sees—was seen as a major witness to the truth of catholic Christianity (as opposed to Gnosticism). But, at the same time, no provincial council of bishops—and certainly not the councils regularly meeting in Carthage—was ready to give up easily its convictions and accept external authority in the field of doctrine. The issue of the baptism of heretics and later the case of the presbyter Apiarius, who was sanctioned in Carthage but admitted to communion in Rome, are classic illustrations of that provincial—or regional—self-consciousness which reacted against incipient Roman centralization.

The regional competence of provincial councils was formally codified in the fourth century. Nicaea (canons 4 and 5) gave them the ultimate authority in appointing bishops, creating "metropolitan districts"—a basic and embryonic pattern of church polity, of which there will be numerous variations in subsequent centuries. The original episcopal council reflected an ecclesiological necessity: It was "ecclesial" in nature. However, the principle adopted at Nicaea of having ecclesiastical organization coincide with the administrative divisions of the empire ("provinces") implied the beginning of secularization. Certainly, the Church could not avoid the practical necessities of its new situation (and its new mission) in the empire, but the trend which consisted in a gradual process of identification of the ecclesiastical and the imperial administrations tended to confuse the old ecclesiological criteria with legal patterns prevailing in the state.

The next step in that process included the establishment of groupings of several provinces, coinciding with the larger imperial administrative units, called "dioceses" (see particularly canon 2 of I Constantinople, 381 A.D.). The principal bishops or primates of such bigger groupings were even at first called by the purely civil title of "exarch" (cf. the "exarch of the diocese" in canons 9 and 17 of Chalcedon, 451 A.D.), which then continued to designate some high ecclesiastical officials as well as imperial administrators throughout the

Byzantine period. However, the biblical title of "patriarch" was eventually chosen for the major sees of Rome, Constantinople, Alexandria, Antioch and Jerusalem (which eventually constituted the famous "pentarchy"), as well as for the newer patriarchates of Georgia, Bulgaria, Serbia and Russia.

Ecclesiologically, these developments were justified by the same logic which originally led to regular provincial episcopal synods. The full integrity and catholicity of each local church required its communion with all the churches. The initial form of this communion was normally realized with neighboring churches in the framework of existing political structures. These canonical groupings were meant to serve unity, not create divisions. And in addition, the universal unity of the Church, which—at the time of Irenaeus, Tertullian and Cyprian—was seen as a unity in a common faith going back to the apostles, with so-called "apostolic" churches enjoying a particular degree of authenticity and prestige, was now also secured in practice through services offered by the empire: The emperor acted as the convenor of ecumenical councils and legally secured the enforcement of their decrees.

The late Francis Dvornik has clearly described the contrast which gradually developed between East and West in interpreting the meaning of regional primacies.[2] In the East, the power of the major sees or patriarchates was interpreted pragmatically, as an expression of the prestige of cities around which local churches gathered themselves quite naturally and whose leadership, at first taken for granted, was later formally defined in conciliar legislation. Thus, Constantinople owed its rise to the fact of being the new imperial captial. In the West, meanwhile, the early collapse of imperial administration and the fact that Rome was the only "apostolic" see led to the development of papal primacy, which claimed a divinely-established origin and frequently served as a healthy balance to secularistic and caesaropapistic trends in Byzantium.

It is interesting that the collapse of imperial Byzantium in the late medieval period gave rise to a similar "primacy

<hr>

[2] Cf. particularly F. Dvornik, *The Idea of Apostolicity in Byzantium and the Legend of the Apostle Andrew* (Cambridge, Mass., 1958), and also J. Meyendorff, *Orthodoxy and Catholicity* (New York, 1966), pp. 49-78.

phenomenon" in the East. Since the emperors of the Palaeologan period, besieged in their capital by invading Turks, were not in a position to act as unifying agents in world Christendom as their predecessors had done, the patriarch of Constantinople became much more explicit in his own claims of exercising world leadership. In fact, he found himself in the position which in the West was that of Pope Gregory the Great in the seventh century. The idea of a Christian empire was reduced to mere symbolism. The Church was left on its own in maintaining its universal witness in a world divided between a multiplicity of "barbarian" states or power-centers. So the patriarchs of Constantinople acted very much like the popes at the time of the barbarian invasions. To quote only one example, Patriarch Philotheus Coccinus, writing in 1370 to Russian princes who were refusing to comply with the policies of the patriarchal administration in Russia, defined his own position and authority in terms that went beyond the idea of primacy found in early popes, and which could have been used by Gregory VII (or Pius XII). Actually it implied a sort of "universal episcopate" of the patriarch:

Since God has appointed Our Humility as leader of all Christians found anywhere in the inhabited earth, as solicitor and guardian of their souls, all of them depend on me (πάντες εἰς ἐμὲ ἀνάκεινται), the father and teacher of them all. If that were possible, therefore, it would have been my duty to walk everywhere on earth by the cities and countries, and to teach there the Word of God. I would have had to do so unfailingly, since this is my duty. However, since it is beyond the possibility of one weak and powerless man to walk around the entire inhabited earth, Our Humility chooses the best among men, the most eminent in virtue, establishes and ordains them as pastors, teachers and high priests, and sends them to the ends of the universe. One of them goes to your great country, to the multitudes which inhabit it, another reaches other areas of the earth, and still another goes elsewhere, so that each one, in the country and place which was appointed for him, enjoys territorial rights, an episcopal chair, and all the rights of Our Humility.[3]

There were no direct challenges to these claims of Philotheus at the time when they were made. On the contrary, the leadership provided by the strong "hesychast" patriarchs of the fourteenth century exercised a lasting influence throughout the Orthodox world during the dark centuries of Ottoman rule in the Balkans and the Middle East. The Orthodox East clearly felt the need for universal leadership, and the exceptional personalities of some patriarchs like Philotheus provided it. However, this was done without any formal ecclesiological or canonical basis. The canonical definitions of Constantinople's rights (especially the canons of I Constantinople, Chalcedon and Quinisext) were clearly limited in scope and could certainly not justify the views on universal authority expressed by Patriarch Philotheus. Consequently, the attempt at an Eastern "papism" failed and institutional regionalism eventually prevailed in the East.

There is no necessity to discuss here the origin and development of "national" churches in the medieval period. At least from the fifth century, beyond the borders of the empire, there were independent churches, each headed by a primate who often carried the title of *catholicos*.[4] Very early, the identity of these churches was defined primarily along cultural or ethnic lines. On the other hand, the Slavic churches of Bulgaria and Serbia also secured *patriarchal* titles for their primates. Although the original ideology of the Bulgarian and Serbian states was Byzantine and therefore accepted the principle of a united universal Christian empire centered in Constantinople, the failure of Bulgarian and Serbian leaders to secure the imperial throne for themselves led in practice to the creation of regional monarchies and regional patriarchates.

[3]Ed. F. Miklosich and J. Müller, *Acta Patriarchatus Constantinopolitani* 1 (Vienna, 1860), p. 521; on the issue see also Part V Chapter 3 below, and my *Byzantium and the Rise of Russia* (Cambridge, 1980).

[4]The Armenian catholicos was Monophysite. The catholicos of Seleucia-Ktesiphon was Nestorian. But the catholicos of Georgia had remained faithful to the Council of Chalcedon and Byzantine Orthodoxy.

There were no canonical obstacles to the existence of this patriarchal pluralism. On the contrary, the ancient canons of Nicaea and subsequent councils were still serving as the backbone of Orthodox canon law, and these ancient rules sanctioned ecclesiastical regionalism in the framework of a universal unity of faith, secured by councils. Actually, this credal unity remained quite effective and allowed for the occasional emergence of universal leadership as well, as happened particularly in the case of Philotheus Coccinus; but institutionally and structurally, regionalism clearly prevailed.

However, the character and meaning of regionalism underwent radical change with the rise of modern nationalism.

2. Nationalism as a divisive force

In our time, the universal Orthodox Church presents itself as a loose fellowship of fully independent or autocephalous churches, united in faith and a common canonical tradition. Formally, it is possible to affirm that this situation is in conformity with early Christian canonical polity. The legislation of the Council of Nicaea provides for the election of bishops by the synods of each province (canons 4 and 5) and knows of no formal authority over the bishop of the provincial capital, or "metropolitan." It is true that Nicaea also acknowledges the *de facto* traditional authority of some churches—Alexandria, Antioch, Rome (cf. canon 6)—over a wider area, but the content of this authority is not very precise and it is always clearly limited territorially. The Byzantine canonist Balsamon (twelfth century) in his commentary on canon 2 of Constantinople was right in saying that "formerly all the heads of provinces were autocephalous, and were elected by their respective synods."[5] However, this ancient regionalism was meant only to secure an effective functioning of local pro-

---

[5] Ed. G. A. Rhallis and M. Potles, Σύνταγμα τῶν θείων καὶ ἱερῶν κανόνων 2 (Athens, 1852), p. 171. On the various meanings of the term "autocephalous," which only gradually, and very recently, became the terminus technicus designating an administratively independent church, see Pierre L'Huillier, "Problems Concerning Autocephaly," *The Greek Orthodox Theological Review* 24 (1979), pp. 166-168.

vincial synods. It also *presupposed* a sense of universal unity and interaction of the episcopate, to which the provincial "autocephalies" were never meant to be an obstacle. Nothing was more foreign to early church structure than some modern understandings of autocephaly according to which "in the sphere of international relations, every autocephalous church is a full and equal subject of international law."[6]

Clearly, modern nationalism has effected a transformation of legitimate ecclesiastical regionalism into a cover for ethnic separatism.

For a historian, it is easy to detect where and how this transformation took place. It occurred as a direct consequence of the great revival of nationalities which started in Western Europe in the second half of the eighteenth century and determined the entire history of the nineteenth. The new nationalist ideology identified the *nation*—understood in both linguistic and racial terms—as the object of basic social and cultural loyalties. It is not universal Christendom, as the Middle Ages conceived it, and certainly not the sacramental community created by the new birth of baptism, as the Christian Gospel required, which was seen as the determining factor of human life, but the nation. And it was also implied that each nation had a right to separate statehood, so that the old European empires, inadequate remnants of Roman or Byzantine universalism, crumbled one after another.

In Greece and in the other Balkan countries of Bulgaria, Serbia and Romania, nationalism was generally promoted by a western-trained and western-oriented secularized *intelligentsia* which had no real interest in Orthodoxy and the Church except as a useful tool for achieving secular nationalistic goals. When the various nationalistic movements began, the leadership of the Church often expressed skepticism and was instinctively afraid of the new secular and divisive spirit which had taken over the formerly united Christian *millet* in the Ottoman Empire. But the Church obviously lacked the intellectual strength, the theological discernment and the institutional structures which could have exorcised the demons of

[6]S. V. Troitsky in *Zhurnal Moskovskoi Patriarkhii*, 1948, no. 7, p. 48.

the nationalistic revolution. On the other hand, the Church had no reason to support the *status quo,* which implied the continuation of a hated Turkish or Austrian rule over the Orthodox population of the Balkans. So patriarchs, bishops and indeed the parish clergy—sometimes enthusiastically, at other times wearily—joined the sweeping nationalistic movement, becoming directly involved in its political success but also—more dangerously—accepting its ideological positions.

The immediate result was divisiveness. Indeed, if Greek nationalism rebelled against Turkish rule, Bulgarian nationalism could not tolerate the Greek dominance in the Church. Similarily, in the Hapsburg Empire, Hungarians rebelled against Austrians, but Serbs resented Hungarian supremacy and, further down the line. Romanians opposed the canonical primacy of the Serbian patriarchate of Karlovci. So nationalism erupted among the Orthodox of all nationalities and was directed not only against Islamic or Roman Catholic (Austrian or Hungarian) overlords, but against fellow Orthodox as well. And since the political goal of all the nationalities consisted in seeking the creation of nation-states—which were seen as the ultimate fulfillment of cultural growth and maturity—the idea of "autocephaly" came to be thought of as the nation's ecclesiastical equivalent: each nation had to establish its own autocephalous church. The ecumenical patriarchate of Constantinople opposed the trend, but unsuccessfully, partly because it itself had become the symbol, and occasionally the tool, of Greek nationalism, which—as all nationalisms—was necessarily blind and deaf to the nationalism of others and therefore unable to transcend the vicious circle of ethnic strife.[7]

[7]Source materials and secondary literature on Balkan nationalism are abundant. Among books in Western languages, the following can be noted as of direct relevance to the ecclesiastical dimensions of the crisis: E. Picot, *Les Serbes de Hongrie: leur histoire, leurs privilèges, leur église, leur état politique et social* (Prague, 1873); Stephen Runciman, *The Great Church in Captivity: A Study of the Patriarchate of Constantinople from the Eve of the Turkish Conquest to the Greek War of Independence* (Cambridge, 1968); K. Hitchins, *Orthodoxy and Nationality: Andreiu Saguna and the Rumanians of Transylvania, 1846-1873* (Cambridge, Mass., 1977); R. W. Seton-Watson, *The Rise of Nationality in the Balkans* (New York, 1966); and C. A. Frazee, *The Orthodox Church and Independent Greece, 1821-1852* (Cambridge, 1969).

Thus, the legitimate and canonical regionalism sanctioned by the canons of the early church was transformed, in modern Orthodoxy, into divisive ecclesiastical nationalism.

I have said earlier that Orthodox ecclesiastical authority remained generally unaware of this dangerous development and often became, in practice, the main spokesman of nationalistic ideology. However, there is a major and very fortunate exception: the Council of 1872 held in Constantinople on the occasion of the so-called "Bulgarian schism." I do not want to discuss here the rather self-righteous character of the decrees which condemned the Bulgarians, as if they alone were guilty of ecclesiastical nationalism, but the text itself makes clear ecclesiological statements of a general nature and of paramount importance for contemporary Orthodoxy. It condemns the heresy of "phyletism" (φυλετισμός), which is defined as "the establishment of particular churches, accepting members of the same nationality and refusing the members of other nationalities, being administered by pastors of the same nationality," and as "a coexistence of nationally defined churches of the same faith, but independent from each other, in the same territory, city or village."[8] Ecclesiologically, the decree implies that the Church cannot adopt, as criteria of its structure and organization, the divisive realities of the fallen world (including nationalism); that, as a eucharistic community, it is called to transcend those divisions and reunite the separated. In its structure itself, it must witness to Christ's victory over the world.

Very poorly followed in practice (to say the least!) the decisions of 1872 witness very fortunately to a strong residual ecclesiological awareness without which the Orthodox Church could not be termed *orthodox* anymore.

In discussing divisive nationalism, I have referred so far primarily to the Orthodox churches in the Balkans, and I have not mentioned the largest Orthodox national church, the church of Russia. The historical fate of that church has obviously been different, but the results, in the question which occupies us now, are the same. The universalist imperial ideol-

---

[8]Quoted in Maximus of Sardis, Τὸ Οἰκουμενικὸν Πατριαρχεῖον ἐν τῇ Ὀρθοδόξῳ Ἐκκλησίᾳ (Thessaloniki, 1972), pp. 323-325.

ogy inherited by Moscow from Byzantium became nationalized and secularized in the sixteenth, seventeenth and eighteenth centuries by a process well described by the late Fr. Georges Florovsky.[9] The one major difference—and perhaps advantage —enjoyed by the Russian church, in terms of preserving a "catholic" and therefore supranational consciousness, was the possibility of continuing missionary activity and thus maintaining a certain practice (and not only the principle) of Christian universality. Also, the emergence in Russia in the nineteenth century of critical scholarship and, more recently, of a church-oriented *intelligentsia* (of which Florovsky himself is a foremost representative) allows for self-examination and self-criticism. But these factors still remain quite insufficient in overcoming ecclesiastical nationalism in practice and in the consciousness of many people.

3. Issues for dialogue

The metamorphosis of regionalism into nationalism in modern Orthodoxy requires a critical evaluation on the basis of what the Orthodox claim to be their ecclesiological position. Such an evaluation is a clear precondition for dialogue with Rome, which also has attempted to reexamine its own ecclesiastical *praxis* in the light of its ecclesiology.

Indeed, it cannot be denied that the primacy of the Roman bishop, as it is witnessed by early Christian writers and the practice of the early church, also went through a metamorphosis. Having first filled the political and cultural void created by the fall of the Western Empire and, later, struggling for spiritual supremacy and political independence against the German emperors, the bishop of Rome became a "supreme pontiff" with secular power on a universal scale. Later, as he lost much of the political recognition which he had achieved in the Middle Ages, the pope's pastoral and doctrinal powers were defined in terms borrowed from medieval legal vocabulary (*plena potestas*). In this new form, the

[9]Particularly in *Puti russkago bogosloviia* (Paris, 1937).

papacy has played a significant role in the spiritual make-up of Christianity in the West. Understood by some as a necessary and indeed God-established foundation of doctrinal security, ecclesiastical discipline and consistent pastoral guidance, it has been seen by others as an antichristian substitute for Christ or, in any case, as a major opponent to human freedom and personal responsibility.

The dialogue between Roman Catholicism and Orthodoxy necessarily includes the issue of regionalism vs. universalism. Both sides agree that these always were essential aspects of Christian witness and Christian unity, and that they are still essential today. If everyone also accepts a measure of self-criticism and recognizes that Eastern Christian regionalism and Western universalism have often in the past taken forms which were ecclesiologically and ethnically unjustifiable, the search for the true solution might become easier.

However, as we discover in joint research the relative and changing realities of history, another basic theological issue arises: the question of the role of the Holy Spirit in history, *i.e.*, the issue of continuous revelation or doctrinal development. Indeed, one can easily agree that forms and structures of the Church can and should adapt themselves to the changing conditions of history. We have referred earlier to the wide acceptance of imperial political structures as *de facto* criteria for church organization in the East and also to the nearly "papal" self-affirmations by eastern prelates, both in Byzantium and later in Russia, in times when the Church had to maintain its witness in conditions of political chaos and disunity. The question may legitimately be asked, therefore, whether similar—although much more prolonged and more consistent—developments in the West, which led the Roman bishop to assume universal leadership, can not be explained and justified in the same manner, as a legitimate response of the Church to concrete demands of history? And if this is so, is it not the Holy Spirit who guided the Roman church along the way?

Clearly, the issue of doctrinal development, particularly in its application to church institutions, has been raised since Newman, but it clearly involves even wider problems today with the adoption by so many of a "process" approach to theology. Indeed, change is recognized as the very sign of truth and as an intrinsic factor of revelation. In the field of ecclesiology, this method is, of course, able to explain the emergence of an institution like the papacy, but also able to neutralize it in practice by referring to on-going and necessary change in the present and the future.

Generally speaking, the Orthodox approach to ecclesiology is rather uncomfortable with the "process" method, which seems to overlook the historical uniqueness (ἅπαξ) of the Christ-event and, therefore, the completeness of the apostolic witness, enshrined forever in the New Testament and preserved by the *apostolic* Church. Without rejecting the idea of development, Orthodox theology would rather describe it in terms of novelty of formulation, not of content. Consequently, any historical change would be evaluated in terms of its *consistency* with the apostolic witness and with tradition, and only secondarily in terms of its relevance to the needs of the historical moment when it occurs. It remains, however, that this Orthodox concern for continuity easily transforms itself into frozen conservatism of almost anecdotal character. Moreover, blind fear of any change leads to a gradual drifting into sectarianism: As opposed to sects, "catholic" Christianity is both faithful to the *depositum fidei* and open to the realities of history . . .

It seems therefore that if the Orthodox-Roman Catholic dialogue is to handle the issue of doctrinal development, it should—especially in the field of ecclesiology—rediscover its *antinomical* and ultimately mysterious character: the antinomy between divine revelation and human perception, between grace and freedom, between the universal and the local. The major discovery which might occur is that the antinomy—always challenging logical and legalistic thinking—is actually not a form of agnosticism but a liberating contemplation of divine truth uncovered in the *sensus ecclesiae* shared by all.

Speaking concretely, the Orthodox clearly have no right to object to Roman primacy solely on the basis of the ethnic provincialism of their national autocephalous churches as they exist today. These are undoubtedly covers for separatism.

Moreover, they need to recognize that if regional unions of local churches are realized through institutional interdependence (regional synods), the universal unity of the Church can also receive an institutionalized form, implying defined channels of interdependence and a form of primacy, models of which existed in the apostolic college and among the local churches of early Christendom.

If, by the grace of God, a union council ever meets, it will have to take up in its agenda the issue of "autocephaly"—as it is practiced now in the Orthodox Church—and of course the issue of Roman primacy. These issues will have to be debated theologically, not only in terms of the content of the New Testament revelation but also by asking the question of what is legitimate "doctrinal development." The Orthodox side will undoubtedly try to interpret development in terms of *jus ecclesiasticum* only, but will also have to formulate ways by which the universality of the Christian message can be maintained on a permanent basis and in an institutional form, as a necessary expression of the nature of the Church.

Then, the debate will have to include practical matters. What happens *in practice* in Western Christendom when papal primacy is either denied or reduced in its real effectiveness? Did not conciliarism evolve into the Reformation, and the new emphasis on conciliarity at Vatican II into a critical breakdown of doctrine and structures?

On the other hand, what would happen *concretely* in the Orthodox world if the present autocephalous churches accepted the existence of a real center of authority, even if this center is defined only *jure ecclesiastico?*

It seems to me that relationships between Orthodoxy and Roman Catholicism will not advance much unless a competent team makes the attempt of drafting an agenda which would include questions challenging for both sides and testing their awareness of being members of the *Catholic Church* of Christ. Both sides will be ready to recognize

—that such membership is fully realized locally, in the
    eucharist;

—that it also implies a regional (*i.e.,* also cultural, national and social) mission;

—that regionalism is not always consistent with universalism, which nevertheless also belongs to the very *nature* of Christ's message.

On these three levels, a common *sensus* will have to be developed. Otherwise, no doctrinal agreements on particular theological issues, and certainly no symbolic gestures or diplomacy will be able to realize the unity we seek.

3

The Ecumenical Patriarchate, Yesterday and Today*

Initiated primarily by the ecumenical patriarchate, the various activities which involve the preparation of an Orthodox council inevitably raise the issue of the exact position of that patriarchate among the local Orthodox churches. If—by the grace of God—the council takes place, or if—also by the grace of God—the various consultations and commissions presently working towards an Orthodox consensus on the issues of the day simply result in formal agreements which will lay the basis for progress and greater unity, the position of the ecumenical patriarchate will certainly come up in a clearer form, whether it is maintained and reinforced, or reduced, or given new forms of operation. Inasmuch as the issues facing the Orthodox Church today are primarily those of a united witness in a changing world and of adequate ecclesial structures which would make such a witness more meaningful, and inasmuch as the traditional role of the ecumenical patriarchate consisted precisely in exercising leadership in those areas, the success or failure of its recent initiatives will determine the patriarchate's own historical future.

As we all know, present realities in the Orthodox Church are not created by theological factors only. They are also

*Paper originally presented under the title "The Ecumenical Patriarch, Seen in the Light of Orthodox Ecclesiology and History" at the Third International Congress of Orthodox Theologians, Brookline, Mass., 1978, and published in *The Greek Orthodox Theological Review* 24 (1979), pp. 227-244.

shaped by historical realities of the past and by purely empirical—primarily political—circumstances of the present. We
will all agree, however, that the particular task of *theologians*
consists in distinguishing permanent and absolute values from
historical contingencies; in helping the Church to keep its
identity unadulterated by the inevitable changes of conditions
in which its witness is to be presented to the world; in defining
what is Holy Tradition and what are human traditions, of
which some are legitimate and valuable and some can harm
the witness of the Church and, as such, are to be rejected. It
is precisely theology that must provide the determining factor
in conciliar decisions. If the forthcoming council is determined
only by politics, it will undoubtedly be a pseudo-council! So,
theologians can render the Church a liberating service, and
should not fail to do so. The present paper on the ecumenical
patriarchate does not pretend to great originality. It is not,
as far as I can see, very controversial. Its only goal is to bring
to our attention those theological and historical considerations
without which a discussion of the role of the ecumenical
patriarchate leads inevitably to a dead end, both in its pan-
Orthodox and in its ecumenical dimensions.

1. Primacy in Early Christian Ecclesiology

It is a well-recognized fact that neither the New Testament nor the sub-apostolic writings provide a clear formal
description of church structure. During the first two centuries
of the Christian era, there existed nothing really similar to
later formulae of canon law. Of course, the Pastoral Epistles
and such documents as the *Didache* or even, in the third
century, the *Apostolic Tradition* of Hippolytus contain precious information, but they refer to local communities and
local situations, so that scholarship, using formal historical
methods, is generally reluctant to accept this information as
a generalized pattern. This means, however, that to understand the realities of the early church, one must go beyond
the careful agnosticism of "pure historians." One must also
appeal to the *theological* content of the New Testament and

to the writings of such fathers as Ignatius, Irenaeus and Cyprian. Here one discovers the authentic ecclesial experience of the early Christian communities, the soteriological and eschatological meaning of the sacramental mystery performed in each community, and the fact that the structure of the Church was not shaped by some authoritarian decree or some special legislative foresight of Christ or His apostles, but that it came into existence in virtue of the very nature of the Church, by divine will, after Pentecost.

Therefore, to understand and to agree upon the character of the ministries in the early church and upon the structure of early church polity, one should first acquire a common sense of the Church itself. This prerequisite constitutes the major difficulty in contemporary ecumenical discussions, which often result in formal, conceptual agreements on particular issues but lack the basic reference to a common perception of the Church itself and, therefore, fail to lead towards real unity.

In Orthodox ecclesiology, the fundamental importance of the local community, centered around the eucharist and manifesting the reality of the Kingdom of God in its totality, in its universality, in its catholicity, has remained consistent with the tradition found in Ignatius, Irenaeus and Cyprian. In particular, it provides the basis for the Orthodox understanding of the episcopate, which presupposes the inseparable unity between each bishop and his community, as well as the identity and, therefore, the equality of all bishops. I will not describe again the fundamentals of that early Christian and Orthodox understanding of the Church, which has been—with individual nuances, but brilliantly—expounded by several contemporary Orthodox theologians, including particularly Nicholas Afanassieff and John Zizioulas. One should note also that the recently published, authoritative work by the metropolitan of Sardis, Maximus, on the ecumenical patriarchate also accepts these fundamental historical and ecclesiological presuppositions as the starting point for its description of the rise of the Constantinopolitan primacy. Indeed, an Orthodox theologian or historian cannot do otherwise. The eucharistic assembly, presided by the bishop, is the fullest manifestation of the Church catholic, although it is always a *local* event. It gathers all the Orthodox Christians living in a given place. Its authenticity is conditioned by *three factors*: unity of faith with the apostles and fathers of the past, unity with all the other Orthodox communities of the present, and *real communion* in the Kingdom of God which is still to come and which is anticipated in the eucharistic mystery. Without those three elements there can be no true Church.

If there is no continuity in the apostolic faith, there is a denial of the redemptive fullness given in Christ "once for all" (*hapax*). If there is no concern for "horizonal" unity in truth with the entire Church universal, there is only congregationalism. And finally, if there is no real communion in the Kingdom to come, in the Bread which comes from heaven, and in the Cup of the new and everlasting covenant, there is only a gathering for Bible study, a theological lecture or friendly emotions.

There is no doubt that the early church was eminently concerned with these three ecclesiological aspects—the apostolic, the "horizontal," the eschatological—and did not tend, as so many Christians have done in later centuries, to *reduce* ecclesiality to only one of these three dimensions. These reductions, as we all know, have resulted in either formal dogmatic conservatism, or institutional authoritarianism, or in various forms of charismatic, or pseudo-charismatic apocalypticisms.

Inasmuch as I am concerned with a particular aspect of early Christian ecclesiology—the development of *primacies* on the local and universal levels—I will briefly discuss here only the two first dimensions, since they were so often (and inevitably) connected with the primacies: the preservation of the apostolic witness, and the "horizontal" unity in faith between the local churches.

The necessity for every local church to maintain continuity with the apostolic faith and witness is the basis of what we call "apostolic succession." In interpreting that essential aspect of Christian ecclesiology, some unfortunate reductions have also taken place among which the gradual—almost imperceptible—growth of a new consciousness in the church of Rome of being more particularly "apostolic" than others. It is not necessary to recall here the age-old debate between East and West about the nature of the Roman primacy. But it is certainly useful to remind ourselves once more of the polarity between two ideas of "apostolicity," the Roman and the Eastern, well defined by a man, Fr. Francis Dvornik, who was not a theologian but was able to unveil important theological truths by simply being a good historian. Whereas Rome developed the idea that certain local churches possessed primacy in virtue of their "apostolic foundation," the East remained quite aloof to that idea. Jerusalem, the "mother of all the churches," contented itself in the fourth century with its pagan name of *Aelia Capitolina* and acquired a certain prestige (which remained local) only when in the fourth century it became a center of pilgrimage. On the other hand, the great centers of Alexandria and Constantinople—which superseded not only Jerusalem but also the unquestionably "apostolic" church of Antioch—did so without any pretense to apostolic foundation. The legends about St. Mark founding Christianity in Alexandria or St. Andrew as a preacher in Byzantium were exploited much later, primarily as arguments (very weak arguments indeed!) against papal claims. But anyone familiar with the writings of Athanasius or Cyril of Alexandria, or with those of Chrysostom or Photius or Philotheus Coccinus of Constantinople, and with the historical circumstances of their activity, knows well that neither St. Mark nor St. Andrew had anything to do with their awareness of being leaders among their fellow bishops.

Quite allergic to the idea that God could have kept Jerusalem, or established any other place, as a divinely established, permanent center of the universal Church, they rather recognized as decisive the *pragmatic realities of history* which have led Alexandria and Constantinople to become economic, political and intellectual centers. Since all local churches (and not only such venerable and apostolic sees as Jerusalem, Antioch, Ephesus, Corinth *etc.*) were manifesting the *same* Kingdom in the *same* fullness, celebrating the *same* eucharist and holding the *same* faith, it was only natural to recognize the leadership of those bishops who presided over churches with material and intellectual means to substantiate that leadership, to make it real and constructive.

Since the most obvious and even overwhelming pragmatic reality of the fourth century was the universal Christian empire of Constantine and his successors, it was inevitable that the imperial capital would eventually supersede Alexandria and would become in the late sixth century an "ecumenical patriarchate." However, since the empire had remained technically "Roman," the bishop of the "Old Rome" continued to be considered as the "first bishop" of the universal Church. But Rome also happened to be one of the churches founded by the apostles themselves. This gave an opportunity to many Byzantines—especially those who were in conflict with their own emperors and patriarchs—to use occasionally arguments which the bishop of Rome particularly appreciated, which referred to the apostolic foundation of Roman Christianity by St. Peter and St. Paul, the *koryphaioi* of the apostolic college.

Thus, for several centuries before the schism, an ambiguous situation prevailed which allowed for a coexistence in the universal Church of the Western "apostolic" criterion of primacy and the Eastern "pragmatic" interpretation. The contrast which appears between this "pragmaticism" of the early Eastern church and of medieval Orthodox on the one hand, and on the other, the honorary primacy held in our own contemporary church by the ancient patriarchates of the East, whereas the historical reasons which justified that primacy in the past have disappeared, is obvious. However, I will not insist on it, because I believe that the role played by the empire in shaping the structures of the Byzantine church (including the elevation of the Eastern patriarchates to the position of primacy) should not and cannot serve as model for us today. Orthodox ecclesiology certainly presupposes the equality of all local churches and therefore allows, so to say, an equal opportunity for any one of them to assume a leading role. But it would be a real catastrophe if sociopolitical factors were officially admitted again as the only decisive criterion for such elevation, as they were at the time of the empire. In fact, the identification of the Church with secular values is

already with us—particularly in the form of "phyletism"—
but fortunately it is not sanctioned by any canonical criterion
and therefore can be opposed and fought against.

So, apostolicity, apostolic tradition, and apostolic faith
cannot be monopolized by any church or any bishop. Such is
the legacy of the early Christian and patristic periods. The
various forms of primacy of certain bishops above their peers
—the metropolitan in a province, the patriarch in a wider area,
as well as the universal primacy of the ecumenical patriarch
—follow no other criterion than the historical or pragmatic
one. However, this pragmatic realism was not a form of
capitulation before secular norms, an easy adaptation to political structures, but a dynamic and living ability of the Church
to preserve her own norms, her own principles of polity, her
own divinely established eucharistic structures in the midst of
contemporary realities. In Orthodoxy today, this dynamism
still exists on the level of popular piety, liturgy and even
theology, whereas on the level of wider church structures there
unfortunately is either an adaptation to historical realities of
one thousand years ago, or else to most unacceptable aspects
of the politics and nationalism of modern states, which are
shamelessly using the Church in their own egotistic and con-
flicting interests.

The task of the future council—if it takes place, and if it
is a true Orthodox council and not a pseudo-council—is to lay
the ground for a gradual restoration of the dynamic relationship between theology and reality, between the eucharistic
community and church structures, between the task of saving
souls, for which the Church exists, and the image offered by
contemporary Orthodoxy to the world around it.

The second essential dimension of early Christian ecclesiology, which also motivates the existence of primacies, is concern for Church unity, particularly through the episcopate.
Although the clergy and laity of each local church undoubtedly have the right to nominate candidates to the episcopal
dignity in that church, the consecration of each new bishop
is a concern of all local churches and requires the participation, at least through proxy, of the *whole* episcopate of the

Church. In practice, only the neighboring bishops, at least two or three of them, participate in the laying on of hands. Their participation always implied (and still implies today) that the newly consecrated bishop becomes a member of the universal college of bishops, because, as St. Cyprian wrote, "the episcopate is one" (*episcopatus unus est*) and each bishop, when he is enthroned in his particular church, acquires the fullness of the dignity which belongs to all (*in solidum pars tenetur*).

The necessity for the participation of several bishops in each new episcopal consecration served as the basic motivation for regular meetings of bishops (*synodoi*), which became canonically institutionalized in the fourth century. In each province of the empire, all the bishops were required to meet twice a year, under the presidency of the bishop of the main city of the province (*metropolis*), and solve doctrinal or disciplinary issues which required a common witness. The canonical legislation of the fourth century, especially that of the Council of Nicaea, was clearly aiming at preserving the integrity of each local church and securing the unity of all churches by assuring territorial unity everywhere and by following pragmatically the administrative divisions of the empire. In each province, there was now a church enjoying full administrative independence and following in its organization no other criterion than the evangelical principle of "neighborhood." The Orthodox Church today is supposed to apply the same model in each of its so-called "autocephalies." In fact, however, there exists today major and very disturbing ecclesiological and canonical departures from the Nicaean model: (1) Some of the present "provinces" (*i.e.,* the "autocephalous" churches) are so large that true episcopal conciliarity is impracticable and is replaced by a system of patriarchal bureaucracy (the restoration of the old pattern of ecclesiastical provinces was widely discussed in Russia in 1905-1917 but never saw light). (2) In some churches (particularly Constantinople and Russia) not all the ruling bishops are members of the "synod"; the so-called "permanent synod" ceased to promote conciliarity and has become an organ of bureaucratic administration exercising power *over* other bishops. (3) Some national churches practically replaced the territorial principle of church unity with an ethnic one: this is the heresy of "phyletism" condemned by the Council of Constantinople in 1872. (4) In some churches, "titular" bishops, as members of synods, play a role totally detached from the pastoral and sacramental responsibilities which ecclesiologically justify the very existence of the episcopal ministry. I consider these factors as substantial departures from Orthodox ecclesiology itself. They should be squarely faced, condemned and, if possible, corrected by the future council.

But let us take a step further in our discussion of primacy. We have seen that the idea of divine or apostolic establishment of primacy in particular places was foreign to early Christian ecclesiology, at least in the East. The same point can be made in reference to the provincial primacies of "metropolitans": with a very few exceptions, the importance of cities determined the place of residence of ancient metropolitans. Pragmaticism prevailed here, too. However, the very *idea* of primacy was very much a part of ecclesiology itself: the provincial episcopal synods needed a president, without whose sanction no decision was valid. Similarly, there existed an "order" (*taxis*) in the apostolic college itself. Such is indeed an inevitable requirement of the very existence of the Church in the world. It must present a united witness, and this unity must be channeled and symbolized by concrete canonical structures.

The regional "primacies," which united several provinces and eventually developed into so-called "patriarchates," have played a great role in history, but their form, number, authority and importance have varied greatly. For example, the mythical system of "pentarchy," which was formally sanctioned by Emperor Justinian at a time when it had practically already ceased to exist, is something used as an Orthodox alternative to the papacy, but its ecclesiological meaning is impossible to define and its importance is limited to being a sort of symbolic model of universal conciliarity.

Much more significant is the issue of universal primacy, which does possess a scriptural and ecclesiological basis. Orthodox anti-Latin polemics have rightly emphasized the pragmatic and political origin of all the primacies, including the primacy "among equals" held by the pope of Rome before the schism. It is a fact, however, that there has never been a time when the Church did not recognize a certain "order" among first the apostles, then the bishops, and that, in this order, one apostle, St. Peter, and later, one bishop, heading a particular church, occupied the place of a "primate" ("first Simon, who is called Peter," Matt. 10:2; cf. Mk. 3:16). During the years which followed Pentecost, the mother church of Jerusalem clearly occupied that position and was presided, first, by Peter and the twelve, and later by James, when the twelve became itinerant apostles. The eventual disappearance of the Judaeo-Christian community in Jerusalem ended the primacy of that original mother church, and as we have seen earlier, it was not claimed by the new church of Jerusalem, made up of Gentiles, which was reestablished under Constantine. By that time, through ways difficult to follow in detail, the church of Rome had acquired a primacy which is witnessed in a variety of ways by early writers, including (perhaps) Clement and Ignatius, and certainly Irenaeus and Cyprian. Historically, the Byzantine (and Orthodox) interpretation of that process—Rome was the capital and the major city—is probably right. It is difficult to imagine that the tradition about Peter's death in Rome would have been in itself sufficient to justify Rome's primacy, as the later papal tradition claims. In any case, the Roman bishop did become the "first bishop" of the universal Church: his seniority was always maintained, especially in the canons (I Constantinople canon 3; Chalcedon canon 28) which defined the position of "New Rome," Constantinople. However, and this is the real ecclesiological difference between Orthodoxy and Roman Catholicism, the Roman primacy had no indelible character. It was *conditioned* by the pope's doctrinal orthodoxy and was not the source of that orthodoxy. The schism occurred precisely because the West believed that the pope, in virtue of his primacy, was doctrinally always right, and that primacy would never be removed from Rome. After the schism, Constantinople was left with primacy in Orthodoxy.

I would venture to affirm here that the universal primacy

of one bishop—the one of Jerusalem, the one of Rome, or the one of "New Rome"—was not simply a historical accident, reflecting "pragmatic" requirements. A united witness of the universal episcopate of the Church is not simply a pragmatic necessity but a sign that the Holy Spirit did not abandon the Church, which remains eternally as the "column and foundation of truth." The apostles and, after them, all the disciples of Christ were sent into the world to be Christ's *witnesses*: the unity and coherence of that witness, the service to the world which it implies, the common action which it requires, can be assured only if the episcopate remains *one*. The function of the "first bishop" is *to serve* that unity on the world scale, just as the function of a regional primate is to be the agent of unity on a regional scale.

However, none of these forms of primacy is a primacy "over the eucharist," and, therefore, no primate has *power over* the other bishops; he is one of them, sacramentally equal to them, fallible as they are. They have the right and the duty to oppose him when he is wrong, and this very opposition is a service rendered to him, for his errors can lead not only to his personal catastrophe but also to the catastrophe of his church as well. Truth is no one's monopoly, but every Christian, and indeed every bishop, is called to manifest it in the various capacities or ministries which exist in the Church of God. There is no ultimate guarantee, no ultimate security. The search for guarantees and securities has led the entire Christian West to the tragic dead end which is apparent today in a form clearer than ever. But we Orthodox still do recognize that there is a special ministry, a special *diakonia* of universal primacy and that such a *diakonia* implies a particular divine *charisma*. Our problem with Roman Catholicism is that we disagree with the immovability, the infallibility of the Roman idea of primacy and therefore with the very particular and indeed disastrous way in which the Christian West later interpreted the exercise of primacy by such men as St. Leo, St. Martin, St. Gregory the Great and other great Roman bishops. And we believe that the *charisma* was indeed transferred to Constantinople.

However, during the entire medieval period, most Byzantine churchmen considered that, in case of union with the West on the basis of the Orthodox faith, the Orthodox bishops of Rome would recover their primacy. So, again, they did not consider universal primacy as being attached to a particular place, but saw it as a *diakonia* necessary for the universal witness of the Church in the world.

2. The Ecumenical Patriarchate Yesterday and Today

In spite of the revival of Byzantine studies in the West which has taken place in this century, the idea that the Byzantine Empire was essentially a system of caesaropapism is widely maintained by most reputable scholars and printed in widely used college textbooks.[1] The theory is obviously wrong: Byzantine Orthodox Christianity could not recognize the emperor as an absolute power over the Christian faith and the Christian Church simply because any such power—even held by a bishop, a patriarch, or a pope, not to speak of an emperor—was excluded by the very nature of Orthodoxy. Orthodoxy did not know "caesaropapism" because it was allergic to "papism" in the first place. And so our Church venerates heroes of the faith who have opposed the heretical emperors of their day—St. Athanasius, St. John Chrysostom, St. Maximus the Confessor, St. Theodore the Studite and so many others—and hails martyrs who "overthrew Copronymus with the sword of faith." What remains true, however, is that during the entire Byzantine period, the exercise of primacy by the ecumenical patriarchate was tightly connected with the "symphony" between the empire and the Church which had been formulated by Justinian and remained the basis for Byzantine political thinking until the end of Byzantium. Even the monks and fathers of the Church who challenged heretical emperors did not challenge the system itself. Patriarchs could often oppose heresies and uncanonical procedures promoted by emperors, but they were aiming at restoring the "symphony," not at destroying it. They were always taking for

[1]Cf. for example W. Ullmann, *Medieval Political Thought* (New York, 1976).

granted that the Christian faith itself implied the existence either of a universal empire or at least of a "commonwealth" of Orthodox states and peoples which recognized the emperor and patriarch of the "New Rome" as universal leaders. It is that system which led to the Christianization of Eastern Europe, transmitting to Slavs, Romanians, Georgians and many others not only the Orthodox faith, but also the immense wealth of Byzantine civilization—liturgy, theology, hymnography, iconography, hagiography—and made the Orthodox Church today a universal Church, and not simply the national religion of the Greek nation.

The specific role of the patriarchate in that process became even more prominent during the last centuries of the Byzantine Empire. The empire had become a negligible political entity, beseiged by the Turks and limited to the city of Constantinople and its suburbs. The patriarchate meanwhile had preserved its immense administrative and canonical powers throughout Eastern Europe. Throughout most of the fourteenth century, it was led by men who came from the monastic, hesychast background and were zealots for universal Orthodoxy. Probably the greatest of them all, Patriarch Philotheus Coccinus, was a Thessalonican Jew converted to Christianity; others—for example, Patriarch Joseph II, or the brilliant diplomat Metropolitan Cyprian of Kiev, or the less reputable Metropolitan Isidore—were of Bulgarian background. In the midst of most tragic political disintegration, Greek and Slavic churchmen and monks worked together—in Constantinople itself, on Mount Athos, in Trnovo, Ohrid, Pec, Moscow and Novgorod—in a common commitment to preserve an Orthodox Christian *oikoumene*. Very interestingly, that late Byzantine period presents a striking analogy with the events happening in the West almost a millenium earlier, when the fall of the Roman Empire provided the Roman bishop with an opportunity to assume responsibility not only for the Church but for society as a whole. It was then, in the fifth, sixth and seventh centuries, that the popes of Rome took over the task of imperial Rome, civilized the barbarian invaders and became the real heads of Western Christianity.

In the East, the almost total weakening of imperial power

in the thirteenth-fifteenth centuries led to similar consequences. We have contemporary documents about ecumenical
patriarchs ruling on political matters in Russia, giving birth
to independent Romanian ecclesiastical provinces, and cor-
responding with the pagan princes of Lithuania and the
Roman Catholic kings of Poland on behalf of their Orthodox
subjects. All these diplomatic and administrative tasks would
undoubtedly have been performed by the emperors in former
times. So, when Byzantium finally fell under the Turkish on-
slaught, the task of becoming the *millet-bashi*—the administrative ruler of the Christian population of the empire of all
nationalities—was not entirely new for the patriarch. The
radical difference was only that he had to perform it now
under Turkish supervision.

The peculiar situation in which the Roman pope found
himself after the fall of Rome in 476 led to his assumption
of the title of "supreme pontiff" (*pontifex maximus*)—the
religious title of the Roman emperors—and to the development
of his well-known claims to absolute monarchy in the Church.
There is no doubt that this development happened historically
when there was concrete need of impressing the Roman
Christian tradition upon the barbarians in terms as absolute
as possible. And the method was not equivalent to simple
power-seeking: its purpose was authentically missionary
and reflected very sincere convictions, especially in such great
personalities as Pope St. Gregory the Great.

It is indeed extremely interesting to discover that a similar
development was taking place in Constantinople during the
late Byzantine period. The main difference was, of course,
that Constantinople could not—and did not—claim any primacy of divine establishment or of apostolic origin. However,
it was indeed enhancing its authority—especially in letters to
"barbarians" intended to assure the perpetuation of the "Byzantine commonwealth" and of Orthodox universality—in
terms quite reminiscent of papal claims. Here is what Patriarch Philotheus Coccinus writes in 1370 to Russian princes
who had politically seceded from their Metropolitan Alexis
(who was then also the regent of the Moscovite grand-prin-
cipality):

Since God has appointed Our Humility as leader of all Christians found anywhere in the inhabited earth, as solicitor and guardian of their souls, all of them depend on me (πάντες εἰς ἐμὲ ἀνάκεινται), the father and teacher of them all. If that were possible, therefore, it would have been my duty to walk everywhere on earth by the cities and countries, and to teach there the Word of God. I would have had to do so unfailingly, since this is my duty. However, since it is beyond the possibility of one weak and powerless man to walk around the entire inhabited earth, Our Humility chooses the best among men, the most eminent in virtue, establishes and ordains them as pastors, teachers, and high-priests, and sends them to the ends of the universe. One of them goes to your great country, to the multitudes which inhabit it, another reaches other areas of the earth, and still another goes elsewhere, so that each one, in the country and place which was appointed for him, enjoys territorial rights, an episcopal chair and all the rights of Our Humility.[2]

Such a text, if used in a Western document, should undoubtedly have to be interpreted as an extreme form of medieval papal claims. When found in the letter of a Byzantine patriarch, provision should be made for usual methods of diplomatic rhetoric. There is no doubt that Patriarch Philotheus would have readily subscribed, on ecclesiological grounds, to a condemnation of papal primacy. Another Byzantine author, Nicetas of Ancyra, who also often uses such titles as "common judge" when he writes about the ecumenical patriarch, immediately qualifies his statement by the following warning:

Do not exaggerate the importance of the title of patriarch which is given to him. For every bishop is also called "patriarch" . . . [He then quotes St. Gregory of Nazianzus referring to his own father, a bishop, as

[2]Ed. F. Miklosich and J. Müller, *Acta Patriarchatus Constantinopolitani* 1 (Vienna, 1860), p. 521.

"patriarch"[3]] and the titles of precedence are common
to all of us [bishops] since all the bishops are fathers,
shepherds and teachers, and it is clear that there are
no special canons for metropolitans distinct from those
which apply to archbishops or bishops. For the laying
on of hands is the same for all, and our participation
in the divine liturgy is identical and all pronounce the
same prayers.[4]

It is extraordinary to discover how precise, responsible
and accurate the Byzantines were when they theologized about
issues of faith or ecclesiology, and also how free they felt
when they composed diplomatic or rhetorical documents and
acted to preserve the integrity of the commonwealth! For it
is quite clear that Patriarch Philotheus, when writing to the
Russian princes, was defining not his ecclesiological position
but his role in the framework of the universal community of
nations—a late Byzantine substitute for the universal Roman
Empire—which he wanted to maintain against its enemies of
East and West. Similarly, after the fall of Byzantium, the
ecumenical patriarch will accept the same identification between Church and society. Without changing anything in
Orthodox ecclesiology, he will *de facto* use the civil power
with which he was vested by the Ottomans to rule all the
Eastern patriarchates from the Phanar and even to suppress
completely the autocephalous churches of Bulgaria and
Serbia.

I have tried to define earlier the *ecclesiological* framework
in which the primacy of Constantinople in the Orthodox
Church was shaped and also the reasons why, in my
opinion, it remains even today a necessity for the universal
witness of Orthodoxy. However, all institutions—even those
which are founded by God Himself—are *historical* phenomena
and reflect the inevitable imperfections of the historical process. One cannot maintain them unless one makes the constant
effort of distinguishing the essential from the peripheral. One

[3]*Or.* 43, 37, PG 36, col. 545C.
[4]J. Darrouzès, *Documents inédits d'ecclésiologie byzantine* (Paris, 1966),
pp. 222-224.

cannot study history, or use it for one's own benefit, without criticism—indeed, a loving and devoted criticism, if one is a Christian and if one discusses the history of the Church.

In the case of the ecumenical patriarchate, it is unquestionable that, between 381 and 1453, it exercised its primacy in an *imperial* Byzantine framework, which implied an identification of the Church with a particular society, a particular civilization. As all historical frameworks, this one involved positive and negative consequences. For example, on the negative side, one can refer to the cultural rebellion against Byzantium of the non-Greek speaking Christians of the Middle East—Egyptian Copts, Armenians, Syrians—which lead into the monophysite schism. On the positive side, one must recognize the tremendous success of Byzantium in converting, educating and civilizing the Slavic nations of Eastern Europe, which are thus indebted to Byzantium not only for the content but also for the forms of their Orthodox culture.

Did this entire Byzantine imperial framework disappear when Byzantium fell under the Turks? It did not. It only took different forms, and this is why the Byzantine model of church organization and mentality continued to flourish: monasticism, spirituality, martyrdom. Also, the medieval concept of pentarchy was maintained and even extended in the case of the establishment of the patriarchate in Russia. The Romanian scholar Nicholas Iorga was right to discover "Byzance après Byzance" in various parts of Eastern Europe, surviving until the nineteenth century.

It is only *in the past one hundred and fifty years* that Byzantine civilization really collapsed in a most drastic, revolutionary and universal way and was replaced with a variety of ideologies, in various combinations, which dominate our own societies today. They are all connected with the Enlightenment and the French Revolution. In the Orthodox East, their most obvious expression is nationalism, which took forms utterly incompatible with the mental and social structures of the Byzantine Middle Ages. Basically, this nationalism can be reduced to such concepts as the "will of the people" or "national interest," considered as supreme and unquestionable values. Of course, throughout the Christian Middle

Ages, there were also wars between nations and tribes, but, ideologically, medieval society was ruled by the notion of a universal Kingdom of God, reflected a universal Christian empire. It is that universal political ideology, and not any "national interest," which rightly or wrongly had received the sanction of the Church. It is also that imperial ideology which sustained and justified the primacy of a patriarch residing precisely in the capital of the empire, Constantinople, the "queen of cities."

How did the ecumenical patriarchate react to that revolutionary change which involved the very *raison d'être* of its existence? To answer this question fairly, one would need volumes of historical research. Some facts are well known, however. For example, the patriarchate rather strongly reacted against the secular national ideology which inspired the creation of the new Greek state in Greece proper. But, of course, it had no power to prevent its further progress. Actually, the internal debate about the identity of modern "Greece" is still continuing among the Greeks themselves: Is Greece called to continue the Byzantine traditions of the Ῥωμαιωσύνη, or is it to be the resurrection of a secular Ἑλλάς? For the Greeks, the patriarchate remains a symbol of the first option, but only a symbol, which has been long bypassed by historical realities.

But the patriarchate was faced not only with Greek nationalism but also with its equivalents among the other traditionally Orthodox nations. And here, one should frankly recognize that it did not succeed in riding the storm. To maintain its authority, it became fiercely defensive, capitulating only under duress and, in its struggle for survival, gradually and unconsciously identified its own fate with that of the Greek nation. The events led the leaders of the Phanar to forget in practice what they had themselves initially discovered at the time of the Greek Revolution, that Greek nationalism was an enemy, not a friend of the patriarchate, that it was incompatible with Constantinople's universal mission, that successors of Chrysostom, of Photius, of Philotheus Coccinus could not identify their fate with that of a heroic, dignified and respectable, but small Balkan nation; that, in order to keep its credibility as leader of world Orthodoxy, the ecumenical patriarch had to remain *recognizable* as father and teacher by the ninety percent of Orthodox Christians who did not speak Greek.

This recognizability was initially and for centuries provided by the fact that Constantinople and the Byzantine Christian tradition were the guide and matrix of world Orthodoxy, unquestionably the center and the guide in theology, art, canon law and all other forms of Christian civilization. At that time, Constantinople was also promoting the translation and diffusion of its heritage in all languages throughout the world. Today this is not the case anymore, and the Church cannot live by simply remembering ancient symbols. So, it is inevitable that, from time to time, some voices are heard denying the primacy of Constantinople, describing the Orthodox Church simply as a federation of national autocephalous churches, or else suggesting the transfer of the primacy to places like Moscow or New York.

Dear friends, perhaps some of you think that it is improper for me, not being a Greek, to criticize Greek nationalism. But, believe me, I am ready here and now to anathematize other nationalisms—including particularly the Russian and also the American—as equally abominable phenomena. By scholarly interest and vocation, I am a *Romaios*—or Byzantine—who firmly believes that the Orthodox Church cannot prosper today without assuming and developing what Florovsky called the "patristic mind," *i.e.,* the vision of Christian truth present in the writings of the Greek fathers, in the traditions of Byzantine art and liturgy, in the catholic spirit of Christian Byzantium.

But it is precisely to *maintain* that tradition, to be *consistent* with it—and therefore truly faithful to its contents—that one should prevent the ecumenical patriarchate from being simply strangled by the Turks in a dirty ghetto of Istanbul. It is with that in mind that I offer to your attention the following conclusions of my paper:

1. Orthodox ecclesiology demands that the Church manifest its unity and catholicity through one bishop in each place, one synod of bishops, presided by a regional primate in each

country (or region), and finally that, on the world scale, the witness of Orthodoxy be a reality through the unity of the world episcopate: this last unity also requires that there be a "first bishop," who would not be a pope with administrative powers *over* his peers but would possess sufficient authority to organize, channel and, in a sense, represent the conciliarity of the Church. It is clear that a definition of such an Orthodox primacy is essential not only for our own internal affairs but also for a meaningful dialogue with Roman Catholicism. In the past, we have always been strictly negative, refuting papal privileges, and we have failed—and unfortunately still fail— to project meaningful alternatives. Most of the time, we were rather simply defending ecclesiastical particularism and nationalism, whereas the issue placed by the papacy before the consciousness of all Christians is that of a world Christian witness. In the Orthodox perspective, the essential functions of the "first bishop" consist in assuring that a constant consultation and conciliarity takes place between all Orthodox churches and that ecclesiastical order—*especially* local and regional unity of all the Orthodox—be secured.

2. In substance, the above functions were precisely those of the church of Constantinople during the Byzantine period. But since Byzantium does not exist anymore, it is simply meaningless to attempt a definition of the rights of the ecumenical patriarchate in Byzantine terms. Nothing can be more harmful to the prestige of the patriarchate than constantly to invoke canon 28 of Chalcedon as a definition of these rights. Even a casual reader of that canon can see that a primacy established in the "New Rome" because it was the "seat of the emperor and the senate" is irrelevent to our situation and that there are no "barbarian lands" in the sense in which this term was used in the fifth century. But there is indeed the need for an Orthodox primate, acting as the bishop of Rome acted in the first centuries and, indeed, as Constantinople itself functioned in the framework of the now defunct Byzantine Empire.

3. The normal functioning of an Orthodox primacy in the modern world would clearly require a permanent representation of all Orthodox churches in a consultative body around

the patriarch and, in general, an international staff. This suggestion is, of course, not new, but it becomes increasingly relevent for reasons which should be obvious to all of us. It would, of course, be much preferable for the patriarchate to remain in the inimitable glorious historical setting of Constantinople, but its very survival as an institution is more important than those historical considerations, and it is clear that the organization of a real world center would be much easier to realize elsewhere.

Finally, let me express my sincere hope that the present preconciliar activities—initiated by the ecumenical patriarchate and which do find sympathy and response in all Orthodox churches, and also great (perhaps too great) expectations in the entire world—will lead to a process matching these three conclusions. It appears to me that the patriarchate stands on a threshold and hesitates between two attitudes: frank and fearless continuation of the conciliar initiative—which, in order to succeed, must of course become much wider, much more open and involve a greater number of competent participants—or return to fearful isolation, to an identification of its own interests with those of modern Hellenism and to a stubborn and defensive restatement of medieval titles. This last alternative would be lethal and would reinforce those who believe that the ecumenical patriarchate is simply a relic of the past and hope that the Turks will finally put an end to its existence. The first one, on the contrary, could revive the dormant potential of contemporary Orthodoxy, while preserving continuity with the past, consistency with the existing canonical tradition (in its essential *meaning*, if not in all its formulations) and make the Church ready to face the challenges of today.

Select Bibliography

The Byzantine Church: Andreev, K., *Konstantinopol'skie patriarkhi ot vremeni khalhidonskogo sobora do Fotiia*, Sergiev Posad, 1895.— Basile (Krivochéine), *St. Syméon le Nouveau Théologien*, Chévetogne, 1980.—Baumstark, A., *Liturgie comparée*, Chévetogne, 1953.— Beck, H.-G., *Kirche und theologische Literatur im Byzantinischen Reich*, München, 1959.—Beck, H.-G., *Vorsehung und Vorherbestimmung in der theologische Literatur der Byzantiner*, Rome, 1937.—Berkhof, H., *Kirche und Kaiser. Eine Untersuchung der Entstehung der byzantinischen und theokratischen Staatsauffassung im vierten Jahrhundert*, Zürich, 1947.—Bornaert, R., *Les commentaires byzantins de la divine liturgie du VIIe au XVe siècle*, Paris, 1966.—Bréhier, L., *Le Monde Byzantin. II. Les Institutions de l'Empire byzantin*, Paris, 1949, 430-570.—Constantelos, D. J., *Byzantine Philanthropy and Social Welfare*, New Brunswick, N.J., 1968.—Delehaye, H., "Byzantine monasticism," *Byzantium*, ed. H. N. Baynes and H. St. L. B. Moss, Oxford, 1948, 136-165.—Dmitrievsky, A., *Opisanie Liturgicheskikh Rukopisei, I-II*, Kiev, 1901.—Dobroklonsky, A., *Prepodobny Theodor, igumen Studiisky*, 2 vols. Odessa, 1913-1914.—Dvornik, F., *Byzantine Missions among the Slavs*, New Brunswick, N.J., 1970.—Dvornik, F., *The Idea of Apostolicity in Byzantium and the Legend of the Apostle Andrew*, Cambridge, Mass., 1958.—Dvornik, F., *The Photian Schism. History and Legend*, Cambridge, 1948.—Erhardt, A., *Überlieferung und Bestand der hagiographischen und homiletischen Literatur der griechischen Kirche von den Anfängen bis zu Ende des 16. Jahrhunderts. Erste Teil. Die Überlieferung. III. Band, 1. Lieferung*, Leipzig, 1943.—Every, G., *The Byzantine Patriarchate (451-1204)*, 2nd ed. London, 1962.—Fliche, A., and Martin, V., *Histoire de l'Église, depuis les origines jusqu'à nos jours*, 21 vols., Paris, 1934.—Follieri, E., *Initia hymnorum Ecclesiae Graecae*, 4 vols., Vatican, 1960-1963.—Gill, J., *Byzantium and the Papacy, 1198-1400*, New Brunswick, N.J., 1979.—Gill, J., *The Council of Florence*, Cambridge, Mass., 1959.—Grumel, V., *Les Régestes des Actes du Patriarcat de Constantinople*, fasc. I-IV, Paris, 1932ff.—Hajjar, J., *Le Synode permanent* (σύνοδος ἐνδημοῦσα) *dans l'église byzantine des origines au XIe siècle*, Orientalia Christiana Analecta 164, Rome, 1962.—Hergenröther, J., *Photius, Patriarch von Constantinopel, Sein*

258   THE BYZANTINE LEGACY IN THE ORTHODOX CHURCH

Leben, seine Schriften und das griechische Schisma, 3 vols., Regens-
burg, 1867 (repr. Darmstadt, 1966).—Hussey, J. M., ed., *The Cambridge Medieval History. Vol. IV. The Byzantine Empire. Part II.
Government, Church and Civilisation,* Cambridge, 1967, 105-134,
135-184.—Hussey, J. M., *Church and Learning in the Byzantine Empire, 867-1185,* London, 1937.—Jugie, M., *Le Schisme Byzantin,*
Paris, 1941.—King, A. A., *The Rites of Eastern Christendom,* 2nd.
ed. Rome, 1947.—Kirchhoff, K., *Die Ostkirche betet. Hymnen aus
den Tagzeiten der byzantinischen Kirche,* 4 vols.—Laurent, V., *Les
"Mémoires" du grand ecclésiarque de l'église de Constantinople,
Sylvestre Syropoulos sur le Concile de Florence (1438-1439),* Paris,
1971.—Lebon, J., *Le Monophysisme sévérien, étude historique, littéraire et théologique sur la resistance monophysite au Concile de
Chalcédoine jusqu'à la constitution de l'église jacobite,* Louvain, 1909.
—Meyendorff, J., *Byzantium and the Rise of Russia,* Cambridge,
1980.—Meyendorff, J., *Orthodoxy and Catholicity,* New York, 1966
(Fr. ed. Paris, 1965).—Michel, A., *Die Kaisermacht in der Ostkirche
(843-1204),* Darmstadt, 1959.—Miklosich, F., and Müller, J., *Acta
et diplomata graeca medii aevi sacra et profana,* 2 vols., Vienna,
1860-1862.—Möhler, L., *Kardinal Bessarion als Theologe, Humanist
und Staatsman,* 3 vols., Paderborn, 1923-1942.—Obolensky, D., *The
Byzantine Commonwealth: Eastern Europe, 500-1453,* London, 1971.
—Pargoire, J., *L'église byzantine de 527 à 847,* Paris, 1905.—Raes, A.,
Introductio in liturgiam orientalem, Rome, 1947.—Runciman, S., *The
Eastern Schism,* Oxford, 1955.—Schmemann, A., *Introduction to
Liturgical Theology,* London, 1966.—Setton, K. M., *The Papacy and
the Levant (1204-1571),* vols. 1-2, Philadelphia, 1976-1979.—Skaba-
lanovich, N., *Vizantiiskoe Gosudarstvo i tserkov' v XI veke,* St. Peters-
burg, 1884.—Syrku, P., *K istorii ispravlenia knig v Bolgarii v XIV v.,*
St. Petersburg, 1898.—Tachiaos, A. E., Ἐπιδράσεις τοῦ ἡσυχασμοῦ εἰς τὴν ἐκκλησιαστικὴν πολιτικὴν ἐν Ῥωσίᾳ,
1328-1406, Thessaloniki, 1962.—Treitinger, O., *Die oströmische
Kaiser- und Reichsidee nach ihrer Gestaltung im höfischen Zeremo-
niell,* Jena, 1938 (repr. Darmstadt, 1956).—Wellesz, E., *History of
Byzantine Music and Hymnography,* 2nd ed., Oxford, 1961.

Theological trends: Dauvillier, J., and De Clercq, C., *Le mariage en
droit canonique oriental,* Paris, 1936.—Diekamp, F., *Die origenis-
tische Streitigkeiten im sechsten Jahrhundert und das fünfte allge-
meine Konzil,* Münster, 1898.—Dörries, H., *Symeon von Mesopota-
mien: die Überlieferung des messalianische "Makarios"-Schriften,*
Leipzig, 1941.—Elert, W., *Der Ausgang der altkirchliche Christolo-
gie: Untersuchung über Theodor von Pharan und seine Zeit als Ein-
fürung in die alte Dogmengeschichte,* Berlin, 1957.—Garrigues, J. M.,
Maxime le Confesseur. La Charité. Avenir divin de l'Homme, Paris,
1976.—Gero, S., *Byzantine Iconoclasm during the Reign of Leo III,*

Louvain, 1973.—Gouillard, J., "Le Synodikon de l'Orthodoxie. Edition et commentaire," *Travaux et Mémoires* 2, Paris, 1967.—Grabar, A., *L'iconoclasme byzantin: dossier archéologique*, Paris, 1957.—Guillaumont, A., *Les "Kephalaia Gnostica" d'Evagre le Pontique et l'histoire de l'Origénisme chez les Grecs et les Syriens*, Paris, 1962.—Haugh, R., *Photius and the Carolingians. The Trinitarian Controversy*, Belmont, Mass., 1975.—Holl, K., *Enthusiasmus und Bussgewalt beim griechischen Mönchtum*, Leipzig, 1898.—Jugie, M., *Theologia dogmatica Christianorum orientalium ab Ecclesia Catholica dissidentium*, 5 vols., Paris, 1926-1935.—Kirchhoff, K., *Symeon, Licht vom Licht. Hymnen*, Helleray, 1930.—Krivochéine, B., "The Most Enthusiastic Zealot: St. Symeon the New Theologian as Abbot and Spiritual Instructor," *Ostkirchliche Studien* 4, 1955, 108-128.—Ledit, J., *Marie dans la Liturgie de Byzance*, Paris, 1976.—Lossky, V., *In the Image and Likeness of God*, New York, 1973.—Lossky, V., *Vision of God*, London, 1963.—Lossky, V., *The Mystical Theology of the Eastern Church*, London 1967 (2nd ed., New York, 1975).—Mascall, E. L., ed., *The Mother of God. A Symposium*, London, 1949.—Medvedev, I., *Vizantiisky Gumanizm XIV-XV vv.*, Leningrad, 1976.—Meyendorff, J., *Byzantine Theology. Historical Trends and Doctrinal Themes*, New York, 1974 (Fr. ed. Paris, 1974).—Meyendorff, J., *Byzantine Hesychasm: Historical, Theological and Social Problems*, London, 1974.—Meyendorff, J., *Christ in Eastern Christian Thought*, 2nd ed., New York—London, 1975 (Fr. ed. Paris, 1969).—Meyendorff, J., *Introduction à l'étude de Grégoire Palamas*, Paris, 1959 (Engl. tr. London, 1964).—Meyendorff, J., Afanassieff, N., Schmemann, A., Koulomzine, N., *The Primacy of Peter in the Orthodox Church*, London, 1963.—Meyendorff, J., *Marriage: An Orthodox Perspective*, 2nd ed., New York, 1974.—Milash, N., *Das Kirchenrecht des morgenländischen Kirche*, 2nd ed., Mostar, 1905.—Ostrogorsky, G., *Studien zur Geschichte des byzantinischen Bilderstreites*, Breslau, 1929 (repr. Amsterdam, 1964).—Pelikan, J., *The Christian Tradition: A History of the Development of Doctrine. I. The Emergence of the Catholic Tradition (100-600)*, and *II. The Spirit of Eastern Christendom (600-1700)*, Chicago, 1971-1974.—Régnon, Th. de, *Études de théologie positive sur la Sainte Trinité*, troisième série, II (Théories grecques des processions divines), Paris, 1893.—Roques, R., *L'Univers dionysien. Structure hiérarchique du monde selon le pseudo-Denys*, Paris, 1954.—Tatakis, B., *La philosophie byzantine*, Paris, 1949.—Tresmontant, C., *La métaphysique du christianisme et la naissance de la philosophie chrétienne*, Paris, 1961.—Wolfson, H. A., *The Philosophy of the Church Fathers*, Cambridge, Mass., 1956.—Zhishman, J., *Das Eherecht der orientalischen Kirche*, Wien, 1864.

Index